Rated Agency: Investee Politics in a Speculative Age

Michel Feher

ZONE BOOKS

near futures

D0209822

© 2018 Michel Feher
ZONE BOOKS
633 Vanderbilt Street, Brooklyn, New York 11218

All rights reserved.

No part of this book may be reproduced, stored in a
retrieval system, or transmitted in any form or by any
means, including electronic, mechanical, photocopying,
microfilming, recording, or otherwise (except for that
copying permitted by Sections 107 and 108 of the U.S.
Copyright Law and except by reviewers for the public
press), without written permission from the Publisher.

Printed in the United States of America.
Distributed by The MIT Press,
Cambridge, Massachusetts, and London, England.

Library of Congress Cataloging-in-Publication Data
Feher, Michel, author.
Title: Rated agency : investee politics in a speculative age /
    Michel Feher ; translated by Gregory Elliott.
Other titles: Temps des investis. English
Description: New York : Zone Books, 2018. | Series:
    Near futures | Translation of: Le temps des investis. |
    Includes bibliographical references and index.
Identifiers: LCCN 2018015515 | ISBN 9781942130123
    (hardcover)
Subjects: LCSH: Finance — Social aspects. | Capitalism —
    Social aspects. | Social change. | Economics —
    Sociological aspects. | Right and left (Political science) |
    Social responsibility of business.
Classification: LCC HG101 .F4413 2018 | DDC 306.2 — dc23
LC record available at https://lccn.loc.gov/2018015515

RATED AGENCY

ALSO IN THE *NEAR FUTURES* SERIES

Undoing the Demos: Neoliberalism's Stealth Revolution
Wendy Brown

Portfolio Society: On the Capitalist Mode of Prediction
Ivan Ascher

*Family Values: Between Neoliberalism
and the New Social Conservatism*
Melinda Cooper

Journeys of Political Despondency

CREEPING SOCIALISM:
THE POSTWAR SPLEEN OF FREE-MARKET ADVOCATES

The Left has not always held a monopoly on melancholy.[1] Without going all the way back to the exiles of the French and Russian Revolutions, the immediate aftermath of the Second World War was arguably a time when the grim mood currently pervading the left side of the political spectrum weighed more heavily on the advocates of free markets. In both cases, we encounter what psychoanalysis diagnoses as melancholia, namely, the inability to mourn a loss. For the Left of today, it is the loss of socialism—made harder to grieve because its once "actually existing" versions were perverted before they were defeated; for yesteryear's stalwarts of economic liberalism, it was the loss of laissez-faire—a motto that originally formed the core of their creed, but was proven unviable by the Great Depression and the war.[2] In each instance, moreover, the same two institutions fuel the gloom: the labor market and the electoral process. While the Left now sees their respective subjection to the dictates of shareholders and government bondholders as the cause of its own decline, postwar liberal Cassandras perceived collective bargaining and universal suffrage as the Trojan horses of socialist totalitarianism.

Emblematic of the depression that engulfed supporters of unfettered markets at the onset of the Cold War, the economist Joseph

Schumpeter devoted his final work—*Capitalism, Socialism, and Democracy*—to showing that capitalism was in critical condition, including in the United States.[3] In his view, what made the impending disappearance of the capitalist mode of production all the more inevitable—yet all the more unfortunate—was that it resulted from its own success. For since the eighteenth century, Schumpeter argued, it was above all to entrepreneurs that the Western world owed its extraordinary development: their boldness had been the prod of scientific progress, their ingenuity had been the driving force that turned inventions and discoveries into innovations, and their determination to profit from the opportunities they created for themselves had served as the engine of economic growth—with benefits that then spread to all social categories. And yet, Schumpeter added, the prosperity brought by entrepreneurial dynamism ended up working against its providers.

The author of *Capitalism, Socialism, and Democracy* traced the decline of economic liberalism to an endogenous—and thus inevitable—evolution in the legal framework of businesses. He stressed that the virtuous cycle of technological progress—whereby improved productivity successively lowered prices, boosted aggregate demand, and stimulated fresh innovations—had not only spurred captains of industry to build factories big enough to harness economies of scale. Since the forces of "creative destruction" unleashed by capitalism required ever-larger investments, companies wholly owned by heads of dynastic families came to be supplanted by publicly traded corporations, where numerous and dispersed shareholders surrendered power to salaried managers.[4]

Within such organizations, the economist went on, the visionary intuitions of entrepreneurs driven by their daring and their greed soon gave way to sensible plans drawn up by technocrats. The latter, Schumpeter conceded, still sought to innovate and to grow the firms they ran; however, instead of risking their fortune to defeat their competitors, as had been the penchant of entrepreneurial daredevils in capitalism's heroic times, they prioritized the perpetuation of their industrial and commercial activities. As internal company growth became their objective, corporate managers relied increasingly on the proprietary technologies developed by their organization, which made them understandably keen to secure the loyalty of their personnel—notably through labor contracts offering job security and social benefits. Yet in doing so, their main concern ceased to be the maximization of profit for capital owners. Instead, they primarily endeavored to reconcile the demands of employees with the interests of shareholders.

While the pursuit of compromise between labor and capital that characterized the management of publicly traded corporations already fostered solidarity among workers, Schumpeter argued that the budding class consciousness of wage earners would not have fed on hostility to employers had it not been for the growing influence of intellectuals. Here again, he explained, the accomplishments of entrepreneurs lay behind the animosity they encountered. For the sciences and technologies that flourished as a result of their initiatives increased the demand for skilled labor, which in turn fostered the vocational appeal of the intellectual professions—teachers, scholars, but also journalists and cultural critics. Yet by themselves, soaring numbers and improved standing did not turn intellectuals into a class endowed with common interests. According to Schumpeter, the feature that actually unified this otherwise loosely defined social group was its antipathy to entrepreneurial values.

Intellectuals, the economist fumed, were typically brimming with purely theoretical knowledge, while business demanded practical skills; they boasted about the disinterested nature of their work, whereas self-interest was the avowed motive of the entrepreneur; they were reluctant to measure success by the yardstick of risk, which was the mainspring of the entrepreneurial spirit; and, above all, they were offended by the contrast between the low remuneration of their contribution to human improvement and the great fortunes selfishly amassed by capitalists. Schumpeter thus contended that resentment had moved intellectuals to use their newfound prestige in public opinion not only to denounce businessmen's vulgarity and venality but also to persuade workers that the exploitation of their labor was the key to their employers' success.

Not content with their role as tribunes of the people, the author of *Capitalism, Socialism, and Democracy* continued, these same intellectuals would soon offer their services to trade unions. Then, having radicalized organized labor, they would set out to mold socialist politicians and draft the programs of their parties. While aware of the growing hostility to which it was exposed, the liberal bourgeoisie did not alter its principles in response. In particular, it continued to pride itself on protecting freedom of association and extending the principle of free competition to the selection of political representatives. Hence Schumpeter's conviction that its demise was imminent: along with their relative numbers in the electorate and their concentration in assembly lines whose operation they could easily disrupt, the workers' susceptibility to the critique of capitalism formulated by their intellectual mentors seemed to him incompatible with the survival of the free world.

As anachronistic as it seems today, the gloom in which Schumpeter wallowed harbors an invaluable suggestion. Indeed, to recall that despondency has not always dwelled in the same camp invites us to imagine that it could switch sides once again. Such is the premise of this book's remaining pages, which will consider what conditions might cause melancholy to revert to the Right. By way of introduction, however, a few lessons must be drawn from the previous episode of the black bile's travels.

There is certainly no dearth of excellent work devoted to the circumstances that, over the course of the 1970s, darkened prospects for transcending or even just containing capitalism: some accounts emphasize the stagnation that resulted from the completion of Europe's economic reconstruction; others, the concomitant exhaustion of Fordism and the social movements to which it gave rise; others still, the opportunities that oil crises and floating currencies afforded to capital owners. Yet regardless of their focus, the authors who attribute the waning of socialist ideals to these various factors tend to couch them in two overlapping narratives—one centered on neoliberalism, the other on the financialization of developed economies—that they sometimes use interchangeably but seldom bother to disentangle.

Neoliberal reforms—especially those pertaining to market deregulation—have certainly been instrumental in the empowerment of financial institutions. However, according to their promoters, these reforms were meant to restore entrepreneurialism, not to establish the hegemony of finance. In other words, what they eventually delivered does not coincide with their alleged purpose. Far from being a purely academic issue, the divergence between the neoliberal project and its unintended—or at least unannounced—consequences has crucial political implications. For if the process of capital accumulation has investors, rather than revamped entrepreneurs, in the driver's seat, the effectiveness, but also the morale, of its challengers are likely to depend on their willingness and ability to adjust their resistance to the power of their foes. Therefore, taking stock of what separates the neoliberal agenda from the "actually existing" regime created by its implementation may go some way toward dispelling the melancholy of the Left.

ENTREPRENEURSHIP FOR ALL: THE NEOLIBERAL PRESCRIPTION FOR MELANCHOLY

The term "neoliberal" refers to the doctrinal revisions and strategic innovations that enabled some die-hard custodians of the classical liberal creed to chase away the feeling that history was not going their way.[5] Brought together by Friedrich Hayek, the international group of scholars who founded the Mont Pelerin Society in 1947—and whose other leading figures included the German editors of the journal

Ordo and Milton Friedman's circle at the Chicago School of Economics[6] — adamantly refused to give in to the Schumpeterian pessimism that was then prevailing in their camp. Yet at the same time, they shared Schumpeter's worries about the deficiencies of the free world's immune system. Though begrudgingly conceding that as integral parts of the liberal heritage, freedom of association and universal suffrage could not be altogether forsaken,[7] they feared that the confiscation of the former by trade unions and the sway of demagogy over the latter were speeding Western societies down the socialist "road to serfdom." To avert such a tragic fate, the economists, jurists, and historians later called "neoliberals" by their critics[8] made it their mission to design the safeguards that would protect representative democracies from the heedless use of the civil and political liberties they granted.

In their view, the threat faced by liberal societies had less to do with the revolutionary fervor of the masses than with the corrosive incidence of Keynesian countercyclical policies — fiscal stimuli and lowered interest rates to ward off recession as well as temporary price and salary indexation to tame inflation. The affiliates of the Mont Pelerin Society certainly recognized that such measures were not meant to deliver socialism: on the contrary, their promoters intended to prevent market failures and, by that token, sustain the faith of Western citizens in their liberal institutions. However, the consensus among what the economic historian Philip Mirowski aptly calls the neoliberal "thought collective" was that, goodwill notwithstanding, attempts to fine-tune the business cycle always proved far more damaging than the flaws they were purported to mend.

Hayek, in particular, charged that, far from protecting markets against themselves, the Keynesian propensity to tinker with the price mechanism rendered them fatally dysfunctional. As he saw it, market prices are precious signals indicating in real time to each member of a society what the others want and have to offer. By contrast, when public authorities interfere with price negotiations, economic agents no longer can gather the information they need to make their own plans autonomously, which in turn makes them more likely to tolerate and ultimately require more intervention on the part of the state. Typically, Hayek argued, when governments endeavor to counter business-cycle downturns, either by boosting domestic demand or by maintaining salaries artificially high, their intrusiveness scrambles the signals sent by prices. Because the ensuing confusion deprives their constituents of the ability to make informed choices on their own, public officials will then feel justified to tighten the grip of central planning at the expense of individual freedom and self-reliance.

Determined to save the free world from what the author of *The Road to Serfdom* labeled "creeping socialism," neoliberal luminaries devised a coherent set of measures that the leaders of the "conservative revolution" would begin to implement at the turn of 1980s. More than just to rehabilitate the original spirit of capitalism, their ultimate goal was to extend the purchase of the entrepreneurial ethos. The latter, they vowed, had to be brought back to the heart of business management so as to curb the technocratic drift of corporate culture already deplored by Schumpeter, but also actively sustained by public authorities—rather than just sheltered from their meddling—and, most importantly, adopted by people who were not professional entrepreneurs. The members of the Mont Pelerin Society wagered that once retrained by the reforms they championed, even people who supported themselves by selling their labor power would be enticed to treat their life as a business: in the face of any given choice, instead of looking to the state, special-interest groups, or intellectual mentors for guidance, they would estimate the costs and benefits that could reasonably be expected from all their available options and select what appeared to be the most profitable course of action.

Insofar as neoliberal reformers assigned governments the task of dissolving the class consciousness of workers—instead of either urging them to keep out of private business matters or, conversely, condoning the use of their resources to appease the working class—they strayed as much from previous upholders of economic liberalism as from Keynesian supporters of the welfare state. Their agenda thus broke new ground in two major respects.

First, as Michel Foucault famously stressed in his 1979 lectures on neoliberalism, Mont Pelerin doctrinaires lay laissez-faire to rest once and for all by showing that the restoration of the liberal order was less about getting the state out of people's lives than about getting public officials to govern in the interest of the market.[9] Indeed, for them, a good government was not primarily meant to refrain from encroaching upon civil liberties and was certainly not supposed to shelter the governed from the hazards and harshness of the capitalist mode of production: instead of protecting the most fragile sectors of the population against the violence inherent in market competition, it should assume the task of preserving the fragile mechanisms of the market from the impatience of the crowd and its exploitation by demagogues.

To keep public officials on the right track, the neoliberal thought collective advocated the creation of a legal and institutional environment wherein elected representatives would be shielded from the temptation to tamper with real prices in order to win votes. The measures purported to contain the trustees of popular sovereignty included constitutional provisions limiting or prohibiting fiscal deficits—a guideline often referred to as the "golden rule";[10] the devolution of monetary policy to central bankers, whose alleged independence was limited only by their mandate to ward off inflation;[11] the privatization of all the public goods and utilities that private investors were eager to fund;[12] and the substitution, whenever possible, of contractual settlements for compulsory regulations—especially with regard to what economists call "externalities," the incidence of commercial transactions on third parties.[13]

Second, instead of envisioning class conflict as a fact to reckon with—whether by seeking compromises or by taking sides—the intellectuals associated with the Mont Pelerin Society endeavored to make it obsolete by achieving what one of them called the "de-proletarianization" of the wage earner.[14] Designed to help workers and employees embrace the mindset and behavior of entrepreneurs, neoliberal social engineering involved access to home ownership for as many people as possible;[15] contractual, rather than socialized, systems of protection against risks, such as funded pensions and private health care coverage;[16] vouchers given directly to needy families instead of public investments in schools and low-income housing;[17] and consolidation of all other types of public assistance into a negative income tax, set at a level low enough so as not to "incentivize laziness" among its beneficiaries.[18]

Getting middle-class and working-class households in the habits of paying off their mortgages, of honoring their insurance contracts, and of managing the resources provided to them in the forms of vouchers and negative taxes was not meant only as a disciplinary exercise: more than simply compelling people living off the sale of their labor power to trade their "socialist" ideals of solidarity and wealth redistribution for the liberal principles of individual freedom and accountability, neoliberal trailblazers wished to convert them to the entrepreneurial virtues, thereby eroding their sense of belonging to a social class whose interests clashed with those of entrepreneurs.

Back in 1947, when Friedrich Hayek founded the Mont Pelerin Society, most of the economists, social scientists, and legal scholars who joined him in the Swiss Alps were perceived as outlandish figures dwelling at the right end of the political spectrum—among the participants, only the German ordoliberals were influential in their own country. Their relative marginalization lasted almost thirty years: things began to look better for them in 1974, when Hayek received the Nobel Memorial Prize in Economic Sciences and Augusto Pinochet invited a group of Milton Friedman's disciples to help him make "Chile not a nation of proletarians, but a nation of entrepreneurs." Yet in the developed world, it would be up to the British and American leaders of the "conservative revolution" to fully embrace the neoliberal art of governing.

Respectively elected in May 1979 and November 1980, Margaret Thatcher and Ronald Reagan were determined to enact the two prongs of the Mont Pelerin program—that is, mobilize the resources of the state to bolster markets and induce their constituents to manage their lives as businesses. Though initially perceived as revolutionary, insofar as they inverted Keynesian priorities, neoliberal policies soon came to express the new orthodoxy—even beyond the United Kingdom and the United States and irrespective of whether conservative or social-democratic parties were in power.

Confronted with neoliberalism's gradual takeover of common sense—at least among mainstream politicians, economic elites, and media pundits—its detractors on the Left were understandably inclined to attribute their own disarray to the successful implementation of the neoliberal project. On the one hand, they blamed the impoverishment of democratic debates on the combined effects of the shackling of fiscal and monetary policies, the transfer of formerly public goods and services to private capital, and the replacement of mandatory regulations by contractual settlements predicated on the issuance of tradable claims. On the other hand, they came to impute the growing impotence of their own critiques and ideals to the corrosive impact that representations of the individual as self-entrepreneur had on wage earners' class consciousness and capacity for indignation.

RAISING EXPECTATIONS: LIFE UNDER FINANCIALIZED CAPITALISM

While scholarly studies of neoliberalism describe the anatomy and triumphal march of an art of governing, the literature on the hypertrophy of finance recounts the emergence of a new regime of capital accumulation.[19] Since the late 1970s, Western economies have experi-

back" shares of their own company. Absurd as a commercial or industrial strategy, this practice is nevertheless sound when, in order to be "competitive," a CEO must attract investors whose sole concern is the shareholder value of the firms they finance.

The primacy of credit is not confined to the private sector. Meeting the preferences of the holders of their public debt has also become the main preoccupation of national governments. Rather than reviving growth or forwarding the transition of their economies toward sustainable energy sources, public officials are primarily committed to boosting the attractiveness of their territory to bond markets. To avert the distrust of bondholders — which is expressed by a rising interest rate on treasury bills and bonds — political rulers who want to appear responsible cater to their creditors' famously predictable tastes by increasing the flexibility of their labor market, cutting social programs, slashing corporate and capital-gains taxes, and putting off any serious regulation of financial institutions.[23]

Finally, the pursuit of creditworthiness also informs the conduct of individuals,[24] including those who once staked their economic security on stable jobs, regular pay raises, and guaranteed social benefits. Since both corporations and states have made it their priority to sustain the confidence of investors, employers and governments are no longer in a position to promise lifelong careers to their employees and constituents. It is now up to job applicants to make themselves valuable, either by advertising highly prized skills and an appealing address book or, failing that, by displaying unlimited availability and flexibility. Altogether, their ability to find work depends more on the credit attributed to their human capital than on collective agreements about salaries and labor conditions.[25]

The material precarity created by this alteration in the conditions of recruitment forces large swaths of the population to borrow, whether in order to access real estate, continue their studies, acquire consumer durables, or simply survive. Yet anyone hoping to obtain a loan must

enced what the sociologist Gerald Davis characterizes as a Cop
revolution. They no longer revolve around the industrial corp
wagering its prosperity on vertical integration and internal gro
in the Fordist era. Instead, both the corporations and the econo
which they are a part revolve around financial markets domin
large universal banks and institutional investors.[20]

The financialization of developed economies can be meas
the relative size of the financial sector in their GDP, the volume
its made by financial companies compared with those of othe
prises, and the proportion of portfolio income—relative to com
cash flow—in the accounts of nonfinancial firms.[21] Howev
and above such indicators—the examination of which corre
the thesis of a massive transfer of funds from the "real econe
speculative financial circuits—what truly manifests the ascene
credit suppliers is their ability to select the projects that deser
financed. Ultimately, their power consists more in deciding v
real economy will comprise than in draining it of resources. Th
mony of finance is therefore bound to modify the conduct and
tations of those who experience it. For if economic agents a
primarily intent on making themselves attractive to investor
they pursue is arguably less the profit yielded by their profe
activity than the credit necessary to exercise it.[22]

Initial evidence for this behavioral shift comes from the
of publicly traded firms. What for more than three decades h
called "corporate governance" does not aim to maximize the di
between sales revenues and production costs over the long te
sole objective is eliciting an increase, in the very near future
value assigned by financial markets to the stock held by share
A corporation's real success does not reside in the profits ge
by the sale of the goods or services it produces but in the capi
resulting from its next share sale. That is why practitioners of
governance so often use a substantial portion of their resources

offer guarantees. In the absence of sizeable assets, aspiring borrowers generally rely both on prospective collaterals—such as the market value of the house they wish to buy or the income that the degree they want to get is purported to generate—and on the reputation for reliability they have acquired by repaying previous loans. Demonstrating their solvency, whether predicated on actual resources, a reputable record, or wise projects, enables borrowers to sustain their creditworthiness—moral, as much as financial—thereby persuading creditors to keep lending to them.[26]

Historically, the ascent of financial capitalism has largely resulted from the implementation of the Mont Pelerin agenda. Even prior to Margaret Thatcher and Ronald Reagan's conservative revolution, a group of economists and legal scholars of neoliberal observance—the founders of the Law and Economics Program at the University of Chicago—were instrumental in legitimizing the claim that the pursuit of shareholder value should be the focus of corporate governance.[27] Worried about the technocratic drift of corporate culture already denounced by Schumpeter, these disciples of Milton Friedman blamed the declining productivity of the American economy on the disconnection between power and ownership within corporations. In their view, once they were empowered by the dispersion of stockholders, managers had ceased to assume that maximizing the distribution of profits to capital owners was their mission. Instead, they prioritized the development of the firm's productive capacities—which meant that maintaining a high rate of reinvestment took precedence over satisfying employees but also over shareholders' demands. Furthermore, in order to keep both labor and capital providers acquiescent, they attended to the reinforcement of their own power by filling their board of directors with cronies and negotiating mutually beneficial deals with public authorities.

Law and Economics scholars charged that the strategic priorities characteristic of managerial capitalism were conducive to a progressive interpenetration of the private and public sectors: they argued that on account of the cultural affinities between the salaried managers of large corporations and senior civil servants, the former were not only prone to behave like the latter—thereby entrenching the technocratic turn of business culture—but also relied on their assistance to evade competition. To reverse these unfortunate tendencies, neoliberal reformers called for the creation of an institutional environment wherein corporate managers would be once again compelled to do the bidding of their employers. As Milton Friedman wrote in a famous opinion piece, those entrusted with the task of managing a company they do not own must be made to recognize that their only "social responsibility" is to meet the expectations of shareholders.[28]

For the promoters of the Law and Economics agenda, restoring the subordination of corporate managers to capital owners called for a new type of competition. Henry Manne, in particular, argued that preventing salaried CEOs from imposing their agenda and personal ambitions—however dressed up as the firm's best interests—required the institution of a "market for corporate control." Such a market, he claimed, would enable actual and potential shareholders to choose, keep, or replace a managerial team based on its ability to increase the value of the capital under its care.[29] In other words, the kind of corporate governance Manne promoted would subject the fate of managers to the impact of their decisions on the price of the corporation's stock.

By the mid-1970s, the Law and Economics approach to governance had already made major headways in business schools. Its growing prestige was largely due to the declining profitability of Fordist vertically integrated firms in search of the economies of scale.[30] However, it was not until the election of Ronald Reagan that a propitious environment for generalizing the new mode of governance was created. Guided by neoliberal precepts, the new Republican administration hastened to remove the obstacles to hostile tender offers and leveraged buyouts, thereby enabling "raiders" to take control of underperforming firms—underperforming with respect to their shareholder value. By virtue of deregulating capital markets, US authorities were thus instrumental in impressing upon corporate managers that raising the stock price of their company was their only mandate.

While helping corporate managers understand that their job was to create value for the shareholders, the deregulatory measures pioneered by the Reagan administration—and gradually replicated throughout the Euro-Atlantic world—rapidly proved equally transformative of statecraft. Indeed, the involvement of governments inspired by the neoliberal doctrine in the emergence of corporate governance would soon affect the definition of their own economic agendas. For if they were to enhance the competitiveness of their country's private sector in a global environment where financial capital could travel freely, public officials had to make the territory under their jurisdiction as attractive as possible to international investors. They thus staked the success of their own tenure on their capacity to lure liquidity handlers with a business-friendly tax code, a flexible labor market, and strong property rights.

While such perks did draw the desired flows of financial capital, governments quickly realized that offering them had a cost: for the measures that were appealing to investors deprived their own budgets of a significant portion of the tax revenue hitherto allocated to their citizens' welfare. Though unwilling to question the wisdom of market deregulation, they still feared that their new priorities could make them unpopular enough to darken their prospects for reelection. Eager to sustain the reputation of their territory among creditors without losing their appeal among voters, elected leaders increasingly opted to substitute borrowing for taxation. In other words, they assumed that the clash between investors' wishes and their constituents' needs could be avoided only through a swelling public debt. Yet by resorting to bond markets to balance their budgets, the heads of states and governments whose deregulatory initiatives had subjected the fate of corporate managers to the whims of the stock market ended up putting themselves in a similar situation. For once reliant on borrowed funds to fulfill their missions as providers of public goods and social protection, they too became dependent on the confidence of their creditors.[31]

As had already been the case with corporate governance, the sway of investors' tastes on political representatives was justified in neoliberal terms: financial markets were praised for the discipline they allegedly imparted to economic agents. Making governments accountable to bondholders, the reasoning went, would keep their propensities to overspend and overreach in check: instead of indulging the demands of "special-interest groups" to secure their own reelection, the fear of jeopardizing the trustworthiness of their treasury bills and bonds would persuade them to exercise the same kind of restraint that the threat of hostile takeovers had imposed on power-hungry managers.

The argument of accountability loomed even larger in the third phase of financialization, when public officials endeavored to curb their ever-increasing reliance on debt by facilitating the access of their citizens to commercial credit. Throughout the 1980s, issuing bonds had enabled governments to honor the preference of investors for lower taxes while still attending to the welfare of their constituents. However, by the beginning of the following decade, the deficits they had incurred to compensate for the loss of fiscal revenues became large enough to make creditors anxious about their solvency. Loath to see their public debt downgraded by the markets but still afraid of being voted out of office, representatives of the state devised a new compromise, which amounted to sharing the burden of living on credit with the people under their administration: since appeasing bondholders involved major cuts in the budgets devoted to the weaving of a social safety net, households and individuals who had hitherto depended on public grants, subsidies, or benefits were now actively encouraged to borrow the funds they no longer could apply for or collect. To justify the substitution of commercial loans for social transfers, its promoters argued, in typical neoliberal fashion, that the former would train their recipients in the discipline of managing their own lives as a business, autonomously and responsibly, whereas the latter could breed only dependency and sloth.

There is thus ample evidence that over the last four decades, neoliberal reforms and their proclaimed objectives have, respectively, tightened and legitimized the grip of finance on the economy. Furthermore, the beneficiaries of financialization and the intellectual heirs of Hayek and Friedman essentially live in harmony. On the one hand, the efforts deployed by neoliberal governments to make labor markets more flexible, tax codes more business friendly, and public sectors leaner can only elicit investors' enthusiasm. On the other hand, the discipline imposed by financial markets and institutions powerfully contributes to the enforcement of the neoliberal agenda: the pursuit of shareholder value prevents corporate managers from giving in to labor unions, the fear of losing the confidence of bondholders deters public officials from spending their way to reelection, and personal indebtedness dissuades private borrowers from supporting political agendas that are likely to drive up interest rates.

Should we then assume that the prescriptions initially formulated by the leading members of the Mont Pelerin Society are perfectly consistent with the empowerment of investors—that financialization was part of the neoliberal plan and is now the condition under which the neoliberal agenda continues to prevail? Friedrich Hayek liked to quote Adam Ferguson, a distinguished representative of the eighteenth-century Scottish Enlightenment, for whom human societies are "the result of human action, but not the execution of any human design."[32] Ironically enough, Ferguson's pronouncement applies especially well to the societies that have been exposed to the implementation of neoliberal policies. For while governments looking to control inflation and stimulate supply have undeniably shaped our brave new financialized world, the people who have to reside in it hardly fit the type that neoliberal social engineering was intent on fashioning.

To protect liberal polities against "creeping socialism," Mont Pelerin luminaries devised measures that were meant to restore the appeal and, more decisively, extend the reach of the entrepreneurial ethos. As they saw it, enticing individuals, regardless of their occupation, to treat their lives as a business would go a long way toward realigning their aspirations with the interests—and the political representatives—of the business community. However, for economic agents who are subjected to the selecting power and continuous ratings of investors, the prevailing concern is not so much the profitability of their endeavors as the cultivation of their creditworthiness. Required to divine and striving to inflect the expectations of potential funders, they are less prone to act and think like entrepreneurs seeking commercial profit than like asset managers speculating on the value of their portfolios. Though hardly indifferent to the revenues that their activities generate, the attractiveness on which their welfare depends derives primarily from the appreciation of their resources—real estate, equity, but also skills and social connections. Neoliberal reforms purported to fashion individuals who would rely on utilitarian calculus—rather than on collective bargaining and vested rights—to maximize their income. By contrast, the subjects of financialized capitalism tend to wager their prosperity on the continuously rated value of the assets—material and immaterial—that make up their capital.

Because market deregulations featured prominently in their program, neoliberal reformers played a decisive role in freeing up finance. In return, the hegemony of the financial markets has largely fulfilled their hopes. Thanks to investors, upholding time-honored institutions such as freedom of association and universal suffrage no longer amounts to putting the socialist fox in charge of the liberal henhouse. Yet in spite of what neoliberalism and financialization provide to and owe each other, it is hardly inconsequential that the latter breeds credit-seeking traders keen on speculative wagers instead of the profit-seeking entrepreneurs driven by rational expectations that the former sought to fashion. The identification of wage earners with either character type would have doubtless proved equally damaging to their class consciousness and thus to their involvement in social struggles about the distribution of the wealth created by the labor process. However, contrary to their conversion to the entrepreneurial ethos, the subscription of economic agents to the dictates of financial markets and institutions does not deactivate the polarity between employers and employees without fostering another kind of conflict—one that involves the allocation of credit and that pits investors against the "investees" who depend on their largesse.

Faced with what they interpret as the success of the "de-proletarianization" program devised by neoliberal intellectuals and implemented by governments converted to their viewpoint, political parties formerly characterized as progressive are today split into two irreconcilable camps. In the wake of 1990s "third way" reformers such as Bill Clinton, Tony Blair, and Gerhard Schröder, most custodians of the social-democratic creed assume—either with pitiful sighs of resignation or sometimes with the brazen ardor typical of recent converts—that "there is no alternative" to the pursuit of what corporate and new public managements call "competitiveness." As for unrepentant advocates of a break with capitalism, they paradoxically spend most of their time and energy defending the remaining scraps of the postwar social compact that earlier generations of anticapitalists used to denounce as the most alienating of snares. Caught between the opportunistic capitulation of the former and the nostalgic resistance of the latter, it is no wonder that left-leaning voters find refuge in melancholy, when they do not give up on politics altogether.

At first glance, there is little solace to be found in the fact that the stakes and expectations molded by the ascendency of finance diverge from what neoliberal social engineering purported to achieve. If anything, the empowerment of investors provides an even more efficient bulwark against "lax" fiscal policies, "rigid" labor markets, and "sloth-inducing" social benefits than the conversion of wage earners to the entrepreneurial ethos. Yet in contrast with the project of weeding out class warfare by means of turning virtually anyone into a profit-seeking and utility-maximizing entrepreneur, the fashioning of credit-seeking traders prone to speculative wagers on their assets delineates a new divide, predicated on capital valorization, rather than on income distribution.

Now what remains to be shown is that seizing on the conflicts whose main protagonists are no longer the employer and the employee, but the investor and the investee[33] will actually help the Left shake its melancholy. In order to test this claim, the next chapters will successively examine the challenges that stakeholders might issue to companies exclusively concerned with increasing the value of their shares, the initiatives that the governed can take to counter the subservience of their governments to the ratings of bond markets, and the political aspirations and imagination that financialized economies impart to those investees who seek to alter the conditions under which credit is allocated.

1. On the elective affinities between the Left and melancholy, see Enzo Traverso, *Left-Wing Melancholia: Marxism, History, and Memory* (New York: Columbia University Press, 2017). For a call to dispel left-wing melancholia, see Wendy Brown, "Resisting Left Melancholy," *Boundary 2* 26.3 (1999).

2. Sigmund Freud, "Mourning and Melancholia" (1915), *The Standard Edition of the Complete Psychological Works of Sigmund Freud*, vol. 14 (London: Vintage, 2001). On melancholia, mourning, and politics, see Judith Butler, *The Psychic Life of Power* (Stanford: Stanford University Press, 1997), pp. 167–98; and Butler, *Precarious Life: The Powers of Mourning and Violence* (London: Verso, 2004), pp. 19–39.

3. Joseph A. Schumpeter, *Capitalism, Socialism, and Democracy* (New York: HarperPerennial, 2008). See, in particular, part 2, "Can Capitalism Survive?" as well as the prefaces to the 1947 and 1949 editions and "The March into Socialism," published as an appendix.

4. Schumpeter echoed the famous thesis of Adolf A. Berle and Gardiner Means in their 1932 book, *The Modern Corporation and Private Property* (New Brunswick: Harcourt, Brace and World, 1991).

5. The trajectory of neoliberal ideas—from the seminal 1938 Walter Lippmann Colloquium, where they were first formulated, to their conquest of the common sense of political leaders, which began at the turn of the 1980s—has been the subject of numerous works, especially in the wake of the 2008 financial crisis. These include, notably, Philip Mirowski and Dieter Plehwe (eds.), *The Road from Mont Pelerin: The Making of the Neoliberal Thought Collective* (Cambridge, MA: Harvard University Press, 2009); Daniel Stedman Jones, *Masters of the Universe: Hayek, Friedman, and the Birth of Neoliberal Politics* (Princeton: Princeton University Press, 2012); Angus Burgin, *The Great Persuasion: Reinventing Free Markets since the Depression* (Cambridge, MA: Harvard University Press, 2012); Jamie Peck, *Constructions of Neoliberal Reason* (New York: Oxford University Press, 2010); Pierre Dardot and Christian Laval, *La nouvelle raison du monde: Essai sur la société néolibérale* (Paris: Éditions La Découverte, 2009); Serge Audier, *Néolibéralisme(s): Une archéologie intellectuelle* (Paris: Grasset, 2012); Christopher

Payne, *The Consumer, Credit and Neoliberalism: Governing the Modern Economy* (London: Routledge, 2012). Other books have sought to shed light on the remarkable resilience of neoliberal rationality. See, in particular, Colin Crouch, *The Strange Non-Death of Neoliberalism* (Cambridge: Polity, 2012); Philip Mirowski, *Never Let a Serious Crisis Go to Waste: How Neoliberalism Survived the Financial Meltdown* (London: Verso, 2013); Wendy Brown, *Undoing the Demos: Neoliberalism's Stealth Revolution* (New York: Zone Books, 2015); and, drawing on Brown's work, Pierre Dardot and Christian Laval, *Unending Nightmare: How Neoliberalism Undoes Democracy*, trans. Gregory Elliott (London: Verso, 2018).

6. The neoliberal constellation also included Austrian, Swiss, French, and a significant contingent of British members, including Lionel Robbins, Michael Polanyi, and John Jewkes, who played a decisive role in shaping the views of Margaret Thatcher. Among the German ordoliberals, who exerted considerable influence over the governments of Konrad Adenauer (1945–1957) and Ludwig Erhard (1957–1963), major figures included Walter Eucken, Wilhelm Röpke, Alfred Müller-Armack, and Franz Böhm. In addition to Milton Friedman, the most eminent members of the Chicago School's second generation were George Stigler, Aaron Director, and Gary Becker. Either trained at or influenced by Chicago School economists, the founders of the Center for the Study of Public Choice (James Buchanan and Gordon Tullock) and of the Law and Economics Program (also known as the "economic analysis of law"), Ronald Coase and Richard Posner, also counted among the most influential affiliates of the Mont Pelerin Society.

7. Neoliberal path breakers usually presented themselves as unrelenting, yet benign advocates of an integrally liberal agenda. Sometimes, however, they did venture into somewhat riskier distinctions: for instance, when asked how he reconciled his liberal creed with his active support of Augusto Pinochet's regime in Chile, Hayek argued that in order to prevent democracy from paving the road to totalitarian serfdom, liberals were entitled to indulge in a measure of authoritarianism.

8. As early as the 1938 Lippmann Colloquium, "neoliberalism" was the term chosen by the future founding members of the Mont Pelerin Society to qualify

their sensibility. However, Hayek—who liked to call himself an "Old Whig"—and his associates did not identify with it subsequently, with the exception of Milton Friedman, who claimed neoliberalism in one 1951 article ("Neoliberalism and Its Prospects," *Farmand*, February 17, 1951, pp. 89-93), only to repudiate it in the following years and to pose as guardian of authentic liberalism. In the 1980s, "neoliberal" would reappear on the Left as a polemical concept to characterize both the nature of the regime instituted by Ronald Reagan and Margaret Thatcher's "conservative revolution" and the shapers of its agenda.

9. Michel Foucault, *The Birth of Biopolitics: Lectures at the Collège de France 1978–1979*, ed. Michel Senellart, trans. Graham Burchell (New York: Palgrave Macmillan, 2008), pp. 129-58.

10. Hayek saw the best shield against lax fiscal policies in the institution of a new type of bicameralism. According to him, what distinguished a liberal society from its socialist antithesis was that the former submitted individuals to common rules but allowed them to define and endeavor to attain their own objectives, whereas the latter required their members to pursue common goals, regardless of their personal preferences. For the constituents of a liberal polity, Hayek added, the preservation of their civil right to conduct their lives according to their own choices was just as paramount as the exercise of their political right to select their representatives. Thus, in order to avert any conflict between these two fundamental dimensions of liberty, the Austrian economist suggested that their respective protections be devolved to two distinct assemblies.

On the one hand, it would be the mission of what he called a "Legislative Assembly" to establish the universal rules that everyone should follow when pursuing his or her privately defined objectives. Applying equally to all and barring anyone, including the agents of the state, from imposing a goal to others would be the essential properties of these rules. On the other hand, what Hayek called the "Governmental Assembly" would be endowed with the power and responsibility to manage and allocate public resources—tax revenues and borrowed funds—but within the regulatory framework defined by the Legislative Assembly. Though composed of elected representatives belonging to rival political parties, the Governmental Assembly would differ from "existing parliamentary bodies" in one major way: "bound by the rules of just conduct laid down by the Legislative Assembly...it could not issue any orders to private citizens which did not follow directly and necessarily from the rules laid down by the latter." Friedrich Hayek, *Law, Legislation and Liberty*, vol. 3, *The Political Order of a Free People* (Chicago: Chicago University Press, 1979), p. 119.

Committed to contain the illiberal potential of popular sovereignty yet reluctant to promote an authoritarian implementation of what he saw as the liberal rule of law, Hayek argued that the proper way to prevent elected representatives from subjecting their constituents to the mandatory pursuit of common goals was to entrust another democratically elected body with the exclusive task of legislating against such abuse of governmental power. Though less inclined to rely on ideal models than their Austrian colleague, ordoliberal economists were also sympathetic to constitutional protections against democratic overreach. To prevent governments from engaging in what they saw as demagogical policies, they were the main champions of the so-called golden rule either forbidding or limiting fiscal deficits that would later become a key tenet of European institutions.

11. Alongside constitutional amendments prohibiting unbalanced budgets, the German ordoliberals also championed the institution of an "independent" central bank—by which they meant unaccountable to voters and their representatives—that would be constitutionally mandated to make price stability its sole preoccupation. Altogether, the architects of Germany's "social market economy" argued for both the containment of elected officials' initiatives, such as taxing and spending, through legislative provisions, and the transfer of some of their traditional prerogatives, such as acting on interest rates, to allegedly apolitical institutions.

While equally determined to keep representative governments on the liberal track, Milton Friedman found the approach of European neoliberals too rigid and cumbersome. For him, if instead of involving themselves in the manipulation of interest rates, central bankers were to carry out a monetary policy exclusively designed to ensure the regular growth of the quantity of money in circulation, the signals that they would send would prove thoroughgoing enough in terms of preventing the alteration of market prices. At once suspicious of additional constitutional amendments, especially in the case of a "golden rule" that could get in the way of tax cuts, and confident in the capabilities of the Federal Reserve—provided that its priorities were straightened up—the leading figure of the Chicago School believed that his brand of monetarism was not only efficient enough, but also discreet enough, as a policy tool, to deter elected politicians from foregoing fiscal discipline.

12. To determine whether a public administration or a private firm is better suited to supply a service, Hayek argued that the relevant perspective is that of the consumer. And from that standpoint, he then contended, governmental agencies are generally suboptimal providers for two reasons: acting as an unchallengeable monopoly, they have no incentive to heed consumers' wishes, and, being financed by taxpayers money, they do not have to care about satisfying investors' demands. Deprived of the proper enticements, the author of *Law, Legislation and Liberty* concluded, the public sector was condemned to inefficiency: consequently, a drastic reduction of its size and scope would not only be in the interest of business, but also of the people that a good government is supposed to serve.

At the same time, Hayek's position was not that of a libertarian: he believed that a service should be provided by the state when consumers' choices and investors' demands were unlikely to lower its cost—or, to put it differently, when providing it to everyone proved cheaper than letting people choose whether to purchase it and when financing it with fiscal revenues proved more realistic than attracting private investments. Yet in his view, these two conditions are met in relatively few cases: among them, he mentioned "obvious instances as the protection against violence, epidemics, or such natural forces as floods or avalanches, but also many of the amenities which make life in modern cities tolerable, most roads (except some long-distance highways where tolls can be charged), the provision of standards of measure, and of many kinds of information ranging from land registers, maps, and statistics to the certification of the quality of some goods or services offered in the market." Hayek, *Law, Legislation and Liberty*, vol. 3, p. 44.

13. The neoliberal approach to regulation stems from a famous article by Ronald Coase, "The Problem of Social Cost," *Journal of Law and Economics* 3 (October 1960), pp. 1–44. Coase took aim at what was then the most widely accepted form of state regulatory intervention, the so-called Pigouvian tax, named after the British economist Arthur Pigou, the author of *The Economics of Welfare*. According to Pigou, public authorities should be entitled to alter the spontaneous formation of market prices whenever a contractual transaction between two consenting economic agents proved harmful to a third party, thereby incurring a social cost that would offset the private benefits resulting from the deal.

Pollution was and remains the textbook illustration of what Pigou meant. Resorting to an environmentally noxious technology, the economist claimed back in 1920, may leave the manufacturers and the consumers of a commodity, respectively, satisfied with the ensuing production costs and retail price; yet the damage inflicted on the victims of pollution—and by extension on society at large—justifies the introduction of a tax on the industrial technology responsible for the nuisance. Ostensibly, a Pigouvian tax is meant to compensate the harmed third parties. However, its real purpose is to make the cost of polluting production processes prohibitive, thereby encouraging producers to look for alternative solutions.

For Ronald Coase, however, Pigouvian taxes were wrongheaded as a guiding principle and almost always unnecessary in practice. The author of "The Problem of Social Cost" began by questioning Pigou's way of assessing and pricing externalities. That the neighbors of a polluting factory are negatively affected, Coase contended, does not necessarily mean that the harm they suffer is greater than what a Pigouvian tax would cause to the various stakeholders of the penalized manufacturer—losses for the owners, higher prices for the consumers, jobs in jeopardy for the workers. Thus, to the extent that, according to Pigou himself, governments are entitled to interfere with the price mechanism only when the social cost of unregulated market relations exceeds the benefits that a governmental intervention would suppress, it would be unwise to introduce a tax before examining its incidence on all the parties that may be directly or indirectly affected by its implementation. Caution in such matters is all the more important, Coase would then conclude, because, in a majority of instances, it is impossible to establish a comprehensive comparison between the ripple effects of taxing and of overlooking a potential nuisance.

At the same time, the mastermind of the Law and Economics Program did not advocate inaction. Far from simply questioning the merit of Pigouvian taxes in order to promote laissez-faire, his purpose was to legitimize a radically new approach whereby, as a rule, private transactions between alleged victims and producers of negative externalities would be deemed preferable to discretionary measures—the latter being envisioned only when a mutually satisfactory outcome could not be found. Faced with the objections that transaction costs are generally too high to make the substitution of private deals for public rulings economically efficient but also that the conflicts over nuisances cannot always be translated into bargains about tradable rights, Coase replied by calling for reforms that would help alleviate these problems—state-sanctioned incentives to generalize contractual resolutions of disputes over externalities and a more expansive definition of private property rights to enlarge the realm of tradable claims.

14. Wilhelm Röpke, *The Social Crisis of Our Time* (Chicago: Chicago University Press, 1950), pp. 218–22.

15. The various members of the Mont Pelerin Society agreed that wage earners who do not own their dwellings tend to be supporters of public housing and rent control—thereby favoring those political candidates who show little regard for fiscal discipline and the price mechanism in the real estate market. In contrast, home-owning workers and employees were seen as primarily concerned with the value of their property and the affordability of their mortgage, making them contemplate price control and high taxes with suspicion.

Of course, neoliberal reformers were hardly the first advocates of widespread home ownership. In the United States, especially, promoting access to real estate property had been a constant trend for Republican as well as Democratic administrations, at least since the time of Calvin Coolidge. His successors Herbert Hoover and Franklin D. Roosevelt proved equally adamant in presenting home owning as a key element of the American dream. Yet what made the neoliberal promotion of home ownership distinctive was that it primarily aimed at warding off class conflict. As Röpke professed in *The Social Crisis of Our Time* (p. 221), "The proletarian [sic] must in all circumstances be divested of his chief material characteristic, viz., his unpropertied state, he must be given the chance of attaining that degree of relative independence and security...which only property can give." For the German economist, a good society is one where a productive sphere composed of efficiently managed and privately owned enterprises is mirrored by a domestic sphere populated by a myriad of more or less affluent, but also efficiently managed and privately owned, homes.

While equally committed to increase home ownership, Chicago School scholars set out to radicalize the conditions under which it should be made available. Motivated by their suspicion of New Deal institutions, they deplored the price distortion caused by the mandates that Roosevelt and his successors had given to the Federal Housing Administration (FHA) and the Federal National Mortgage Association (FNMA). According to Friedman and his colleagues, allowing public institutions to select and support deserving home owners was a serious mistake: the selection process would end up excluding a sizable portion of potential buyers from the real estate market, while the protection provided to selected mortgage holders would have a negative effect on their sense of personal responsibility. To prevent this twofold flaw, Chicago School economists simply recommended that future governments turn the allocation of mortgages into a fully commercial process: they claimed that letting the private sector set its own criteria of selection would increase the accessibility of loans, whereas preventing the public sector from acting as collateral would improve the accountability of borrowers.

16. According to Röpke, wage earners should be endowed with the ability to "acquire freely disposable funds and become a 'small capitalist,' possibly by being given the opportunity of acquiring stocks." Wilhelm Röpke, *Mass und Mitte* (Zürich: Rentsch, 1950), p. 154, quoted in Werner Bonefeld, "German Neoliberalism and the Idea of a Social Market Economy: Free Economy and the Strong State," *Journal of Social Sciences* 8.1 (2012), p. 154. Short of making

the stock market accessible to everyone, he contended, social policy needed to enable its beneficiaries to perceive the funds set aside for their pension and health insurance as the building blocks of a personal capital.

In contrast to the spirit of the welfare state, according to which individual contributions to the institutions providing health care and pension benefits were to weave a collective safety net shielded from market competition, ordo-liberals held governments' responsibilities in these matters to be twofold: the purpose of public initiatives should be, on the one hand, to empower all able citizens to save enough money for their impending retirement and to purchase an insurance policy from a private health care provider and, on the other hand, to devote a fraction of tax revenues to the segments of the population either too poor or too disabled to handle the anticipation of their old age and the management of their medical costs without the direct assistance of the state.

That people would save exclusively for their own individual health care and pension—instead of contributing to a collective pool redistributed as benefits by a public institution—did not necessarily mean that they managed the "capital" purported to cover their medical costs and secure their livelihood once they retired: indeed, when social services are privatized, insurance companies and pension funds are in charge of investing their clients' money—and also in a position to dictate the terms of the contracts they issue. But then again, ordo-liberal reformers did not really intend to turn wage earners into autonomous investors. As Röpke repeated time and again, the real objective of the reforms he advocated was to undo the proletariat, and the means to that end was to dissuade wage earners from identifying as proletarians. He thus argued that if workers and employees were made to trust private providers of social benefits, they would cease to stake the improvement of their safety on welfare programs obtained thanks to the bargaining power of confrontational unions and identify instead with the hopes and fears of the handlers of their capital.

There again, Chicago School economists agreed yet they went further than their German colleagues. Convinced that in all circumstances individuals are at once better off and more likely to behave responsibly if they are entitled to call the resources at their disposal their own, Friedman, Stigler, Becker, and like-minded scholars advocated the complete privatization of health care and pensions: contrary to ordoliberals, who maintained that the neediest portion of the population requires assistance in the form of tax-collected and state-managed funds, they claimed that help of that sort only serves to thwart the entrepreneurial dispositions of the poor—thereby keeping them endlessly needy—and thus called for the transfer of social security programs to the private sector.

17. Starting in the 1960s, Milton Friedman advocated a complete overhaul of the public housing programs initiated under Roosevelt's New Deal, advanced by Harry Truman's 1949 Housing Act, and further developed in the context of Lyndon B. Johnson's "War on Poverty." Instead of spending money on the construction of rent-controlled projects in poor neighborhoods, the author of *Capitalism and Freedom* contended, public authorities were to allocate the funds purported to help disadvantaged people to the people themselves. "Surely," he wrote, "the families being helped would rather have a given sum in cash than in the form of housing." Milton Friedman, *Capitalism and Freedom* (Chicago: University of Chicago Press, 1962), p. 178. According to Friedman and his followers, the recipients of such funds should use them as they saw fit: instead of being assigned to specific dwellings alongside people facing identical predicaments—and thus being deprived of any incentive to develop their enterprising dispositions—they should be free to look for a place to live of their own choosing with a budget that they managed on their own.

Meanwhile, on the supply side, recipients of vouchers would give the private sector the opportunity to compete for their resources—provided that real estate developers were given the proper tax incentives to make investments in low-income housing profitable for them. The same reasoning led Chicago School economists to call for a sweeping reassessment of the government's approach to education. Instead of keeping tax money invested in public schools, Friedman famously championed the generalization of tuition vouchers, which, in his view, would both empower parents, regardless of their financial means, to choose the school of their children and oblige public institutions of education to compete with the private sector—though the author of *Capitalism and Freedom* readily confessed that the ultimate purpose of his proposal was the demise of the public school system.

With regard to higher education, Chicago School economists were, not surprisingly, very much in favor of substituting student loans for publicly funded grants and scholarships. Though the increasingly large share of Guaranteed Student Loans (GSL) in the programs covered by the Higher Education Act seemed to move in that direction, Friedman and his followers objected to the fact that these were government-backed loans—for the same reasons that they objected to subsidized mortgages: the price distortion and the diminished accountability caused by subsidies.

Gary Becker, in particular, argued for the feasibility of a fully commercial student loan system: while conceding that a defaulting former student could not be "repossessed" by lenders—in other words, that, unlike a mortgaged house, a person's human capital could not be treated as collateral—he contended that there were ways around such difficulty, such as deducting interest on student loans from taxable income, prohibiting personal bankruptcy, or indexing the rate of reimbursement on the eventual earnings of the borrower. Gary Becker, *Human Capital: A Theoretical and Empirical Analysis with Special Reference to Education*, 3rd ed. (Chicago: University of Chicago Press, 1993), pp. 93–94.

18. While Milton Friedman and his followers recognized that welfare benefits could not be left, as they were in the past, to private charities, they claimed that the perverse effects of social programs on the character of their recipients could be partially alleviated if allowances were to be supplied in the form of a "negative income tax." There again, as with the voucher system, the rationale was that the poor lack money rather than protection. Thus, to the extent that the tax rate was calculated so as to avoid making such a subsidy more advantageous than even the minimum level of "positively" taxable labor income, the advocates of the negative income tax contended that the latter would be the optimal way of curbing the dependency of the unemployed poor on welfare benefits—short of letting them fend for themselves.

19. Post-Keynesian and Regulation School economists, in particular, attribute the rise of finance to the crisis of Fordism in the context of a globalization

of trade. For the former, see Engelbert Stockhammer, "Financialisation and the Slowdown of Accumulation," *Cambridge Journal of Economics* 28 (2004), pp. 719-41; Özgür Orhangazi, "Financialization and Capital Accumulation in the Nonfinancial Corporate Sector: A Theoretical and Empirical Investigation on the US Economy, 1973-2003," *Cambridge Journal of Economics* 32 (2008), pp. 863-86; Gerald Epstein (ed.), *Financialization and the World Economy* (Cheltenham: Edward Elgar, 2005). For the second, see Michel Aglietta and Laurent Berrebi, *Désordres dans le capitalisme mondial* (Paris: Odile Jacob, 2007); Michel Aglietta and Antoine Rebérioux, *Dérives du capitalisme financier* (Paris: Albin Michel, 2004); Michel Aglietta and Sandra Rigot, *Crise et renovation de la finance* (Paris: Odile Jacob, 2008); Robert Boyer, "Is a Finance-Led Growth Regime a Viable Alternative to Fordism?: A Preliminary Analysis," *Economy and Society* 29 (2000), pp. 111-45; El Mouhoub Mouhoud and Dominique Plihon, *Le savoir et la finance, liaisons dangereuses au coeur du capitalisme contemporain* (Paris: Éditions La Découverte, 2009).

20. Gerald E. Davis, *Managed by the Markets: How Finance Re-Shaped America* (Oxford: Oxford University Press, 2009), p. 5.

21. On these various measures of financialization in the United States, see Greta A. Krippner's important book, *Capitalizing on Crisis: The Political Origins of the Rise of Finance* (Cambridge, MA: Harvard University Press, 2012), pp. 27-57. For an extension of Krippner's approach to France, the United Kingdom, Germany, and Japan, see Cédric Durand, *Fictitious Capital: How Finance Is Appropriating Our Future*, trans. David Broder (London: Verso, 2017), chapter 6.

22. For an illuminating presentation of this change in priorities from the standpoint of capital, see Ivan Ascher, *Portfolio Society: On the Capitalist Mode of Prediction* (New York: Zone Books, 2016). A useful typology of studies devoted to financialization is provided by Natasha Van der Zwan, "State of the Art: Making Sense of Financialization," *Socio-Economic Review* 12 (2004), pp. 99-129.

23. For an enlightening account of Western states' growing dependency to bondholders, see Wolfgang Streeck, *Buying Time: The Delayed Crisis of Democratic Capitalism*, trans. Patrick Camiller (London: Verso, 2014) and *How Will Capitalism End?: Essays on a Failing System* (London: Verso, 2016). For the United States,

see also Krippner, *Capitalizing on Crisis*, and for France, Benjamin Lemoine, *L'ordre de la dette: Enquête sur les infortunes de l'État et la prosperité du marché* (Paris: Éditions La Découverte, 2016).

24. See Randy Martin, *Financialization of Daily Life* (Philadelphia: Temple University Press, 2002) and Rob Aitken, *Performing Capital: Toward a Cultural Economy of Popular and Global Finance* (New York: Palgrave Macmillan, 2007).

25. On the impact of financialization on employees' terms and conditions of recruitment, see Gerald F. Davis, *The Vanishing American Corporation: Navigating the Hazards of a New Economy* (San Francisco: Berrett-Koehler, 2016), pp. 139–50, and Davis, *Managed by the Markets*, pp. 191–208. See also David Weil, *The Fissured Workplace: Why Work Became So Bad for So Many and What Can Be Done to Improve It* (Cambridge, MA: Harvard University Press, 2015); Randy Martin, Michael Rafferty, and Dick Bryan, "Financialization, Risk and Labour," *Competition and Change* 12 (2008), pp. 120–32; Melinda Cooper, "Shadow Money and the Shadow Workforce: Rethinking Labor and Liquidity," *South Atlantic Quarterly* 114 (2015), pp. 395–423.

26. See, in particular, Martha Poon, "From New Deal Institutions to Capital Markets: Commercial Consumer Risk Scores and the Making of Subprime Mortgage Finance," in "Tracking the Numbers: Across Accounting and Finance, Organizations, Markets and Cultures, Models and Realities," special issue, *Accounting, Organizations and Society* 35.5 (2008), pp. 654–74; Doncha Marron, *Consumer Credit in the United States: A Sociological Perspective from the Nineteenth Century to the Present* (New York: Palgrave Macmillan, 2009); Paul Langley, *The Everyday Life of Global Finance: Saving and Borrowing in Anglo-America* (Oxford: Oxford University Press, 2009), and Langley, "The Uncertain Subjects of Anglo-American Financialization," *Cultural Critique* 65 (2007), pp. 67–91.

27. The first generation of Law and Economics scholars included Ronald Coase, George Stigler, Henry Manne, Robert Bork, and Richard Posner.

28. "There is one and only one social responsibility of business—to use its resources and engage in activities designed to increase its profits so long as it stays within the rules of the game, which is to say, engages in open and free competition without deception or fraud." Milton Friedman, "The Social Responsibility

of Business Is to Increase Its Profits," *New York Times Magazine*, 13 September 1970.

29. Henry Manne: "Mergers and the Market for Corporate Control," *Journal of Political Economy* 73 (1965), pp. 110-20. In *Managed by the Markets* (pp. 59-101), Davis underscores the importance of Manne's article.

30. The beginning of the shareholder-value era can be traced to the publication of an influential article by Michael C. Jensen and William H. Meckling, "Theory of the Firm: Managerial Behavior, Agency Cost and Ownership Structure," *Journal of Financial Economics* 3 (1976), pp. 305-60.

31. On the transition from the "tax state" to the "debt state," see Streeck, *Buying Time*, chapter 2.

32. Adam Ferguson, *An Essay on the History of Civil Society* (Cambridge: Cambridge University Press, 1996), p. 119, quoted in Friedrich Hayek, *New Studies in Philosophy, Economics and the History of Ideas* (London: Routledge and Kegan Paul, 1978), p. 264.

33. For a similar use of the notion of investee, see Jacques-Olivier Charron, "Toward Investee's Capitalism," *Futures* 68 (2015), pp. 19-30.

CHAPTER ONE

The Stakes of Corporate Governance

EMPLOYERS AND INVESTORS

A gradual yet decisive change of emphasis has recently transformed the critique of capitalism. Previously centered on the *profits* reaped by multinational corporations, grievances are now primarily directed at the conditions under which financial institutions allocate *credit*. Although the exploitation of wage earners by their *employers* has by no means receded, *investors'* demands are arguably what fuel the most vehement and widespread outrage—if only because increasing job scarcity and precarious working conditions are ultimately attributed to them.[1] The main locus of criticism has thus shifted from the market where labor is made into a commodity and priced accordingly to the market where resources and endeavors are turned into assets and evaluated as such.[2]

The various "occupation" movements of 2011—May 15 (15-M) in Spain and Occupy in the United States and the United Kingdom— already substantiated this change of target, as did the US and French presidential campaigns of Barack Obama in 2008 and François Hollande in 2012. Once in charge, of course, both former candidates were quick to renege on their campaign trail promises, yet their commitment to stand up to the speculators arguably played a considerable role in their electoral success. While Obama vowed to defend the interests of Main Street against the predatory ways of Wall Street, Hollande famously announced that his true opponent was "faceless" finance.[3]

The perception of financial institutions as unscrupulous predators is hardly new. Back in the 1980s, banks and investment funds
already had earned a bad name through hostile takeover bids, the junk
bonds scandal, and the fraud and collapse of a third of the savings-
and-loan associations in the United States. Henceforth, their reputation only worsened, courtesy of the banking crises in Scandinavia
and Japan at the start of the 1990s, the monetary crises in Mexico in
1994 and Southeast Asia three years later, the collapse of the hedge
fund Long-Term Capital Management (LTCM) in 1998, the bursting
of the dot-com bubble in 2001, and the scandal-ridden bankruptcies of
WorldCom and Enron in 2002.

Public animosity toward financial institutions peaked in the
months following the stock market crash of summer 2008.[4] By then,
money handlers were not merely reviled for their greed and cynicism,
they were also accused of dangerously irrational behavior. Correctly
blamed on the toxic assets developed and disseminated by the banks,
the 2009 Great Recession revealed that left to their own devices, financial markets were anything but efficient. Though interpretations of the
crisis vary—some merely focus on the recklessness of an insufficiently
supervised profession, whereas others point to an irreversible trend
affecting capitalism itself—none leave asset managers unscathed.

Yet in practical terms, financial institutions themselves have barely
suffered from the universal opprobrium heaped upon them. The social
movements that sought to bring them to account have faded away with
little or no tangible results, while the very elected officials mandated
with the task of regulating the financial industry actually endeavored
to restore its hegemony. Unless we believe that the next crash will be
the vector of immanent justice, the remarkable resilience of a world
subjected to finance poses the question of how capitalism can be
resisted, once investors are in charge.

According to Marx's definition, to which social democrats are no
less beholden than their revolutionary rivals, capitalist exploitation

is predicated on the condition of wage labor, the socioeconomic relationship between a "free" worker and an employer. The so-called free workers, whose labor power is constituted as a commodity for sale, are exploited insofar as their wages are inferior to the exchange value of the wealth they produce, thereby enabling their employers to make a profit. Thus, in Marx's account, capitalism's core relationship involves employers who exploit and workers who are exploited. The former are exploiters because the profit they make proceeds from an appropriation of the value created by their employees. The latter are exploited because they are dispossessed of both the means and the product of their activity and are paid a salary that reflects only the market price of their labor power.[5]

Investors do not easily fit into this account of capitalist exploitation. Charges lodged against financial institutions do not involve the fees they pay to their employees—market traders hardly qualify as exploited workers. Instead, they involve the criteria to which they subject the allocation of human and material resources. While liquidity providers are rightly accused of collecting exorbitant returns on their investments, thereby depriving producers of a large part of the income they produce, focusing on the share of the surplus value that investors manage to appropriate does not do justice to their significant role and power. The dividends, interest payments, and other premiums they collect certainly add up to outrageous sums. Yet this is an accusation that can be levied against any segment of the propertied classes. What is specific to investors as such is their ability to select the kinds of endeavors that deserve resources. Put another way, the distinctive prerogative of investors resides not in the extortion of income, but in the allocation of capital: more than appropriation, *accreditation* is their specific business.

In light of this functional difference between employers and investors, the argument that capitalism today revolves around financial markets is bound to have major implications for its detractors. For if critics are to give precedence to conditions of credit allocation over modalities of profit extraction, they will stress a specific harm that must be distinct from exploitation in Marx's sense of the term. Consequently, they will also need to identify an injured party other than the exploited worker whose emancipation was the objective of the labor movement, which, in turn, will require them to imagine another form of resistance than the time-honored struggle against the ruthless boss.

Before going any further, two caveats are in order. First, to claim that the critique of selective investors should take precedence over the critique of exploitative employers is not to assert that the exploitation of labor has decreased—quite the contrary. In the private sector, where corporate governance has become the art of creating value for shareholders, CEOs have wagered the recognition of their talent on their ability to reduce labor costs. Similarly, in the realm of statecraft, the measures that governments take to placate bondholders have translated into increasingly severe cuts in budgets for social programs and public utilities. Altogether, it is thus accurate to associate the last three decades with an unprecedented transfer of income from labor to capital.

Yet to make sense of such a transfer simply by pointing to the rise of new forms of management, public as well as corporate, proves insufficient. For wage stagnation and shrinking welfare programs ultimately derive from the rating power exercised by investors. Thanks to the removal of legal and administrative obstacles both to the circulation of capital (across national borders as well as across types of financial activities) and to the creation of new kinds of assets (derivatives, in particular), liquidity handlers have been empowered to rule as much on the competitiveness of a company as on the attractiveness of a territory. This is why the issue of *accreditation*—the valuation of capital—should be addressed in its own right rather than merely in terms of its consequences for *distribution*—the allotment of income.

Second, to suggest that workers' struggles against exploitation no longer represent the paradigm of social conflict does not mean that such struggles have lost their heuristic value. For even if labor is not the political substance that can be mobilized to challenge the hegemony of investors, the methods and approaches formerly developed by the labor movement to understand and counter the power of employers remain relevant in meeting the challenges faced by social movements today.

Whether informed by Marxist critique or simply by their own experience, working-class activists in the era of industrialization regarded wage labor as the institution responsible for their exploitation. Yet far from simply rejecting the conditions imposed upon all wage earners, they formed labor unions, whose members identified with the shared ordeal and common interests of men and women deprived of any means of subsistence other than the sale of their labor power. As coalitions of salaried workers from different sectors became united and strengthened by the recognition of their common fate, they came to challenge their exploitation in the labor market. Union activists certainly objected to the status of "free worker" whereby wage earners are represented as owners of a commodity called labor power, the sale of which they "freely" negotiate. Following Marx, some union sympathizers denounced such "freedom" as the subjective formation created by liberal law to legitimize workers' exploitation.[6] In practice, however, the labor movement embraced the condition of the free worker—strategically, at least—as part of the collective identity from which the working class would draw its power.

At a time when capital accumulation is driven by finance, reenacting the strategy developed by the labor movement in the age of industrial capitalism entails exposing *and* appropriating the condition to which investors subject the potential recipients of their beneficence. Such reprisal thus has two tenets: it involves identifying the subjective form that financial markets constitute as the object of their assessments—in other words, identifying the "successor" to the free worker that the labor market fashions as the owner and seller of his or her labor power—but also assuming its features in order to challenge financial capitalists on their own turf.

PROFIT EXTRACTION AND CREDIT ALLOCATION

Seen from the standpoint of class identification and conflict, the recent transformations of capitalism bring a fundamental contrast between employers and investors. This appears in differences between what employers and investors actually do—their specific function and prerogatives in the process of capital accumulation—and thus reveals differences between the profiles of the subjects that employers and investors both address and fashion as they exercise their functions.

The functional difference between employers and investors must be traced to the sites where they operate. For employers, it is the labor market, the place where work is commodified—where a commodity called labor power is traded by its owners. Investors, by contrast, primarily dwell in financial markets, the place where ventures of all kinds are turned into assets. The former aspire to make a profit: their purpose is to generate revenues superior to their expenditures by means of pricing appropriately the labor power needed to produce commodities. The latter preside over the allocation of credit: their purpose is to apportion capital by means of selecting the endeavors they deem worthy of investment. Employers are thus in the business of appropriating a share of what workers have produced, whereas investors ultimately get to decide what deserves to be produced.

Modeled on the market in goods and services, the labor market thus hosts only businesspeople. It is meant to coordinate transactions among economic agents who are guided by their self-interest and keen on negotiating the exchange of the commodity called labor power at the best possible price—which, at the end of the bargaining day, will be called the market-clearing price. Employers, who buy labor power in the labor market, use it to produce commodities that they sell in the market of goods and services. Free workers, who sell their labor power to employers in the labor market, use the income from their sale to buy commodities from employers in the market of goods and services. In the classical liberal world constituted by the articulation of these two markets, employers and workers are both commercial traders, or businesspeople, both owners of tradable commodities, equally free to negotiate the price of the commodities they seek to acquire and sell.

By contrast, the subjects that investors perceive and address are no longer traders trying to profit from their transactions by maximizing the price of what they sell and minimizing the cost of what they need to purchase. What investors contemplate are rather *projects* eager to attract financing, or, more generally, projects that seek to bolster their own credit, moral as well as financial.[7] Such projects range from national governments' provisional budgets and corporations' business plans to job seekers' applications, prospective students' statements of purpose, start-up creators' pitches, and loan seekers' credit scores. From the standpoint of financial institutions, companies, states, and people are not perceived as legal or natural entities seeking to profit from their commerce with each other, but as legal or natural entities hoping to be the object of investment, or, better put, hoping to be considered worthy of investment.

The claim that projects are to financial markets what merchants are to markets in goods and services—labor included—immediately faces a major objection. As already mentioned, the liberal conception of human nature upon which classical and neoclassical market economies are predicated endows everyone, whether laborer or capitalist, with the status of utility-maximizing property owner. In a world shaped by hegemonic finance, by contrast, it would seem that only persons, whether physical or legal, in search of backing are turned into projects, whereas putative financers are granted a different status—that of project evaluator. Unlike the liberal condition of the commercial trader, which is equally ascribed to the free workers and their employers—thereby allowing the latter to deny any exploitation of the former by claiming that they are both equally free to pursue their self-interest—there would be no subjective formation common to all inhabitants of the financialized world. Whereas employers and employees are endowed with the dual function of seller and buyer, supplier and client, there seems to be no reversibility between the functions of investor and "investee."

Yet a closer inspection shows that while financial capital in its global, liquid, and anonymous form may itself be regarded as a "pure" investor, the concrete institutions and individuals that actually provide credit must also be included among investees. Indeed, insofar as they are accountable to their own shareholders and have often borrowed the funds they allocate, financial institutions qualify as much as projects as nonfinancial companies, states, and private borrowers. Although imparting creditworthiness is their specific job, they still share the status of credit-seeking ventures with the economic agents that they subject to their assessments. Symmetrically, those legal and natural persons who do not officiate in the financial industry are not merely investees: while endeavoring to get their own projects appreciated, they necessarily contribute to the accreditation of others. They do so either directly, when their savings enable them to invest in various rated initiatives, or indirectly, when their enthusiasm about (or alternatively their distrust of) their fellow investees' initiatives affect the latter's appreciation in the eyes of investors. Consequently, it appears that all the subjects of financialized capitalism, regardless of their profession, are both supplying and demanding credit—are both investors and investees—just as their predecessors were both suppliers and purchasers of commodities.[8]

NEGOTIATION AND SPECULATION

Negotiation is the practice that drives markets where goods, nonfinancial services, and labor power are exchanged. Buyers and sellers negotiate the prices of the commodities in circulation and, as long as competition between producers remains free and undistorted, neoclassical theory predicts that supply and demand will end up finding a meeting point that is optimal for all parties. In capital markets, by contrast, prices are formed much less by negotiation between the partners to the exchange than by the *speculations* of investors whose object is the value that their peers are about to attribute to tradable assets. Whereas the clearing price of a good or nonfinancial service corresponds to the negotiated optimization of sellers' and buyers' satisfaction, the market value of a financial asset expresses the current state of investors' speculations on the attractiveness of that asset in the eyes of their colleagues.

As John Maynard Keynes and his follower Hyman Minsky argued, this is why financial markets are structurally unstable—why their operations do not lead to the formation of an equilibrium price. When a securitized project submitted to the assessments of investors suddenly benefits from a positive rumor, Keynesians explain, the demand for this asset is bound to rise, and so will its price, as is the case in any other market. However, contrary to what occurs with other types of commodities, the appreciation of a financial asset will not reduce but, obversely, increase demand for it, because the initial rumors about the value of the underlying project are confirmed. In short, the soaring price of a security increases its attractiveness to investors. Price and demand rise together in an upward spiral that nothing offsets—not, at any rate, until the emergence of a rumor about the asset's possible overvaluation. Thereafter, to the extent that this new rumor catches on, demand for the security will sag and drag its price into a downward spiral symmetrical to the mutually reinforcing appreciation and attractiveness that preceded it.[9]

The alternation between periods of enthusiasm and periods of distrust, both self-generated, as well as the abruptness and unpredictability of the shifts from one to the other, far from being accidental, accurately describes the ordinary behavior of financial markets. The latter's role is not to coordinate negotiations between traders—that is, to ensure the automatic adjustment of commodity prices to the productive capacity of suppliers and the means of consumption of purchasers—but to provide a sounding board for the speculations of investors—that is, to record the wagers they are constantly placing on the developing mood of their peers. Among purveyors of financial assets, the propensity to imitate, but also the desire to anticipate the enthusiasms and doubts of competitors thus largely replaces the calculations leading to the optimization of costs and benefits that govern transactions in other markets.

In the eyes of employers, employees are not partners engaged in a common enterprise, but traders encountered in the job market who, as such, are entitled to negotiate the price of the sole commodity in their possession—their labor power. The condition of autonomous labor dealers to which employees are assigned enables their exploitation, but also its concealment under what Marxists used to call "formal equality." Indeed, as commodity traders, employers and employees enjoy the same rights (their personhood is inalienable, and they are free to dispose of what they own) as well as the same duties (they must keep their commitments and respect both the personal integrity and the private property of others). The apparent symmetry of the contractual relationship between employers and each of their employees functioned to maximize the former's extortion by hiding it behind the latter's consent. Conversely, the decision of labor unions to negotiate workers' employment conditions and wage levels *collectively* made it possible for them to reach agreements that were less unfavorable to the interests of their members than the individual labor contracts favored by capitalists.

To curb the exploitation inherent in the wage relation, early labor unions did not simply denounce the legal subterfuge that endowed it with the appearance of a fair transaction. In order to wage their struggle in the labor market, unionized workers not only appropriated their status as traders in labor power but also placed their associations under the aegis of the right to freely negotiate the price of the commodities they owned. Since the legal framework required for the operation of a competitive market authorized them to pursue their self-interest using every means consistent with the practice of negotiation, they were able to argue that their solidarity in the face of employers was a legitimate lever for securing better remuneration of their labor power.[10]

Backed by business-friendly governments and legitimized by classical liberal doctrine, bosses long sought to treat wage-earner solidarity as a monopolistic practice, thereby keeping unions illegal. In time, however, the development of industrial capitalism eventually rendered this position untenable. For once concentrated in large factories, workers were in a position to obstruct the production process, whether by going on strike or even by resorting to sabotage. As a result, employers came to understand quickly that it would be more worthwhile, or at any rate less costly, to engage in collective bargaining than to prohibit labor unions.

It should be stressed that the reformist wing of the labor movement was not the only one to opt for the appropriation of the status of free worker in order to negotiate the price of labor power in the job market. Whether they intended to humanize capitalism or sought to hasten the advent of socialism—either by combining their industrial action with the political agenda of socialist parties or by conceiving their movement as the catalyst of a future revolution—all union organizations played the game of wage relations. While the most moderate wanted only to reconcile an improvement in working-class living conditions with corporate profitability, radical militants, in accordance with Marx's prognosis, reckoned that by preventing capitalists from intensifying the exploitation of labor, they were depriving the owners of capital of the only means at their disposal to counter the tendency of profit rates to fall, thereby contributing to the maturation of the revolutionary process.[11]

For the presumptive heirs of either tradition—those who wish to break with capitalism and those who are content with what Karl Polanyi called "embedded markets"—the rekindling of the labor movement's initial inspiration today cannot proceed from the projection of the conflict of interests between labor and capital characteristic of the industrial era onto a social landscape that has been profoundly altered by the ascendancy of financial capital. For once employers are compelled to tailor their decisions to investors' preferences, their disempowerment effectively downgrades the bargaining power of their employees. Rather than revive old modes of industrial action, one should take stock of the strategy developed by early workers' unions, but in an environment where economic activity is dependent on the moods of financial markets, and reenact their resolve to appropriate the condition to which they were assigned. In other words, to follow the example of early labor unions would paradoxically amount to abandoning the status of negotiator over labor power supply on which unions once built their leverage in order to assume the condition of project bearers pursuing the appreciation of their initiatives by speculating on other people's expectations. In short, rediscovering the intelligence of early labor unionism means adapting its strategy of critical appropriation to the condition that credit providers impose on the men and women exposed to their valuations.

When that happens, the focus of investee activism shifts from the extraction of profit to the attribution of credit. The liberty that financial capitalism grants equally to everyone, investors and investees alike, is no longer the freedom to negotiate that industrial capitalism conferred on employers and employees. It is the liberty to speculate—or rather, to speculate on the speculations of others—so as to shape their assessments. More than the apportioning of what has been produced, investee coalitions and activists seek to influence the selection of what gets to be produced. For their purposes, how endeavors are rated takes precedence over how commodities—labor power included—are priced. Rather than income distribution between workers and owners of the means of production, their primary concern is the conditions of capital allocation.

What, in practice, will such investee activism entail? Once again, a comparison with the labor movement is helpful. In order to make income apportionment between labor and capital less lopsided, union activists did not confine themselves to embracing the condition of free workers. In their capacity as commodity dealers endowed with the liberty to bargain, they strove to revise the art of negotiation so as to adapt it to working-class interests. Along with their determination to funnel workers' solidarity into collective agreements, labor activists developed new bargaining techniques, such as various kinds of strikes (mass strike or slowdown, limited or indefinite strike), occupying the workplace, and even sabotage.[12]

Admittedly, from the "Springtime of Peoples" in 1848 through the 1970s, the long succession of extended conflicts and temporary settlements that punctuated the history of industrialized countries did not deliver socialism, whether as the eventual outcome of gradual reforms or as the revolutionary resolution of capitalism's internal contradictions. Nevertheless, a long century of collective bargaining under the aegis of organized labor resulted in a deep transformation of what counted as liberalism. In place of the classical liberal conception of civil society as a collection of individuals pursuing their private interests arose a widely accepted representation of the social world based on the existence of potentially antagonistic classes. Though both depictions identified the pursuit of self-interest as the main subjective motivation with which governing agencies needed to reckon, their respective assessments of how different interests meshed or clashed shifted from cooperation and competition among individuals to group solidarity and rivalry. Accordingly, the model for an optimal social compact strayed from the aggregate utility automatically provided by free and fair markets to brokered agreements painstakingly negotiated by the representatives of wage-earning and capital-owning classes.

Along with this reassessment of proper liberal procedures came a revised role for the state. For the founding fathers of classical liberalism, a government subjected to the rule of law was primarily meant to secure the freedom and fairness of trade and, for that purpose, to see to it that the governed fulfilled their contractual commitments and respected both the personal integrity and the private property of their fellow citizens. Fostering a virtuous circularity between collective bargaining and class-consciousness building, the social-democratic compact gave governments the roles of referee (with regard to conflicts) and guarantor (of deals between wage earners and employers). Rather than compelling wage earners to compete with each other to sell their labor power to employers, state officials were expected to enable negotiations between the representatives of labor and capital, but also to guarantee the enforcement of their eventual agreements, even when these settlements encroached on the full exercise of property rights.

Easily achievable as long as high growth rates facilitated conflict management, the art of brokering acceptable compromises between workers' expectations and capitalists' requirements became excessively challenging once the economies that had been devastated by the Second World War were fully reconstructed. The ensuing stagnation across the developed world offered its political rulers a choice between involving themselves more deeply in the economic administration of their countries in order to preserve the income distribution characteristic of the postwar social compact, and relinquishing the allocation of resources to markets so as to extricate themselves from the pressure exercised by their constituents' competing demands. Western governments eventually opted for the second solution, arguing that it was more in line with liberal values to bank on the enterprising spirit of their citizens than to expose their societies to the perils and abuses of administered economies. In stark contrast with the Keynesian wisdom, according to which "taking an ever greater responsibility for directly organizing investments" was the state's calling, Western governments then embraced the neoliberal faith in the capacity of markets to instill discipline in economic agents and thus to preside efficiently over the way in which credit is awarded.[13]

Initially, endowing financial markets with the license to select deserving projects translated into skyrocketing interest rates: since declining growth had created a seemingly protracted credit crunch, investors could take full advantage of the competition between applicants for their funds to demand exceptionally high returns. The sudden devolution of the "responsibility for directly organizing investments" to the private sector thus played a major role in the brutal recession that struck most Western countries at the turn of the 1980s. However, the same governments that took the lead in handing over the allocation of credit to markets—the Reagan administration and its British partner—combined their disengagement with a widespread relaxation of the regulations that previously hampered the circulation of capital: they opened their borders to financial flows, lowered taxes on capital gains, and gave free reign to financial engineering. As these manifold deregulations made their territories especially attractive to international investors, the resulting influx of liquidity soon brought the price of credit down to less prohibitive levels.[14]

Once interest rates started to decrease, the measures required to attract investors—the free circulation and low taxation of capital but also the strengthening of intellectual property rights, the deregulation of financial professions and operations, and the reduction in labor costs—rapidly became established as the distinctive criteria for a territory's attractiveness and thus as the keystone of a new art of governing. The efforts deployed by postwar governments to reconcile the class interests of national wage earners and national employers—by exhorting both sides to sacrifice some immediate demands in order to preserve social peace and maintain economic growth—gave way to a new prevailing concern.

For public officials as for corporate managers, what mattered primarily was their attractiveness in the eyes of an international community of credit providers. The latter were now in a position to be particularly exacting, to the point of demanding returns on investments that were four or five times higher than the growth rate for production and income. On the one hand, since the United States and the United Kingdom declared the competition for their favors open, investors were free to move around as they saw fit. On the other hand, the range and choice of potentially profitable investments at their disposal was greatly enhanced both by the emergence of industrial powers with an abundant, inexpensive workforce and by the impact of the new information and communication technologies (ICT) on the supply of goods and services. Indeed, thanks to emerging markets and ICT, distributing the production of a commodity over several continents soon became commonplace.

In an environment where employers and political leaders are dependent on investors' evaluations of the competitiveness of their companies and the attractiveness of their territories and where the bargaining techniques used by labor unions to struggle against exploitation and to influence arbitration have arguably lost much of their effectiveness, emulating the militant creativity of the labor movement cannot consist in relying on the procedures it developed at a time when negotiation was at the heart of industrial relations. Confronted with investors who speculate on the short-term appreciation of the projects submitted to them by firms, states, or households, but also faced with managers, politicians, and private individuals who speculate in return on the expectations of credit providers, it is precisely in the art of speculation that today's activists must become proficient if they are to follow in their predecessors' footsteps. Challenging investors on their own ground—as labor unions did with employers—today involves acting on the conditions under which credit is allocated. For in financial markets, the reputations that attract investment are not earned at the end of tough bargaining, but constructed through wagers on the promising character of projects submitted for evaluation.

CALCULATING COSTS AND ASSESSING RISKS

So far, investors on the lookout for short-term capital gains have clearly cornered financial markets. Hence, it is scarcely surprising that their tastes and concerns preside over the evaluation of credit-seeking endeavors. News that typically makes the estimated value of a firm rise includes plans for an imminent reduction in its payroll, rumors about a forthcoming increase in the proportion of its profits distributed as dividends, or a commitment of its research and development department to focus on products that can be patented more rapidly. The same applies to the attractiveness of a territory, which is enhanced by announcements of cuts in public expenditure, reductions in labor protection, and relaxation of control over financial operations. Even the valuation of individuals' human capital depends on similar criteria—speculations about the prospective appreciation of their skills or, failing that, about an increase in their availability and flexibility.

To challenge the monopoly that professional investors hold on the process of accreditation, there is no point bargaining with them over what they deem worthy of investment, and there is little to be gained in merely denouncing the speculative character of their assessments, as if there existed political authorities sufficiently insensitive to their favors to be moved by such denunciation. Just as the labor movement did not expose the exploitation inherent in the condition of wage labor without at the same time endeavoring to invent new techniques for wage negotiations, so today's activists will have to inhabit their condition as investees in such a way as to match their opponents' skills in the art of speculation. In short, investee activism must be about altering the conditions of accreditation. This means fostering the appreciation of alternative projects, both by promoting different evaluative criteria and by working to discredit the type of endeavors that financial capitalists are spontaneously inclined to appreciate.

Investors, as Keynes explained long ago, "are largely concerned, not with making superior long-term forecasts of the probable yield of an investment over its whole life, but with foreseeing changes in the conventional basis of valuation a short time ahead of the general public."[15] Insofar as these changes are themselves a function of wagers on the likelihood of their impending occurrence, speculators soon establish themselves as the main protagonists of the developments they seek to anticipate. Thus, the task of a movement of investees is to participate, for its own purposes, in this game of self-fulfilling prophecies. It is, in other words, a question of "counterspeculating." The purpose of activist counterspeculators is, on the one hand, to make the techniques of corporate governance and public administration currently appreciated by financial markets seem unduly risky and, on the other hand, to increase the attractiveness of practical alternatives—those favoring social rights and reduction of the ecological footprint rather than short-term financial gain or those giving access to knowledge and health care precedence over the reinforcement of intellectual property rights.

There should be no mistake about what counterspeculation purports to achieve: for while investees may be successful enough to get investors to revise their assessments, they can hardly expect to conquer the hearts and minds of credit providers. Once again, their situation is analogous to that of the labor movement of yesteryear, whose representatives never hoped to persuade manufacturers to pursue anything other than the maximization of their profits. Union activists aimed to impose new parameters on the way business executives calculated profitability. This meant conveying to employers that if they persisted in rejecting concessions to labor, the price of their intransigence would prove higher than the increase in wages and improvement in working conditions demanded by their employees. Thus, the actual stake of the arm wrestling involved in collective bargaining between labor and capital was not the emergence of a common purpose—the manifestation of some "general interest" transcending class conflict—but a reassessment of cost and benefit calculations that bosses were compelled to associate with profit maximization.

It is true that short of a genuine consensus about fairness and prosperity for all, the CEOs of the Fordist era did not merely resign themselves to being more accommodating to workers' demands in their budget forecasts. As mass consumption of standardized commodities became the main outlet for industrial production, at least in the most developed countries, the relative prosperity of the wage-earning classes proved indispensable to their employers' enduring profits. Following the all too famous example of Henry Ford, who wanted his workers to be in a position to buy the cars they manufactured, capitalists involved in the mass production of durable consumer goods soon recognized that by offering better wages, by conceding more leisure, and even by helping to finance their employees' pensions and health costs, they were not simply endeavoring to appease the working classes. Because decent salaries, paid vacations, and guaranteed social benefits, respectively, enabled wage earners to purchase the commodities produced by their labor, to find the time to consume them, and to feel sufficiently secure to spend a growing portion of their disposable income, businesses that agreed to these concessions were ensuring the durability of their own turnover as well as improving their workforce's living standards. In short, social progress and capital accumulation both stemmed from the constitution of workers and employees as eager and solvent consumers.

From the employers' standpoint, the virtuous circle between profits and payroll began to unravel in the late 1960s. Even before growth rates started to decline, a widening discrepancy between what the Fordist model of managerial capitalism had to offer and the expectations it was purported to satisfy had put the postwar social compact in jeopardy. The problem was not only that standardized mass-produced commodities no longer met consumer tastes, but also, as the student and worker revolts of the 1960s revealed, that consumerism was failing to fulfill its appeasing function and, most importantly, that demands for equality from women and minorities hitherto sidelined by the affluent society were exposing the limits of welfare capitalism's inclusiveness. Caught short by the evidence of dissatisfaction and making it their priority to avert the politicization of discontent, corporations and governments initially responded with concessions regarding wages, social benefits, and the extension of civil liberties, thereby fueling inflation and confronting capital owners with a rapid devaluation of their assets.

In the end, however, the proliferation of social conflicts generated by the crisis of the Fordist mode of capital accumulation hastened neither the transition from liberal democracy toward socialism nor even the conversion of developed countries to the Scandinavian model of social democracy. Instead, inflation and unrest paved the way for the triumph of the conservative revolution of the early 1980s. Determined to relieve the business community from the increasing pressure exerted by wage earners, the leaders elected at the turn of the decade — Margaret Thatcher in 1979 and Ronald Reagan in 1980 — made it their priority to weaken unions. Yet as swift and brutal as their crackdown on organized labor proved to be, it was made possible only by the decision of their immediate predecessors — the Labor prime minister James Callaghan and the Democratic president Jimmy Carter[16] — to turn their backs on Keynesian fiscal and monetary policy. Once the full implementation of the neoliberal agenda succeeded in taming inflation and disempowering organized labor, businesses were indeed freed from the pressure exercised by their employees throughout the 1960s and 1970s but only to submit to the dictates of investors. Put differently, the governments most committed to the restoration of vibrant and unbridled capitalism did not relieve their job markets from negotiations that were proving increasingly less favorable to employers without taking measures that would shift the balance of power toward investors.

Short of putting an end to collective bargaining, financial deregulation efficiently enabled speculations on the value of capital to preempt negotiations over the price of labor. At the same time, the policies responsible for the ascendency of credit providers over profit extractors have not so much stifled social struggles as shifted their focus. Unhindered capital movements do not deprive employees of the ability to wrest concessions from their employers without delineating a new challenge. Insofar as investors' valuations ultimately determine how managers distribute a company's income, it is only by putting pressure on the assessments of investors that managers' arbitrations can be altered. To that end, investee activists should not only confront speculators in the very arena where endeavors of all kinds are securitized but also join them in the psychic space where they make their wagers.

As already underscored, when organized labor challenged industrial capitalists in the labor market, their purpose was not to persuade employers to abandon their quest for profits, but to compel them to reassess the impact of intransigence on their production costs and thus on their profits. Similarly, today, the mission of a movement of investees is not to divert investors from their pursuit of capital gain, but to make them reevaluate the risks of the projects submitted to their scrutiny, in keeping with their habitual preferences.

WAGES AND CORPORATE SOCIAL RESPONSIBILITY

At once the main target of labor activists' critique and the main object of their demands, wages are at the heart of trade-union struggle. On the one hand, in keeping with Marx's perspective, the very existence of a wage-earning class reveals the exploitative nature of capitalism: salaries reflect what the job market deems necessary for the reproduction of the commodity that wage-earners sell—their labor power—rather than the price that the market for goods and services assigns to the commodities they have produced. On the other hand, however, struggling for higher wages is what labor unions spend much of their time doing. Thus, their activism largely amounts to bargaining for a better remuneration of the commodity that is the vehicle of their exploitation.

Far from representing a flaw or weakness, the ambivalent status of wages in labor activism may be regarded as the cornerstone of its past achievements. For while the radical critique of salaried work became the catalyst of workers' class consciousness—in that it led them to realize that being identified as "free" owners of their labor power was alienating and served only to legitimize their exploitation—workers' demands for pay raises proved a major mobilizing factor and arguably the one most conducive to social progress. From the standpoint of labor unions, denouncing the structural injustice done to wage earners— the commodification of labor sealed by the employment contract—went hand in hand with bargaining over wages, and, as already mentioned, such a dual strategy was no less popular among revolutionary support- ers of a break with capitalism than with reformist defenders of a mar- ket economy tempered by social protection and progressive taxation.

Now, to argue that the prospective subjects of today's social strug- gles are no longer employees, but investees, invites questions about whether the latter have something at their disposal that is equivalent to what salaried work represented for the labor movement—the insti- tutional construct that workers saw both as a wrong causing them to mobilize and as an instrument for conquering their rights. Specifi- cally, we must inquire into the existence of an institution that is both constitutive of the hegemony of investors yet liable to being seized as a locus of activism by militants seeking to alter the current conditions of credit allocation.

Management textbooks prove especially useful when it comes to addressing this question. From them we learn that two types of eco- nomic agent are involved in the valuation of a company's shares. The first includes the owners of the equity but also their peers—that is, the wider community of investors who may include the equity in their portfolios. The second comprises all the physical and legal persons who do not own any part of the stock, but who are nonetheless involved in the firm's operation. Among them are the company's employees, customers, and suppliers, but also the public authorities, local or national, on which the firm depends (as a user of public infrastructure and services) as well as the taxpayers residing in the territory where it is located (inasmuch as they finance the infrastructure and public services it uses), and, finally, the people whose environment is affected by the company's activities.

The first category of agents thus includes both actual and potential "shareholders," while the management literature designates the various components of the second category as "stakeholders." Depending on the context, textbooks either stress the distinction between shareholders and stakeholders or treat the former as a subset of the latter — that is, they classify shareholders as a category of stakeholders. Generally speaking, the clear-cut distinction between the two is maintained when the subject under discussion pertains to legal matters. Indeed, according to the so-called agency theory that Law and Economics scholars have successfully established as the standard doctrine in business management, a firm must no longer be conceived as a full-fledged legal entity, endowed with its own personality and interests, but rather as a bundle of contracts between a "principal" (shareholders) and a set of "agents" (stakeholders) appointed by shareholders to perform a particular task.[17] Yet shareholders are included in the great family of stakeholders when textbooks leave the terrain of legal obligations for that of managerial "best practices." According to its proponents, "corporate governance" is not merely about balancing share valuation with a company's other stakes but also about demonstrating that shareholders' interests are ultimately aligned with that of the "other" stakeholders — and that the implementation of best practices is always a "win-win" strategy.[18]

Until the turn of the 1980s, stakeholders who did not own any stock in the companies in which they had a stake rarely relied on the ability of "best practices" to make their expectations converge with the claims of shareholders. For the most part, the protection of their specific interests was a matter of laws, compulsory regulations, and collective agreements. In addition, throughout the Fordist era, the main concerns of corporate managers were growth and long-term profitability. What stood for good governance among managers involved appeasing both shareholders and wage earners—dissuading the former from selling their stock and the latter from disrupting production by striking, but also persuading both capital and labor providers to restrain their immediate demands. Their goal was to ensure that a sufficient proportion of annual income would be allocated to new investments. Rather than creating the communion of a team under the auspices of "win-win," managers' essential skills involved brokering compromises and urging patience.[19]

However, once the promoters of the Law and Economics agenda prevailed over the custodians of managerial capitalism—in business schools, as well as in business practice—the art of governing a corporation underwent a radical change. Whereas Fordist firms had been endowed with an intentionality equally distinct from the requests of its shareholders and the claims of its employees, companies were now perceived as a bundle of intertwined mandates entrusted by a principal—the owners of the capital, whatever their number—to a multiplicity of agents. Included among the latter, the managers appointed by the board of directors and approved by the shareholders' general assembly would no longer be responsible for the company's commercial sustainability but would be solely accountable to their principal. Practically, this shift of loyalty—from the firm to its shareholders—did not merely result in the distribution of an ever-increasing proportion of dividends at the expense of wages as well as of reinvestments. Companies' executives also had to learn that raising the capital value of the stock—in other words, creating shareholder value—was their true mandate.[20]

What the champions of the agency theory of the firm call "corporate governance" is no longer centered on the pursuit of endogenous growth, which Fordist managers saw as their mission, but instead focuses on the valorization of the financial asset that the firm represents in the eyes of investors. In accordance with this change of perception, bringing about an immediate increase in the credit accorded to a stock by financial backers takes precedence over maximizing the long-term profit a firm can make by selling the commodities it produces. Credit-seeking governance includes a number of novel practices, not only buying back one's own shares to avert a drop in their price, but abandoning activities that are profitable but deemed too labor intensive to attract investors and diverting funds from productive to speculative outlets to protect the next dividend distribution from disappointing order books.[21]

For the mode of governance championed by agency theorists to prevail over the managerial approach to the firm, several conditions had to be met. First, the constraints imposed on investors following the Great Depression and reinforced at the end of the Second World War needed to be lifted—whether fiscal and regulatory impediments to the cross-border circulation of capital, partitions erected between different financial operations and professions, or rules limiting the use and creation of financial derivatives. Managers would wager the success of their company on its credit with actual and potential investors only if the latter were granted a complete freedom of movement and choice.

Second, imposing stock appreciation as the sole indicator of worthy business endeavors called for a theory that would legitimize this mode of selection. Such was the function of the "efficient market hypothesis" (EMH), which mainstream economists were quick to support. According to Eugene Fama, the most indefatigable promoter of the EMH, prices assigned by financial markets, to the extent that information circulates freely enough to make them "fair," accurately reflect the "fundamental value" of the equities on which investors speculate.[22] Though Fama and his peers recognize that in some cases, such as the subprime crisis, facts fail to confirm the efficient-market hypothesis, they contend that these accidents are not frequent enough to justify the intervention of public authorities, except to bail out the credit providers whose ability to function is compromised by the sudden discrepancy between the fair-market price and the fundamental value of their assets.

Third, to reempower shareholders at the expense of all other stakeholders, the resistance of the managerial class needed to be overcome. Hitherto identified with the higher interest of the firm, corporate managers were understandably reluctant to be redefined as "agents" devoted exclusively to fulfilling the wishes of a "principal." Making them settle for their new and humbler mission called for a disqualification of the culture of collective bargaining and endogenous growth distinctive of managerial capitalism. To that end, Law and Economics proselytizers alleged that posing as the loyal caretakers of their company's long-term prosperity merely enabled managers, the salaried directors of large corporations, to reinforce their own power. As they saw it, CEOs took advantage of the dispersion of capital owners to put stockholders' wishes on an equal footing with demands emanating from labor, consumers, and political authorities. By the same token, they granted themselves the right to arbitrate between competing claims, thereby singlehandedly ruling the firms employing them.[23]

At the outset of the conservative revolution, it made good strategic sense for the advocates of radical change in corporate culture to add Fordist managers to the list of "rent-extracting" groups—along with civil servants, unionized workers, and the unemployed. In the end, however, what really converted CEOs to the pursuit of shareholder value was less the critique of their entrenched privileges than their cooptation by and as stockholders. Indeed, it was primarily the indexing of an increasingly large portion of their income to share prices—particularly in the shape of stock options—that persuaded corporate managers to embrace the Law and Economics worldview. Once they were shareholders themselves, business executives were quick to recognize the merits of a type of corporate governance exclusively devoted to the creation of value for their peers.[24]

As the managerial class embraced its new mission, its members changed their views on the legal, regulatory, and conventional protections heretofore enjoyed by those stakeholders who did not own stock. Instead of seeing them as parameters in the construction of a balancing act, managers were inclined to perceive these protections as burdens that "good" governance was meant to minimize. From the mid-1980s on, their new agenda was clearly backed by governments in North America and Western Europe. Having already done their part by delivering emancipated financial markets, public authorities now shared the private sector's desire to attract investments to the territory under their administration and, to that end, they were very much inclined to provide the deregulations and tax cuts that would enhance such attractiveness.

Yet rather than seizing on this propitious conjuncture to demand that previously vested social rights, administrative regulations, and collective agreements be simply rolled back, the practitioners of corporate governance argued that guaranteeing stakeholders' protections was a task they were both willing and able to perform, albeit on a voluntary basis. Taking care of the people and institutions affected by their firms, they explained, fell to them for two reasons: because their allegiance to the "principal" did not prevent them from remaining empathetic individuals as well as good citizens and—professionally speaking, especially—because they believed that the reputation of the company they managed would be enhanced by their solicitude. Managers claimed that offering employees decent wages and working conditions, treating suppliers fairly, ensuring consumer safety, resorting to clean technologies, and acquitting themselves of the fiscal and civic duties required for a harmonious integration into the community were so many ways of improving their firm's corporate image, thereby contributing to its credit.

Promoted by this rhetoric about the convergence among a firm's various "stakes," corporate social—and environmental—responsibility (CSR) soon became an essential component of good governance.[25] While reconciled with their new role of "agent" mandated by shareholders to create value for them, corporate managers still wanted to make sure that the fulfillment of their mission would not unduly expose them to accusations of negligence or irresponsibility vis-à-vis stakeholders, if only because such charges were liable to indirectly affect their own credit. They thus took pains to argue that far from forcing shareholders to lower their expectations, measures meant to satisfy stakeholders' demands were likely, more often than not, to further the pursuit of shareholder value—provided that it would be up to corporate executive to design such measures.

EMPLOYEES AND STAKEHOLDERS

At first glance, the new managers' eagerness to identify with corporate social responsibility would seem a throwback to an earlier era when—instead of all the compulsory constraints that trade unions, consumer groups, and environmentalists have succeeded in imposing on capitalism since the late nineteenth century—social welfare was merely the product of charitable initiatives that entrepreneurs pursued of their own volition. On closer inspection, however, the social responsibility allegedly motivating corporate managers, as long as they are able to exercise it freely, does not amount to the restoration of the order predating the advent of the welfare state. For while the Carnegies and Rockefellers of yesteryear conceived of their good works as disinterested initiatives (in that they were not intended to make a profit for the owners of capital), today's business executives see the attention they pay to the demands of stakeholders as a factor in the valuation of equity. Rather than a good deed, which can be called charitable only if it carries no economic reward, socially responsible management is thought to contribute to the enterprise's credit with individuals and institutions that have the resources to acquire a share in it.[26]

For that very reason, the true judges of the social and environmental responsibility with which a firm can be credited are neither the managers themselves nor the stakeholders whose interests they claim to uphold, much less legislators. They are, rather, the investors who rate the company's efforts by either buying and retaining its shares or, on the contrary, selling or declining to purchase them. In other words, it ultimately falls to financial markets to pronounce on the socially responsible character of a firm's conduct. The company or, more precisely, the agents mandated to govern it are therefore justified in measuring their financial and social "performances" by the same yardstick. For if it is true that their contributions to the enterprise's good reputation—for example, its consumption of natural resources, treatment of the workforce, use of technology, testing of goods and services, or relations with the public authorities—are bound to translate into value for their shareholders, then managers experienced in techniques of good governance may also believe that their own conduct in these various areas ceases to be irreproachable only when doubts about them have an unfavorable impact on share price.

For Marx and the labor movement won over by his analyses, wage labor was to be denounced because, under the guise of giving workers the freedom to negotiate the remuneration of their toil, it deprived them of both the means and the product of their labor. Similarly, today, a movement of investees is justified in exposing the deception harbored by the notion of "corporate social responsibility." On the pretext of voluntarily assuming responsibility for the interests of their stakeholders, firms converted to the cult of shareholder value are in fact intent on divesting themselves of what used to be their legal, regulatory, or conventional obligations. "Socially responsible" enterprises now refer to investors' reactions, rather than to the law, policy regulations, or collective agreements among social partners. Their managers argue that the good standing of their firm's stock shows that the conditions of employment they provide are decent, that the contracts they sign with their suppliers are fair, that the technologies they employ are clean, that the commodities they offer their customers are not defective, and that the sums they pay to the community in the form of contributions and taxes are not insufficient. It can therefore be concluded that "corporate social responsibility" is to social responsibility what the "free worker" was to freedom—an abuse of language intended to legitimize the operations of capitalism.

Yet back in the time of the First International, labor unions had no qualms about encouraging their members to embrace their wage-earning free-worker status, for doing so allowed them to counter their own exploitation and, eventually, to conquer the very rights and protections that corporate governance now aims to suppress and replace with a form of solicitude subject exclusively to the sanction of financial markets. Therefore, if the main task today is challenging shareholders for the power to evaluate the treatment of stakeholders, activists would do well to approach corporate social responsibility in the same way that their predecessors did wage labor: *both* as the instrument of their subordination *and* as the object of their demands.[27] In other words, just as the labor movement simultaneously criticized and espoused the depiction of the worker as the owner of his or her labor power, investee activists should now denounce but also adopt the idea of the enterprise as a team whose well-being is valued by investors.

Making financial markets the arbiters of the measures taken by a corporation to improve the lot of its stakeholders boils down to "securitizing" the social and environmental responsibility claimed by its management.[28] As previously emphasized, managers converted to principles of good governance do not consider the initiatives they take—whether to reduce their ecological footprint, render the work of their employees less burdensome, establish healthy relations with their business partners, or provide better quality guarantees to consumers—as unavoidable yet costly expenses. In their view, insofar as investor confidence (and the shareholder value that expresses it) partially depends on a firm's good reputation, responsible practices should be included among its value-creating assets rather than among its operating costs.

Even so, bolstering the firm's image is not intended to divert practitioners of corporate governance from what, in all circumstances, remains their principal objective—meeting the financial expectations of current as well as potential shareholders. In order to be "competitive" here, no manager is unaware that the most appealing signals sent to investors derive from measures such as cutting the payroll, using cheaper and thus more polluting technologies, resorting to suppliers and subcontractors whose competitiveness stems from unscrupulous labor practices, relaxing quality controls on products, and establishing an efficient mechanism of tax "optimization." In other words, the art of sustaining a firm's shareholder value involves endowing it with an image of responsibility toward stakeholders and at the same time luring investors with the promise of performances that can be achieved only by irresponsible practices.

Concealing the contradiction between these images of the firm is among the most urgent tasks that managers must perform in order to valorize their company in the capital market. Revealing what corporate executives do their best to mask, however, is only part of the stakeholder activist's mission. Exposing the antinomy between the ethical and the financial criteria of asset appreciation makes it possible to awaken stakeholders to the subterfuge involved in the securitization of their interests. Yet for the awareness thus created to translate into activism, stakeholders must still equip themselves with the means to modify the relative degrees of social responsibility and social irresponsibility in investors' conjectures. In other words, stressing the contrast between a firm's actual practices and the reputation its directors seek to build may prove sufficient to unite stakeholders through shared indignation. Yet these indignant stakeholders won't become effective activists until their concrete strategy focuses on perceptions of the risk involved in investing in that enterprise.

Whereas trade unionism in the industrial age gauged the improvement of working conditions by establishing a balance of power with the employers, activists seeking to challenge the sway of shareholder value over managerial decisions must instead strive to target directly what Keynes called the "animal spirits" of investors so as to alter the "conventional basis of valuation" of the assets involved.[29] If our speculative age hinders activism aimed at raising wages because such policies are increasingly shaped by the expectations of financiers, then activists must focus on the volatility of investors' moods. More precisely, they must bank on the speculative character of the decisions made by purveyors of credit such that they reevaluate the hazards of socially and ecologically irresponsible investment policies.

At once the institutional form of industrial extortion and the preferential object of workers' demands, wages endowed their recipients with a consciousness of being an exploited class while providing them with the strategic framework for their fight against exploitation. As the privileged site of capitalist predation shifts from the job market to financial markets, however, corporate social responsibility assumes the dual status hitherto reserved for wages: symptom of shared wrong and index of activist strategy. On the one hand, corporate social responsibility constitutes an asset—a component of the aggregate value of the company's stock—that allows wage earners, customers, suppliers, but also taxpayers and neighbors respectively contributing to and affected by the activity of a firm to recognize themselves as stakeholders subjected to the speculations of investors. On the other hand, the securitization of their lot epitomized by CSR enables these various categories of stakeholders to see that altering the bets on which the treatment of their interests depends is the stake of their joint struggles.

Forging a class consciousness that is shared by the totality of stakeholders is, at first blush, a project full of pitfalls. The diverging interests of wage earners (concerned with averting a decrease in the elements making up what their employers call "labor costs") and consumers (preoccupied by the impact of a price increase on their purchasing power) seem difficult to overcome. The same is true for environmental activists, who—given their focus on the ecological damage caused by the exploitation of natural resources and the use of polluting technologies—seem likely to clash with the priorities of trade unions mandated to safeguard jobs in the very sectors in question. Generally speaking, efforts to reduce the price of commodities in for-profit businesses are bound to sustain competition between different categories of stakeholders.

While such obstacles to stakeholder solidarity cannot be underestimated, the rise of a new mode of corporate governance devoted to shareholder value greatly reduces their relative significance. For once the stock value of the firm becomes its managers' chief concern, it will not be long before this priority harms all economic agents who have a stake in but do not own a share of the company. In other words, the social and environmental impact of measures intended to bolster investor confidence is likely to persuade the various stakeholders that faced with the wrongs they suffer collectively, they would do better to combine their claims than to confine their struggle to their own particular interests.

Though necessary to forge a stakeholder class consciousness, identifying a shared antagonism is not sufficient to convert solidarity into mobilization. To translate a sense of shared grievance into a faith in the effectiveness of coordinated action, it is also incumbent on the organizations defending different stakeholders' rights—labor unions, consumer groups, promoters of fair trade, "green" activists—to help their affiliates recognize the links between their particular causes and, above all, to take initiatives where these affinities manifest themselves.

To influence the wagers that determine an enterprise's shareholder value, stakeholders can resort to a vast array of militant actions. Among them are calls for a boycott of the company's goods, class-action suits against practices of dubious legality, as well as campaigns promoting alternative production techniques or exposing compromising information supplied by whistleblowers. No doubt these various forms of activism have long been part of the repertoire of social movements. Thus, neither their expansion nor their success would require the emergence of a class consciousness common to all categories of stakeholders subjected to securitization. For activists, however, conceiving their own undertakings as stakeholders' struggles over credit allocation has considerable heuristic value with regard to the stakes and significance of their actions.

For example, once reframed as stakeholder activism, calls to boycott a brand associated with sweatshops or to denounce subcontractors that brutally exploit their workforce are no longer primarily aimed at raising consumer awareness.[30] More than seeking to influence the sentiments of a public that might consume the brand's products, activists now target the speculations of shareholders and, beyond them, of financial markets themselves. Better still, organizers can now create a virtuous circle between investor anxiety about the impact of irresponsible practices on the valuation of their portfolio and managers' doubts over the legitimacy of recourse to such practices for boosting the attractiveness of their firm to financiers.

The struggle of the Sioux tribe living in the Standing Rock Reservation clearly illustrates the significance and merit of such a strategic reorientation. Beginning in early 2016, a vast constellation of native and ecological activists from several countries mobilized to stop work on the Dakota Access Pipeline project or, at the very least, to divert the route of the oil pipeline threatening the water spring that irrigates the reservation where the Sioux live. This enormously expensive construction project, spanning over 1,100 miles and four US states, is intensely controversial. The controversy stems both from its environmental impact and from the affront it represents for the Native Americans whose sacred cemeteries adjoin the pipeline. Following a series of mobilizations and a broad-based social-media campaign centered on the efforts of the Sioux and their local allies, the pipeline was suspended in the closing weeks of the Obama administration. The government's authorization to continue the work was given on 7 February 2017, a few days after Donald Trump's investiture.[31]

On the evening of 8 November 2016, once the result of the presidential election was known, activists campaigning against the Dakota Access Pipeline realized that neither their campaign on the ground nor the legal actions they had taken to get the project condemned would be sufficient to prevent construction. Their forecast was soon confirmed: the initial legal decisions went against them, and once resumption of work had been authorized, the police proceeded with a violent evacuation of the activist encampments on the site. Far from withering away, however, the movement was to be relaunched thanks to a new initiative—a disinvestment campaign. Rather than banking everything on public sympathy and court judgments, the activists targeted the keystone of this gargantuan infrastructure project—its financing.

Thus "Defund DAPL" was born. The new campaign seeks to persuade private and institutional investors to withdraw their money from the banks funding the pipeline's construction—in particular, Wells Fargo and Bank of America—but also from the enterprises that co-own the structure.[32] Though the initiative is still young, the results are arguably far from negligible. Several billion dollars have been disinvested from companies linked to the project since early 2017. As one leading figure of the campaign, Native American activist Jackie Fielder, explains: "We have the economic power to show companies that when they finance an environmentally racist project...their bottom line will suffer."[33]

In the United States, activists achieved their first major victory when Seattle's municipal council voted against renewing the city's ties with Wells Fargo because of the bank's involvement in financing the Dakota Access Pipeline, thereby depriving the financial institution's coffers of $3 billion. Following this initial success, hundreds of activists from across the country immediately contacted the protagonists of the Seattle vote to ask for their advice. What the major city's municipal council had done, they believed, was set to become a new model. Out of these consultations came a "strategic guide" book and a website[34] intended to introduce as many people as possible to the art of launching a disinvestment campaign.

Thanks in part to publication of the guide, Seattle had indeed become a model in a very short space of time: in San Francisco, Los Angeles, New York, Bellingham, Raleigh, Albuquerque, Davis, and Santa Monica, but also in far-away Berlin, activists succeeded in putting a proposal to defund DAPL on their municipal council's agenda. And the victories have multiplied.[35] This was particularly the case in San Francisco, where the companies involved in financing and constructing the pipeline account for $1.2 billion of the city's portfolio. The Board of Supervisors adopted a resolution recommending that the city's present and future investments be examined from a social perspective—an optic intended to exclude protagonists of the Dakota Access Pipeline.

Defund DAPL is now spreading across the Atlantic Ocean. Beyond Berlin, the movement has been a striking success in Norway, where Storebrand, the country's largest private investor, managing $68 billion of assets, withdrew from financing the Dakota Access Pipeline. Its managers have sold $34.8 million of shares they held in three enterprises connected to the project: Phillips 66, Marathon Petroleum Corporation, and Enbridge. The Norwegian bank DNB and the investment company Odin Fund Management soon followed Storebrand's example. Likewise, the KLP pension fund, under pressure from the Sami

Parliament, sitting in Lapland and representing the Sami indigenous people, withdrew from the project's financing program. "Divestment is a last resort," conceded Matthew Smith, the head of Storebrand's sustainability team, because "when you divest from companies, you give up your possibility to influence companies to come to a better decision."[36]

Finally, among the infrastructure's creditors, the Dutch bank ING announced that it had sold its shares, worth $120 million, of the $2.5 billion loan that is financing the Dakota Access Pipeline's construction. Once again, disinvestment occurred after the failure of negotiations over rerouting the pipeline. ING not only sold $220 million of shares it owned in companies linked to the project but announced its decision not to do business with them in future.[37]

The campaign started by the Sioux is not an isolated case, especially in the area of fossil fuels. In December 2016, the annual report of investment activists Arabella Advisors, *The Global Fossil Fuel Divestment and Clean Energy Movement*, indicated that $5 billion had been disinvested from fossil fuels in fifteen months in seventy-six countries around the world.[38] In March 2017, a report by the Commonwealth Bank of Australia expressed concern at the fact that twelve coal mine projects in Australia had been temporarily put on hold for want of investors. Among them is Alpha Coal, a gigantic coal mining and extraction project in the Galilee Basin—a project that is particularly devastating to the environment. Here too a failure in the judicial process persuaded activists to switch targets from the corporation to the financiers. In 2014, Alpha Coal's promoters tasked the French bank Société Générale with refining the financial package and finding investors and loans for the mining project. After several months of strong civic pressure steered by three associations—Friends of the Earth, Attac, and Bizi!—Société Générale's director for sustainable development and CSR announced on 5 December 2014 that the bank was definitively withdrawing from the project. Nine years after its launch, Alpha Coal is at a standstill.

In business schools across the United States and Europe, corporate social and environmental responsibility figures among the most frequently debated subjects. On one side of the debate are the followers of Milton Friedman, who treat CSR as a sham, at best. Already in 1970, Friedman's opinion piece in the *New York Times* famously argued that a commercial firm's sole responsibility is to ensure an increase in its profits. On the other side, the proponents of CSR advocate a form of management that accommodates the demands of all the enterprise's stakeholders—those who have shares in it, but also those for whom its proper functioning is an important issue. In this controversy, where the arguments of both camps are as well oiled as they are predictable, it is worth noting that the position defended by disciples of the author of *Capitalism and Freedom* is paradoxically the one that remains closest to the old school of managerial capitalism. For Friedman's supporters are the ones who claim that it is up to public authorities and the law, not agents mandated by shareholders, to concern themselves with the rights and protections of stakeholders. For their part, those who call for the inclusion of stakeholders' interests in the domain of corporate governance show a better understanding of the "agency theory"—despite the fact that the original promoters of the theory were largely inspired by the Chicago School of Economics and trained at the University of Chicago. Indeed, according to supporters of CSR, what entices corporate managers to take good care of their stakeholders is the fact that investors value firms with a reputation for being virtuous.[39]

Now, regardless of where they stand, both sides of the debate over corporate social responsibility concur that there are only two types of actors at play. What they examine are the decisions made by managers mandated to create shareholder value and the judgments that shareholders and creditors pass on such decisions. As for stakeholders, the debate bears on whether their interests should be regarded as an external constraint or, conversely, as a component in the process of share valuation. Yet neither of these perspectives construes them as partners in the guessing game between managers and investors. Consequently, the challenge of stakeholder activism consists in recasting stakeholders and their interests not only as objects but also as subjects of speculation. What is at stake, so to speak, is elevating stakeholders to the status of bettors on the financial impact of a firm's social and environmental performance, alongside investors and managers.

To get a better idea of what such a status involves, it is worth revisiting the conditions that ensured the hegemony of what agency theory calls "corporate governance." The first condition was the removal of all restrictions on takeover bids, including hostile ones, and, more generally, the abolition of regulations intended to protect the integrity of firms from the greed of "raiders"—whether investment bankers or managers of speculative funds. Following the wishes of Law and Economics scholars, the license given to the spearheads of financial capitalism made possible the development of a market in corporate management—that is, a regime of competition where investors were able to replace those managers who were not successful enough at creating shareholder value.

No less than the threat of being dismissed if prospective returns did not match investors' expectations, the reinforcement of the board of directors' control over CEOs also proved significant in reconciling the managerial class with its new calling. Here too the Law and Economics perspective was instrumental in legitimizing tighter supervision over business executives. Proponents of the agency theory of the firm argued that only the appointment of "independent" administrators—by which they meant those attentive to the interests of shareholders rather than loyal to the managerial team—could compensate for the powerlessness of shareholders, who are too numerous and dispersed to influence the governance of their property.

While both the external and internal pressure to which managers are now exposed has compelled them to prioritize their firm's financial performance over other considerations, it is arguably their personal interest in the objectives they are required to pursue that has persuaded them to embrace wholeheartedly the new criteria of good governance. Even more than the growing precariousness of their jobs, what is primarily responsible for the sincere attachment of corporate managers to the pursuit of shareholder value is the increasing proportion of their compensation that takes the form of stock options and other types of income indexed to the share price of the firm they manage.

Finally, once trained in the requirements of their new profession by the stick of professional insecurity and the carrot of bonuses, company executives became able to make further progress thanks to the continuing education provided by rating agencies. The ratings regularly published by Moody's, Standard & Poor's, and Fitch enable managers to ascertain the merits of their recent decisions, since the assessments made by these three leading agencies play a decisive role in shaping investors' confidence in an entrepreneurial project. With time, however, what executives learn is how to tailor the management of their businesses to the preferences of the raters themselves—that is, to select the initiatives they take on the basis of the score they are likely to receive.[40]

Concurrently intended to inform managers about the measures that answer to investors' expectations and to help investors evaluate the near-future prospects of the equities that managers are seeking to valorize, rating agencies play a strategic role in maintaining the hegemony of financial capitalism. For this reason, rating agencies are the institution on which a stakeholders' movement should model itself. Increasing the relative importance of corporate social responsibility in the overall valuation of a share presupposes sending signals that can reorient the wagers of speculators by holding out the promise of returns from investing in projects whose good reputation is not misplaced and, correlatively, by attaching fears of losses to equities that reflect irresponsible choices. Thus, establishing "alternative" rating agencies—true to their model insofar as they play on the same motivations (that is, supplying markers intended to reduce uncertainty) yet alternative because their assessments are based on criteria other than prospective yield—is arguably the most effective way to act on the relationship between investors' anxieties and the efforts deployed by managers to assuage them.

Institutions and indices dedicated to "socially responsible investing" (SRI) have doubtless existed for a long time. Initially linked to churches—Methodist, in the case of the Pax World Fund created in 1971, Catholic in the case of the Credit Cooperative launched by the Catholic Committee against Hunger and for Development in 1983—funds with an ethical reputation diversified and multiplied thereafter. Steering clear of industries involved in manufacturing weapons was the Pax World Fund's raison d'être, but subsequent organizations sought to tap savings for companies or projects that offer other guarantees as well. In particular, they purport to select firms that are attentive to social rights, respectful of "sustainable development" norms, and observant of prudential management rules. In truth, however, these initiatives are largely about providing outlets for investors anxious to reconcile, at the lowest possible cost, their search for profits with their moral scruples as well as helping enterprises position themselves in the socially responsible investment market. In other words, what usually counts as socially responsible investment represents little more than a dash of soul to which financial capitalism treats itself on the cheap, as indicated by the companies listed on the MSCI KLD 400 Social Index—the standard index when it comes to responsible investment.

However, creating a niche for reconciling returns with a good conscience is not the only prospect that nonfinancial rating can proffer.[41] The scope of a social and environmental responsibility index will be very different if its production and publication are undertaken by stakeholders' organizations eager to pool their expertise and share their resources in order to promote their mode of benchmarking so as to rival financial rating agencies in influence. Although Moody's, Standard & Poor's, and Fitch notoriously contravene the most elementary rules of impartial arbitration—being funded by the very firms whose conduct they are assessing—they have nevertheless succeeded in establishing the oracular character of what they modestly call their "opinions."[42] The success of rating agencies stems from the functioning of financial markets: even when investors are aware that conflicts of interests cast a long shadow over the assessments produced by the three major agencies, they still assume that their peers will trust the agencies' ratings. And since they reckon that an asset's market value is a function of speculation, they will be inclined to ratify any judgment that they believe likely to be widely shared. Insofar as such mimetic attitudes are frequent enough to make them consequential, the biases blighting the work of evaluators admittedly do not prevent their evaluations from turning out to be correct.

Confirmed in their practices by the enduring trust of the investing community, credit rating agencies nonetheless trail a long succession of errors behind them, some of them with tragic consequences. Because they are paid to spur investors toward the equities most likely to appreciate in the short term, their appraisals are invariably indulgent toward manipulation of accounts and risky financial arrangements. Thus, it is not surprising that among the most resounding fraudulent collapses of the last two decades are firms to which the agencies had awarded the highest ratings. Even so, poor work and shortcomings in their code of ethics are insufficient to tarnish the authority of their views among savings collectors and thus to diminish their power to intimidate the institutions they assess.

While the hold of the three dispensaries that dominate the ratings market certainly warrants denunciation from the standpoint of stakeholders—but to which body could they be denounced?—what investees should primarily draw from the existence and power of rating agencies is a model for an effective form of activism. For those who seek to offset the influence of shareholder value on corporate management, investors' propensity to make their choices based on the sentiments they attribute to their colleagues is an invitation to get involved in engineering the hopes and fears that preside over the appreciation of an equity.

Need we be afraid that such engagement portends rallying, if not to financial capitalism itself, then at least to the mindset of its abettors? This would be to forget that labor union strategy in the late nineteenth century largely mirrored agreements among bosses to fix the level of wages. Indeed, given that the paradigm of the cartel inspired workers' organizations in their struggle in the labor market, there is no reason why, as the capital market becomes the center of gravity of social struggles, stakeholder activists would be compromised today if they were to borrow the modus operandi of credit rating agencies.

Suited to act upon the conjectures that inhabit the psyche of investors, the militant expertise involved in evaluating the nonfinancial impact of corporate governance will also prove instrumental for the emergence of a condition shared by various types of stakeholders. The research and cooperation required to assess a company's global imprint—to measure the combined impact of its conduct on climate, consumer health, workers' employment conditions, and state and local budgets—lay bare the connections between the various facets of its management. Consequently, constructing a common accreditation index that pools different perspectives and skill sets would prove conducive to the empowerment and solidarity of activists on apparently distinct fronts, such as employment law, environmental protection, consumer protection, and the fight against tax evasion.

Finally, adopting the rating paradigm also enables coalitions of stakeholders to conform to the time frame from which shareholders derive their power. Throughout the Fordist era, the relationship between employers and employees unfolded in a temporality punctuated by occasional conflicts, followed by more or less extended stretches of peace, with terms duly agreed upon or even inscribed in laws and compulsory regulations. The reign of investors is foreign to this segmentation of time. Because share prices are liable to change at any moment, its temporality is one of continuous pressure. While such pressure is exercised on company executives in the first instance, managers do their best to offload it onto stakeholders.

In our post-Fordist era of financialized capitalism, public authorities are still expected to act as referees striving to balance conflicting claims: in particular, governments remain tasked with arbitrating between the demands of credit providers and the interests of the citizens who elect those governments. In practice, however, their concern with preserving the financial attractiveness of their territory, as well as that of their own bills and bonds, leads them to subordinate the wishes of their constituents to the confidence of their creditors. Faced with the decay of states' arbitrating function, social movements can no longer envisage their modus operandi as an alternation between demands and compromises with business executives negotiated under the aegis of a third party deemed impartial. Henceforth, influencing corporate governance consists less in striking temporary deals with managers in the presence of a guarantor than in subjecting managers to the same constant harassment as investors inflect upon them. As we have seen, this is precisely the scope of a new form activism modeled on the operations of rating agencies: the collection of information and the publication of "opinions" on the risks of an investment represent the most efficient way—for those investees who seek to challenge the current hegemony of investors—to intervene in the incessant speculation from which the allocation of capital derives.

Designed to keep the stock market bullish, what Law and Economics scholars call corporate governance has transformed labor relations. On the one hand, due to the continuous pressure exercised by investors, business executives no longer see their job as a succession of balancing acts between the conflicting interests of wage earners and capital owners. As trade unions often charge, payroll is now treated as nothing more than an adjustment variable purported to maximize the returns on capital. Yet on the other hand, the criteria of competitiveness that credit providers impose on corporate managers are becoming the main stake of a new kind of social struggle. The main site of conflict is not the market where negotiations determine the price of labor, but the market where speculations establish the value of stocks. Rather than employees and their employers, stakeholders and shareholders are the protagonists of these struggles. Their privileged object is not wages but rather corporate social responsibility. Finally, while labor unions challenged industrial capitalists by replicating the tactics of bosses' cartels, for stakeholder activists faced with the hegemony of financial capitalism, the valuation techniques developed by rating agencies constitute a more suitable model.

It is not only in the private sector that financialization reshaped social conflicts. As public authorities opt to finance their budgets by issuing bonds instead of raising taxes, they become more anxious about reassuring the holders of their debt than about keeping their commitments to their constituents. The expectations of credit providers thus prove as detrimental to the exercise of popular sovereignty as they do to the bargaining power of labor unions. The next question, which the following chapter attempts to address, is whether investee activism can also be geared toward checking the preemption of political democracy by financial institutions.

1. "Investors" is a very broad category: it includes, on the one hand, individuals, private companies, and public agencies seeking to collect a return on their savings and, on the other hand, institutions whose purpose is satisfying such pursuits. In addition to the distinctions relative to modes of investment (loans, shares, but also options and futures contracts) and to monetary creation, which separates banks from nonmonetary financial intermediaries, Regulation School economists provide a typology of financial intermediation agencies based on their occupational specialty and particular responsibilities. The types include: *banks*, which tend to be "universal" insofar as they convert deposits into credit, help corporations or states raise capital, and manage portfolios on behalf of third parties; *institutional investors*, composed of pension funds (in countries operating the system of funded pension provision) and insurance companies providing life insurance and major risk coverage; *mutual funds* involved in the management of portfolios belonging to individual savers but also to nonfinancial enterprises and institutional investors; *hedge funds*, which pool the funds of selected clients with the promise of higher returns than market indices; *private equity* funds specializing in leveraged buyouts; *venture capitalists*, who finance the creation and development of enterprises—particularly start-ups—not quoted on the stock market; *sovereign funds*, whose resources derive for the most part from the income generated by their country's natural resources and exchange reserves; *university endowment funds*, financed by alumni, companies, or foundations; and *public smoothing funds for pay-as-you-go pension systems* in countries where this system is in operation, which, unlike institutional investors, have no contractual commitments to individual savers. This typology is derived from Tristan Auvray, Thomas Dallery, and Sandra Rigot, *L'entreprise liquidée: La finance contre l'investissement* (Paris: Michalon Éditeur, 2016), pp. 68–76; and Michel Aglietta and Sandra Rigot, *Crise et rénovation de la finance* (Paris: Odile Jacob, 2008), pp. 177–208.

2. Monica Prasad and Greta Krippner stress the fact that in the United States, initial deregulation of financial markets was justified in the name of democratizing credit and supported for that reason by a number of grass-roots movements.

Indeed, throughout the 1970s, both consumer activists such as Ralph Nader and pensioners' groups such as the Gray Panthers rebelled against the conditions of access to markets, which they considered biased toward corporations. In their view, small savers and households seeking loans should enjoy the same opportunities as the managers of large firms. However, once "discriminatory" provisions were done away with, disintermediation did not deliver credit democracy, but an unprecedented hypertrophy and concentration of savings collectors. For instance, Gerald Davis indicates that Fidelity, the largest of the mutual funds, has become the principal shareholder in more than 10 percent of the US companies quoted on the stock market. See Gerald Davis, "A New Finance Capitalism?: Mutual Funds and Ownership Re-Concentration in the United States," *European Management Review* 5 (2008), pp. 11–21; Davis, *Managed by the Markets: How Finance Re-Shaped America* (Oxford: Oxford University Press, 2009), p. 19. On the retrospectively paradoxical "populist" impetus behind financial deregulation, see Monica Prasad, *The Politics of Free Markets: The Rise of Neoliberal Economic Policies in Britain, France, Germany, and the United States* (Chicago: University of Chicago Press, 2006), pp. 66–82; Greta R. Krippner, *Capitalizing on Crisis: The Political Origins of the Rise of Finance* (Cambridge, MA: Harvard University Press, 2012), pp. 80–82.

3. "We cannot only have a plan for Wall Street," proclaimed Democratic candidate Barack Obama on 19 September 2008 during a campaign event in Florida. "We must also help Main Street." Nearly four years later, on 22 January 2012, François Hollande delivered a speech that would haunt him throughout his five-year term: "my real opponent has no name, no face, no party. It will never stand as a candidate, will never be elected, and yet it governs. This opponent is the world of finance." That day, carried away by his own momentum, the Socialist candidate also declared himself in favor of introducing a tax on financial transactions and creating a public rating agency. He even mentioned that once elected, he would ban stock options and regulate bonuses.

4. On the stages and successive accidents of financialization up to the 2008 crisis, see David Harvey, *The Enigma of Capital and the Crises of Capitalism* (New York: Oxford University Press, 2010); David McNally, *Global Slump: The*

Economics and Politics of Crisis and Resistance (Oakland: PM Press, 2011). On the collapse of Long-Term Capital Management—a fund created by two Nobel Prize winners—see Roger Lowenstein, *When Genius Failed: The Rise and Fall of Long-Term Capital Management* (New York: Random House, 2000). On the history of Enron, see Bethany McLean and Peter Elkind, *The Smartest Guys in the Room: The Amazing Rise and Scandalous Fall of Enron* (New York: Portfolio, 2003).

5. See Karl Marx and Frederick Engels, *Collected Works*, vol. 35 (London: Lawrence and Wishart, 1996), pp. 177–86: *Capital*, vol. 1, part 2, chapter 6, "The Buying and Selling of Labour Power."

6. "For the conversion of his money into capital, therefore, the owner of money must meet in the market with the free labourer, free in the double sense, that as a free man he can dispose of his labour power as his own commodity, and that on the other hand he has no other commodity for sale, is short of everything necessary for the realisation of his labour power." Marx and Engels, *Collected Works*, vol. 35, p. 179.

7. This change in condition has already been explored by Luc Boltanski and Ève Chiapello in *The New Spirit of Capitalism* (1999), trans. Gregory Elliott (London: Verso, 2006), chapter 2. Their survey of management literature from the 1990s leads the authors to identify the advent of what they call a "projective city," where individuals no longer identify with an existence compartmentalized between the spheres of work, private life, and citizenship. Instead, these new citizens envision their lives as a portfolio of activities corresponding to so many temporary projects. Moving between projects is thus a way of life whose environmental correlate is the network and where the social, professional, civic, and private spheres tend to blur or at least overlap. While Boltanski and Chiapello underscore the importance of reputation—that is, credit—in managing portfolios of activities, the management literature they study does not yet bring out the role of investors and the market in which they operate as the privileged site of value creation.

8. That the credit-seeking project is to capital markets what the profit-seeking commodity trader is to nonfinancial markets—the profile common to all agents recognized by these markets—does not necessarily entail that the first

has *succeeded* the second as the universal condition ascribed by capitalism. For investors and their worldview admittedly predate the financialization of capitalism distinctive of recent decades, while commercial law continues to govern the relations between buyers and sellers of commodities. Yet by virtue of their conjunction, the emancipation of financial flows, the rise of new industrial powers, and the development of information, communication, and transportation technologies have prompted a deep transformation of the regime of capital accumulation, which has resulted in a genuinely unprecedented subordination of employers' power to investors' preferences. Such is the effect of the revolution described by Gerald Davis in *Managed by the Markets*. See also Michael Useem, *Investor Capitalism: How Money Managers Are Changing the Face of Corporate America* (New York: Basic Books, 1996); William Lazonick, "'Evolution of the New Economy Business Model," *Business and Economic History On-Line* 3 (2005); https://www.thebhc.org/sites/default/files/lazonick.pdf.

9. On the functioning of financial markets, and especially the stock market, see John Maynard Keynes, *The General Theory of Employment, Interest and Money* (1936; London: Macmillan, 1973), chapter 12. On financial markets' structural instability, see Hyman P. Minsky, *Stabilizing an Unstable Economy* (New Haven: Yale University Press, 1986); Minsky, "The Financial Instability Hypothesis," *Working Paper* 74, The Jerome Levy Economics Institute of Bard College, May 1992, http://www.levyinstitute.org/pubs/wp74.pdf; Minsky, "Uncertainty and the Institutional Structure of Capitalist Economies: Remarks upon Receiving the Veblen-Commons Award," *Journal of Economic Issues* 30 (1996), pp. 357–68. On the distinctive mode of valuation of financial markets, see André Orléan, *L'empire de la valeur* (Paris: Éditions du Seuil, 2013), pp. 231–312.

10. See, in particular, Benjamin Coriat, *L'atelier et le chronomètre: Essai sur le taylorisme, le fordisme et la production de masse* (Paris: Christian Bourgois Éditeur, 1979), pp. 89–106; Michel Aglietta, *A Theory of Capitalist Regulation: The US Experience*, trans. David Fernbach (1979; London: Verso, 2000), chapters 2 and 3.

11. See, in particular, Rosa Luxemburg, "Social Reform or Revolution," in Peter Hudis and Kevin B. Anderson (eds.), *The Rosa Luxemburg Reader* (New

York: Monthly Review Press, 2004). On the history of the trade-union movement and its different wings, see Wolfgang Abendroth, *A Short History of the European Working Class*, trans. Nicholas Jacobs and Brian Trench (London: New Left Books, 1972); Marcel van der Linden and Wayne Thorpe (eds.), *Revolutionary Syndicalism: An International Perspective* (Aldershot: Gower/Scolar Press, 1990); Nelson Lichtenstein, *State of the Union: A Century of American Labor* (Princeton: Princeton University Press, 2003); Jean-Louis Robert, Friedhelm Boll, and Antoine Prost (eds.), *L'invention du syndicalisme: Le syndicalisme en Europe occidentale à la fin du 19e siècle* (Paris: Éditions de la Sorbonne, 1997).

12. Edward Shorter and Charles Tilly, *Strikes in France 1830–1968* (Cambridge: Cambridge University Press, 1974); Michelle Perrot, *Jeunesse de la grève: France 1870–1871* (Paris: Éditions du Seuil, Paris, 1984); Coriat, *L'atelier et le chronomètre*; Beverly Silver, *Forces of Labor: Workers' Movements and Globalization since 1870* (Cambridge: Cambridge University Press, 2003); Mario Tronti, *Workers and Capital* (forthcoming, Verso, 2019).

13. Greta Krippner shows how the political and monetary authorities in the United States blamed the stagflation of the 1970s on both excessive and conflicting demands emanating from various sectors of civil society. According to the common sense of the time, consumers, enterprises, municipalities, and labor unions all kept asking for more, even though there was no economic growth to meet their expectations, and credit was becoming increasingly scarce. While some on the Left regarded the growing pressure on liberal regimes and the galloping inflation that it generated as the precursor of a terminal crisis of capitalism, those who would soon be labeled neoconservative lamented the state of "democratic overload" in which Western governments found themselves and thus called for an authoritarian reaction on the part of the state—one that should be modeled on the disciplining intervention of a stern and responsible family head. Eventually, however, political leaders did not heed the call of those who reckoned that too much democracy was killing democracy—for example, the sociologist Daniel Bell, author of *The Cultural Contradictions of Capitalism* (New York: Basic Books, 1976) or Michel Crozier, Samuel Huntington, and Joji Watanuki, authors of *The Crisis of Democracy* (New York: New York University Press,

1975). Instead, by the turn of the 1980s, they let themselves be persuaded by Milton Friedman and his followers in Chicago that the task of sifting demands for resources should be left to the markets. See Krippner, *Capitalizing on Crisis*, pp. 58–85; see also Wolfgang Streeck, *Buying Time: The Delayed Crisis of Democracy Capitalism*, trans. Patrick Camiller (London: Verso, 2014), chapters 1 and 2.

14. Krippner, *Capitalizing on Crisis*, pp. 86–106.

15. Keynes, *The General Theory of Employment, Interest and Money*, p. 154.

16. On the premises of the ascent of financial capitalism in the United States and the United Kingdom in the second half of the 1970s, see Daniel Stedman Jones, *Masters of the Universe: Hayek, Friedman, and the Birth of Neoliberal Politics* (Princeton: Princeton University Press, 2012), pp. 241–53; Krippner, *Capitalizing on Crisis*, pp. 82–85.

17. See the founding article by Michael C. Jensen and William H. Meckling, "The Theory of the Firm: Managerial Behavior, Agency Cost and Ownership Structure," *Journal of Financial Economics* 3 (1976), pp. 305–60. See also Michael Jensen, *Foundations of Organizational Strategy* (Cambridge, MA: Harvard University Press, 1998).

18. R. Edward Freeman, Jeffrey S. Harrison, and Andrew Wicks, *Managing for Stakeholders: Survival, Reputation, and Success* (New Haven: Yale University Press, 2007).

19. Carl Kaysen thus wrote that "management sees itself as responsible to stockholders, employees, customers, the general public and, perhaps most important, the firm itself as an institution." Kaysen, "The Social Significance of the Modern Corporation," *American Economic Review* 47 (1957), pp. 311–19, quoted in Davis, *Managed by the Markets*, p. 74. See also Richard Sennett, *The Culture of the New Capitalism* (New Haven: Yale University Press, 2006), pp. 15–83.

20. It is not only among publicly traded corporations that the pursuit of capital gains takes precedence over sales revenues. The same is true for start-ups financed by venture capitalists (VCs), even if their strategy is predicated on different priorities than what corporate managers identify as "best practices." Indeed, what VCs look for are entrepreneurs who vow to discover and then

dominate new markets. Because such ambitious projects require long periods of returnless investments, the losses that the balance sheets of start-ups display are often registered as positive signals, indicative that the promised conquest is under way. Thus, in the eyes of investors whose main concern is the capital value of their portfolio, the decision of a start-up to refrain from distributing dividends in order to secure its hold on a market is deemed as enticing as the announcement by a corporation that it will spend less on either payroll or research and development in order to increase the remuneration of its shareholders.

21. See, in particular, Tristan Auvray and Thomas Dallery, *L'entreprise liquidée: La finance contre l'investissement* (Paris: Michalon Éditeur, 2016), pp. 99–101; Olivier Weinstein, *Pouvoir, finance et connaissance: Les transformations de l'entreprise capitaliste entre XXe et XXIe siècle* (Paris: Éditions La Découverte, 2010), pp. 97–109; Gerald Davis, "New Directions in Corporate Governance," *Annual Review of Sociology* 31 (2005), pp. 143–62; Davis, *Managed by the Markets*, pp. 93–96.

22. Eugene Fama, "Agency Problems and the Theory of the Firm," *Journal of Political Economy* 88.2 (1980), pp. 163–74. For a Keynesian critique of the efficient market hypothesis, see Robert J. Shiller, "From Efficient Market Theory to Behavioral Finance," *Journal of Economic Perspectives* 17.1 (2003), pp. 83–104.

23. In the United States, during the 1970s, the onslaught against allegedly almighty managers fed on two related motives: the declining productivity of vertically integrated US corporations—especially compared with their German and Japanese competitors—and their propensity to ward off their decline by resorting to horizontal integration: that is, to make up for their waning profitability by becoming tentacular conglomerates in which executives would further their quest for hegemony at the expense of shareholders. See, in particular, Ernie Englander and Alan Kaufman, "The End of Managerial Ideology: From Corporate Social Responsibility to Corporate Social Indifference," *Enterprise and Society*, 5.3 (2004), pp. 404–50.

24. The standard promotion of the new mode of corporate governance can be found in Michael Jensen, "Value Maximization, Stakeholder Theory, the Corporate Objective Function," *Business Ethics Quarterly* 12 (2002). For a historical and

critical account of its rise to prominence, see Englander and Kaufman, "The End of Managerial Ideology"; Gerald Davis, *Managed by the Markets*, pp. 82–87; William Lazonick and Mary O'Sullivan, "Maximizing Shareholder Value: A New Ideology for Corporate Governance," *Economy and Society* 29 (2000), pp. 13–35; William Lazonick, "The Financialization of the U.S. Corporation: What Has Been Lost, and How It Can Be Regained," *Seattle University Law Review* 36 (2012), pp. 857–909.

25. On the history of the notion of corporate social responsibility, see Archie B. Carroll, "A History of Corporate Social Responsibility: Concepts and Practices," in Andrew Crane, Dirk Matten, Abagail McWilliams, Jeremy Moon, and Donald S. Siegel (eds.), *The Oxford Handbook of Corporate Social Responsibility* (Oxford: Oxford University Press, 2008), pp. 19–46. See also David Vogel, *The Market for Virtue: The Potential and Limits of Corporate Social Responsibility* (Washington: Brookings Institution Press, 2005); Michel Capron and Françoise Quairel-Lanoizelée, *La responsabilité sociale d'entreprise* (Paris: Éditions La Découverte, 2010). For a critique of the pretentions of CSR, see Gerard Hanlon, "Rethinking Corporate Social Responsibility and the Role of the Firm—On the Denial of Politics," in *The Oxford Handbook of Corporate Social Responsibility*, pp. 156–72.

26. On the history of measurements of profit and the relations between what pertains to profitable activities and not-for-profit activities in US capitalism, see Jonathan Levy, "Accounting for Profit and the History of Capital," *Critical Historical Studies* 1.2 (2014), pp. 171–214.

27. In his *Pouvoir, finance et connaissance*, Olivier Weinstein reaches the same conclusion (p. 182). See also Michèle Descolonges and Bernard Saincy, *Les entreprises seront-elles un jour responsables?* (Paris: La Dispute, 2004).

28. Securitization is the operation that converts a debt into an alienable financial asset subject to valuation.

29. According to Keynes, the utilitarian psychology that informed neoclassical economics at the time—and that for the most part still does—misunderstands human motivations: "Most, probably, of our decisions to do something positive, the full consequences of which will be drawn out over many days to

come, can only be taken as a result of animal spirits—of a spontaneous urge to action rather than inaction, and not as the outcome of a weighted average of quantitative benefits multiplied by quantitative probabilities." Keynes, *The General Theory of Employment, Interest and Money*, p. 161.

30. On the limits of boycotts directed exclusively at the public, see Timothy M. Devinney, Pat Auger, and Giana M. Eckhardt, *The Myth of the Ethical Consumer* (Cambridge: Cambridge University Press, 2010). However, it can be argued that thanks to the development of social networks, campaigns for boycotts have gained in effectiveness and rapidity. This is attested, in particular, by the misadventures of Abercrombie and Fitch, the multinational casual-wear retailer. The inflammatory managing director of the brand, Mike Jeffries, regularly displays his contempt for those whom he regards as undesirables: the ugly, the fat, the handicapped, and the poor. A target of boycott calls since 2004, the firm was barely affected until May 2013. Yet following publication of an article where an Abercrombie and Fitch manager declared that his enterprise "prefers to burn clothing than to give it to the poor," Greg Karber, a young American author, posted a video on YouTube in which he is seen distributing Abercrombie and Fitch clothing to homeless people and launching a campaign, #FitchThe-Homeless, widely relayed on social networks. At the time of this writing, the video had been viewed more than 8 million times. In 2017, the stock market capitalization of Abercrombie and Fitch stood at $777 million, compared with $5 billion ten years earlier. The share price has likewise fallen nearly 85 percent over the same period. More recently, the election of Donald Trump has given new impetus to boycott calls. In addition to the #GrabYourWallet campaign directly targeting Ivanka Trump and her clothing-and-accessories brand, the startup Uber has been one of the main victims of these boycotts. In late January 2017, whereas the VTC Lyft company promised the sum of $1 million to the American Civil Liberties Union (ACLU) to support its action against Trump's Muslim ban, its main competitor and market leader, Uber was accused not only of breaking a strike at JFK International Airport in New York by taxi drivers who were demonstrating their opposition to the ban on Muslim immigrants sought by the administration, but also of capitalizing on the move. This attitude

occasioned Uber a sizeable number of requests to cancel subscriptions. More than two hundred thousand people cancelled their application in a single weekend. Five days later, Travis Kalanick, then Uber's managing director, announced he was abandoning his participation in the US president's economic council, which he had agreed to take part in a month earlier.

31. During the election campaign, it was revealed that Donald Trump holds between $500,000 and $1 million in shares of Energy Transfer Partners, the enterprise behind the Dakota Access Pipeline, and more than $500,000 in shares of Philips 66, which will own 25 percent of the pipeline when it has been completed. The managing director of Energy Transfer Partners invested more than $100,000 in the Republican candidate's campaign.

32. The defunddapl.org website gives an exhaustive list of the financial institutions that are implicated in the construction of the pipeline and delineates a number of actions that can be taken against these institutions. Activists are urged to write to the CEOs of DAPL sponsors in order to ask them to renounce supporting such a toxic project; publish the letters they have sent on social media and tweet periodically to keep them in the public eye; divest from the incriminated institutions, to the extent that they had their personal savings handled by them, and give as much publicity as possible to their withdrawals; check whether their local governments use the services of financial institutions involved in the financing of DAPL and, if they do, pressure them into switching to other creditors; and keep the defunding movement alive through the organization of public events such as marches and sit-ins in front of the buildings of DAPL financers and city halls of municipalities where mayors refuse to look for alternative credit providers.

33. Julia Carrie Wong, "Private Investor Divests $34,8M from Firms Tied to Dakota Access Pipeline," *The Guardian*, 1 March 2017.

34. Mazaska Talks (Money Talks), "The Boycott: Put Your Money Where Your Solidarity Is," https://mazaskatalks.org.

35. Jimmy Tobias, "These Cities Are Pulling Billions from the Banks That Support the Dakota Access Pipeline," *Nation*, 20 March 2017.

36. Wong, "Private Investor Divests $34.8M from Firms Tied to the Dakota Access Pipeline."

37. Julia Carrie Wong, "Dakota Access Pipeline: ING Sells Stake in Major Victory for Divestment Push," *The Guardian*, 21 March 2017.

38. Arabella Advisors, *The Global Fossil Fuel Divestment and Clean Energy Movement*, December 2016, https://www.arabellaadvisors.com/wp-content/uploads/2016/12/Global_Divestment_Report_2016.pdf.

39. See, especially, Paul C. Godfrey, Craig B. Merrill, and Jared M. Hansen, "The Relationship between Corporate Social Responsibility and Shareholder Value: An Empirical Test of the Risk Management Hypothesis," *Strategic Management Journal* 30 (2009), pp. 425–45; Michael E. Porter and Mark R. Kramer, "Creating Shared Value: How to Reinvent Capitalism—and Unleash a Wave of Innovation and Growth," *Harvard Business Review*, January–February 2011; republishedathttp://www.creativeinnovationglobal.com.au/wp-content/uploads/Shared-value-Harvard-business-review.pdf. For a critique of this model, see Hanlon, "Rethinking Corporate Social Responsibility and the Role of the Firm."

40. On the discipline imposed by the rating agencies, see, especially, Alexandra Ouroussoff, *Wall Street at War: The Secret Struggle for the Global Economy* (Cambridge: Polity, 2010). On the work of the rating agencies and their role in the 2008 financial crisis, see John Ryan, "Credit Rating Agencies: Are They Credible?," *International Journal of Public Policy* 9.1/2 (2013), pp. 4–22.

41. Established in the late 1990s, when the issue of sustainable development became prominent in public debates, the first nonfinancial rating agencies assessed enterprises in accordance with social and environmental criteria. As the number of these agencies has multiplied over the last two decades, they have developed different methods of evaluation. The least demanding among social and environmental rating agencies—of which the French Vigeo Eiris (http://www.vigeo-eiris.com) is a good example—give their rating based on a questionnaire completed by the companies themselves. Managers are thus asked to report on their own practices regarding labor relations, sustainability, and ethics. In March 2017, acting in partnership with the main financial operator in the Eurozone—Euronext—Vigeo Eiris launched an index called "Cac 40 Gouvernance." Illustrative of the agency's reliance on what the firms they rate choose to disclose, major and hardly irreproachable corporations such as

AXA, BNP Paris, Engie, Vinci, Sociéte Générale, and Total figure at the top of the ranking.

Less indulgent toward the firms under scrutiny, the mode of evaluation invented by the startup Provenance (https://www.provenance.org/whitepaper) uses blockchain technology—the transparent, secure technology for storing and transmitting Bitcoin information—to inform consumers about the provenance of commodity as well as about the social and environmental conditions under which it is produced. For example, the site makes it possible to trace the manufacture of a T-shirt from cotton field via the storage shelf to its shipment. Because blockchain technology makes fraud impossible, Provenance can ensure that the transactions submitted to the startup's scrutiny cannot be falsified and are recorded in linear, chronological, and indelible fashion on a public database. There is therefore total transparency. However, the system established by Provenance has no constraining character: only enterprises wishing to display their mode of production transparently adhere to it. But once enrolled in the process, falsification of data is impossible.

Finally, more ambitious initiatives are emerging, such as the Corporate Human Rights Benchmark (https://business-humanrights.org/en/chrb), launched in London on 13 March 2017. The outcome of longstanding collaborative work between NGOs and local communities, this project aims to offer the first large-scale public evaluation of respect for human rights by enterprises along the entirety of their subcontracting chain. The evaluation is made on the basis of a detailed analysis of public documents dealing with child labor, labor-union freedoms, workers' health and security, women's rights, climate justice, and the use of natural resources. Some of the protagonists of Corporate Human Rights Benchmark, such as the Swiss data provider ESG RepRisk, evaluate nearly sixty thousand enterprises in their database. Their assessments are based on reports drafted by about ten thousand NGOs throughout the world, but also on critical examination of media articles and social networks. By way of comparison with agencies such as Vigeo Eiris, among the corporations scrutinized by Corporate Human Rights Benchmark, only six are favorably rated.

42. Accused of having played a significant role in the 2008 financial crisis,

especially because they awarded the highest ratings to the financial products responsible for the crash, the three major agencies invoked freedom of expression and, in particular, the First Amendment of the US Constitution, arguing that their ratings are mere opinions. On this point, see Theresa Nagy, "Credit Ratings Agencies and the First Amendment: Applying Constitutional Journalistic Protections to Subprime Mortgage Litigation," *Minnesota Law Review* 94 (2009), pp. 140–67.

CHAPTER TWO

The Bonds of Governmental Policy

TAX AND DEBT

As financial capitalism becomes hegemonic, the three-way relationship at the heart of the postwar social compact—employees, employers, and representatives of the state—is gradually superseded by a different set of triangular interactions involving shareholders (or more generally, investors), managers, and stakeholders. In this new configuration, governments are conspicuously absent, at least as arbiters of social conflicts between labor and capital. Yet state actors hardly disappear altogether. For while the deregulation of financial transactions and of financial engineering to which they attended considerably dent their capacity to act as mediators between shareholders and stakeholders, public officials nonetheless remain one of the partners in another three-sided game played in the bond market.

Today, as the German sociologist Wolfgang Streeck has shown, the rulers of the most developed states live in a condition of dual dependency. Though pledged to the voters who elect them, they are also subject to the whims of bondholders. The votes of the former confer democratic legitimacy on their salaries and authority, while the choices of the latter dictate the size and shape of the budgets they control. This situation has existed for only a little over three decades.[1] Before the late 1970s, states in the Euro-Atlantic world financed themselves largely through their tax revenues and, as the sociologist Benjamin

Lemoine points out, through the so-called nonnegotiable part of their debt—sums required to be deposited in the treasury account by national financial institutions or direct advances to the government from the state central bank.[2]

Until the late 1960s, this mode of financing enabled public authorities to retain their relative autonomy, thereby ensuring social peace without generating excessive inflation. It was buoyed by strong growth rooted in mass production for domestic markets and consumption by the wage-earning classes. In the subsequent decade, however, both the stagnation affecting industrialized countries (due to the exhaustion of the Fordist mode of capital accumulation) and the new levers at the disposal of capital owners (gained through floating currencies, liberalization of energy prices, and deregulation of financial engineering) resulted in a fateful change of course.

Initially, as Streeck argues, governments of industrialized countries primarily feared rekindling the endemic protests of workers, minorities, and students that had marked the 1960s. State representatives thus relied on indexing salaries to prices in order to shield the purchasing power of wage earners from the declining productivity of the economy.[3] Yet holders of financial assets rapidly grew intolerant of the depreciation of their portfolios brought about by recourse to inflation as a tool of social appeasement. By the mid-1970s, savings could find a home in speculative alternatives to productive investments—courtesy of the 1971 collapse of the Bretton Woods system of fixed exchange rates, the volatility of oil prices in the wake of the 1973 embargo, and the ensuing comeback of derivative financial products that had been banned following the Great Depression. Credit providers, more capable of shielding their liquidities from the vagaries of the real economy, now found themselves in a position to make their grievances heard. Indeed, it took only a few years for the threat of what amounted to an investors' strike to prove effective. In 1979, shortly after his appointment as head of the Federal Reserve, Paul Volcker dramatically switched priorities: appeasing asset owners rather than wage earners was the new order of the day. His decision to clamp down on the money supply caused interest rates to rise dramatically. Drawn from Milton Friedman's monetarist rulebook, the resulting shock put a definitive end to the inflationary consequences of Keynesian policies in a time of declining growth, and by that token, to the complaints of asset owners and managers.[4]

Designed to curb demand, this new monetary policy immediately plunged the United States—and, in its wake, all developed countries—into a violent recession. The social impact of the monetarist turn proved especially harsh at home. This was also due to the considerable strain that mass unemployment put on welfare-state services, a difficult situation that was amplified by Ronald Reagan's decision to make good on his campaign promise to gratify the American people with unprecedented tax cuts. Convinced that Western wage-earning classes were too attached to full employment and decent social benefits to tolerate the neoliberal agenda on both monetary and fiscal matters, many observers forecast a rapid failure for the conservative revolution. Yet Friedman's and Hayek's most ardent disciples not only remained in power until the end of the decade, they also laid the groundwork for a new art of collecting and managing public finance, one that would soon be adopted by all Organisation for Economic Co-operation and Development (OECD) member states.

In *Capitalizing on Crisis*, sociologist Greta Krippner traces the political success of this cocktail—Volcker's monetary asceticism mixed with Reagan's tax rebates—to investors' enthusiasm about such policies around the world. Attracted by high returns on investments and a favorable fiscal regime, holders of liquid assets everywhere rushed into US markets. While the sudden influx of foreign and domestic capital prompted a rapid fall in interest rates, what survived the monetarist shock was the determination of all governments to make the attractiveness of their countries to investors their first priority. Following the lead of the Reagan administration and its British partner, Margaret Thatcher, elected officials of the developed world abandoned both fiscal and monetary Keynesian policies. Instead of pursuing full employment by sustaining demand, they kept up the fight against inflation (even though there was no longer any inflation to quell) and resorted to supply-side measures (such as tax cuts and market deregulation) to stimulate economic growth.[5]

In the 1980s, the first cohort of rulers who made it their priority to create a welcoming environment for financial capital had thus already agreed to deprive themselves of a significant portion of tax revenue formerly devoted to social programs and public utilities. Yet despite their propensity to castigate bureaucracy and denounce governmental handouts, the same "revolutionary" rulers could not afford to discard an essential function of the welfare state: dissipating social conflict. While conservative revolutionaries confronted labor unions, slashed social programs, and privatized public goods, they still sought to maintain the resources necessary to appease their citizens by borrowing in financial markets the revenue lost in tax reductions.

A transition ensued, to adopt Streeck's terminology, from "tax state" to "debt state." Neoliberal rhetoric notwithstanding, this did not revive the classical liberal ideal of small government. Rather than simply reneging on their postwar commitments, elected representatives embarked on a mission to construct a new social compact. Though still about harmonizing divergent interests, the art of governing would now involve balancing the requirements of *international lenders* with the needs of *domestic citizenries* for whom money was borrowed.[6] While these two constituencies harbored conflicting expectations, governments saw room for conciliation between them. On the one hand, institutional investors—pension funds, insurance companies, and mutual funds—were eager to line their portfolios with reliable securities such as treasury bills and bonds issued by trustworthy states. On the other hand, the funds thereby collected enabled public officials to provide services and maintain utilities hitherto primarily financed by fiscal revenues and social contributions. To keep lenders confident in their ability to honor their debt, governments had to warn their citizens that the welfare state must be mended in order to survive.

Though successful enough at keeping social protest and inflation at bay, the increasing substitution of government debt for tax levies afforded rulers but a temporary respite. For while it enabled them to attract investors without alienating voters, the combination of loans and tax cuts resulted in rapidly expanding deficits, which eventually raised the anxiety level of credit providers. To dissuade nervous lenders from turning their back on their bills and bonds, governments had no other choice than to devote an ever-increasing slice of their budget to debt servicing. Yet doing so compelled them to renounce the very programs they had sought to preserve by going into debt.

Still committed to appeasing their constituents, but already too dependent on borrowed funds to question the legitimacy of bondholders' requirements, the political leaders who inherited the predicament of the "debt state" in the early 1990s now sought to preserve the conservative revolution's fledgling social compact by introducing a second innovation. Reckoning that they could not stake their reelection on a new round of debt-financed promises—since swelling deficits would raise the interest rates on their bills and bonds to prohibitive levels—governments decided to support private consumption by encouraging households to follow in their footsteps. Put another way, they sought to foster their citizens' ability to indebt themselves. Facilitating access to personal credit thus became the privileged means by which states sought to curb the expansion of their own debt while keeping taxes low and the living standards of their constituents ostensibly unchanged.

Spearheaded by champions of the "third way" during the 1990s—the Clinton administration in the United States and Tony Blair's government in the United Kingdom—the rapid expansion of private debt made it temporarily possible to contain public deficits. What easy access to consumer credit did not alter, however, was the propensity of governments to choose loans over taxes. Indeed, in the United States, the terrorist attacks of 9/11 impelled the Bush administration to preside over a simultaneous and dramatic increase of both private and public debt. On the one hand, George W. Bush borrowed massively to finance his campaigns in Afghanistan and Iraq—which translated into budget cuts for social programs and public investments other than the military. Yet on the other hand, to elicit the American people's assent to a "war against terror," government agencies did their upmost to further improve the accessibility of private credit.

Remarkably, the ensuing real estate and banking crises, followed by the Great Recession of 2009, did not fundamentally change this dual-track policy. Thereafter, governments have only refrained from relying on public and private debt simultaneously. In the wake of the Lehman Brothers bankruptcy, state authorities resorted first to deficit spending in order to prevent the private banking system from collapsing, then to transferring the cost of their rescue mission to their own citizens by subjecting them to fiscal austerity programs, and finally to offsetting the recessive consequence of these measures by allowing for the gradual reinflation of private debt bubbles.

While treasury bills and bonds are issued to make up for declining fiscal revenues, consumer credit incentives are provided to limit the growth of public deficits. Combined and used in succession, these two ways of financing social demands are what Streeck associates with a transition from "debt state" to "consolidation state."[7] Practitioners of this new mode of government claim that unlike their lax predecessors, they can lighten the tax and debt burdens the state imposes on its taxpayers and their descendants, respectively, while also managing any damage to its credit with investors. Better still, they argue that improving the management of public finances and prioritizing interest payments on already contracted loans protects their nation's independence, thereby justifying the painful reforms that fiscal consolidation necessarily entails.

In truth, however, consolidation states are hardly geared toward freeing future generations from the burden of debt. Intent on persuading financial markets that debt servicing is their primary concern, their representatives actually aim to preserve recourse to borrowing as the preferred mode of supplying the state's treasury. The safety valve provided by ever more commercially accessible loans temporarily softens the social impact of austerity measures, which are required to sustain the confidence of credit providers. Yet the inevitable bursting of speculative bubbles created by the accumulation of risky individual loans reveals the depth of the consolidation state's dependence on bondholders. For once markets crash, whatever public officials have managed to save by enticing their citizens to run up their own debts will be devoted not to helping out indebted households but to bailing out their creditors. In between the bailouts of financial institutions deemed "too big to fail"[8] there is also the ongoing competition between "consolidation states" seeking to attract investors. This translates into permanent one-upmanship in three arenas: lowering capital and corporate taxes, slashing budgets for social programs and public services, and rendering labor markets more flexible. Resulting from this three-part race to the bottom, the agenda of the consolidation state actually entails a gradual depletion of the resources invested in the welfare of its constituents—even as the latter remain nominally sovereign.[9]

How can we make sense of the power imbalance between political and financial credit providers? In principle, state representatives remain accountable to both lenders and voters. That governments addicted to loans cannot afford to lose the confidence of bondholders is easy to understand. However, as long as elections decide who gets to be in charge, public officials are equally dependent on their constituents' loyalty. We thus need to examine what authorizes politicians, if not to ignore completely their electorate's aspirations, then at least to subordinate them to the demands of lenders. We need to understand why the former are persuaded by the latter's requirements—or, in Margaret Thatcher's famous words, by the claim that "there is no alternative."

PERIODIC ELECTIONS AND CONTINUOUS EVALUATION

The asymmetrical relationship between elected representatives and the two groups on whom their ability to govern depends—voters and bondholders—attests both to the porous boundaries between political and financial milieux and to the susceptibility of at least a portion of the electorate to the worldview peddled by the politico-financial elite. Possessing no large fortune of their own, many citizens in developed countries nevertheless chose to identify as taxpayers unduly burdened by taxes (particularly because the obligation to repay their own debts fuels their hostility to taxation) or to identify as savers concerned about the mood of the markets (particularly when their pension and medical coverage doubly depends on the performance of their pension funds and the insurance companies that manage them).

However, neither politicians' elective affinities with the owners of capital nor the diverging perspectives of middle-class citizens regarding their own interests captures such novel phenomena in the history of liberal democracies. Therefore, invoking the collusion of the dominant and the alienation of the dominated fails to explain the unprecedented willingness of political leaders to damage their credit in public opinion in order to maintain the confidence of bond markets. For even if a significant portion of the electorate believes that it is incumbent on the state to honor its debts and to strengthen business competitiveness, elected representatives who yield to these injunctions are increasingly unpopular. To understand why political leaders stubbornly subject themselves to financial capital, then, it is important to remember that what primarily distinguishes the power of investors (whose impact on corporate governance we have already stressed) is the *temporality* in which it is exercised.

Citizens of representative democracies are authorized to exercise their sovereignty periodically through the ballot box. Although their moods are abundantly surveyed from one election to the next, they have few means of influencing the decisions made in their name during their elected leaders' term, and they are even less empowered to recall representatives who have reneged on campaign promises. In addition, even when voters are invited to express their preferences, the neoliberal institutional reforms of recent decades—from the "independence" conferred on central banks to the budget deficit caps enshrined in law—have the effect of considerably reducing the range of issues under debate.[10]

The ways in which lenders make their opinions heard by rulers who seek to retain their trust are very different. Because lenders are able to buy or sell government bonds at any time, they exert a form of pressure on politicians that is not intermittent, like that of the electorate, but continuous. Whereas polls indicating the state of public opinion are essentially intended to inflect the rhetoric of the next electoral campaign, investor moods are the object of incessant evaluations—or better still, anticipations—to which public policy must invariably conform. Indeed, the slightest expression of skepticism on the part of the markets can be enough to affect the ability of the government to borrow and can thereby deprive politicians of the resources considered necessary to ensure reelection.

Because governing largely consists in parrying the most pressing risks, the putative wishes of investors constantly preempt the hopes of voters. While voters cannot be completely ignored—particularly in the months preceding a major election—candidates generally refrain from making pledges that could make credit providers wince. Thus, campaign trail promises are more likely to be about curbing the allegedly exorbitant cost of immigration, welfare programs, public utilities, and social security fraud than about tackling tax evasion and market deregulation. Likewise, vows to bring back jobs and prosperity will generally be associated with the "trickling down" of wealth generated by supply-side incentives rather than with demand-boosting measures such as public investments in education or health care. While voters are generously enticed to ask their representatives to toughen their stance on foreigners' rights, public servant "privileges," and state-sanctioned laziness of the unemployed, they are clearly led to believe that any reform liable to threaten the attractiveness of their country in the eyes of investors—and, for that that reason, to raise the interest rate on government bonds in the secondary market—simply does not belong to the realm of reasonable expectations.

Like corporate managers and businesspeople in general, political leaders may certainly have personal reasons for being sensitive to the requests of investors. The "revolving door" between government and finance, which ensures temporary postings for out-of-work politicians tied to financial institutions, proves as efficient in disseminating "best practices" as the stock options by which shareholders adorn require-ments and admonitions to business executives.[11] Yet quid pro quos notwithstanding, politicians' subservience to bondholders owes less to their entwinement with financial circles—especially given that public perception of such complicity is increasingly costly in terms of popu-larity—than to the contrast between the continuous pressure of the credit markets and the "discrete" or occasional character of ballot-box sanctioning.

In most cases, channeling popular anger into resentment for cul-turally alien foreigners, fraudulent job seekers, and unaccountable state bureaucracies serves the custodians of the status quo well. For the partial legitimacy it gives Extreme Right demagogues, who are then elevated to the status of mouthpiece of excessive, yet understandable protest, enables mainstream political figures to remain in office—both as a rampart against uncouth populists and as "moderate" enforcers of their agenda. Diversion and triangulation, efficient as they may be, are not magic bullets, however. There are various circumstances for designated scapegoats to fail at capturing the animus of the electorate. Yet even when a majority of voters stake their lot with candidates determined to challenge financial creditors, the combined power of the latter to move their funds around and to scare states dependent on the renewal of their loans quickly makes ballot-box verdicts relatively insignificant.

Although mandated to reject the dictates of financial markets, these newly elected leaders are soon forced to acknowledge their limited leeway. As incapable of averting capital flight as they are of extricating themselves unharmed from the loans contracted by their predecessors, they soon fear that their discredit with investors will eventually extend to voters who were initially won over by promises of change. Such was precisely the anxiety that induced Greek Prime Minister Alexis Tsipras to back down in 2015. Elected in January to challenge the austerity program imposed by Greece's creditors, Tsipras then performed a spectacular U-turn only six months into office—even despite a referendum that confirmed popular support of his campaign commitments.[12]

SHELTERING SPACE AND OCCUPYING TIME

In theory, one can envision two different ways of countering the sway of bondholders over public policy. The first aims to restore the effectiveness of the temporality distinctive of representative democracy—in particular, the relevance of periodic elections. This involves sheltering the spaces and institutions in which popular sovereignty is most firmly rooted from the continuous pressure exercised by global financial markets. The second does not seek to establish a safe haven but to occupy the time that creditors have conquered. This requires practitioners who set themselves the task of challenging investors' hold on governmental priorities by emulating their techniques of relentless harassment.

Supporters of the first approach tend to regard the nation-state as the framework most conducive to rehabilitating the sovereign power delegated by the people to their representatives. In their view, the revolutions punctuating Western history since the eighteenth century have gradually constituted the nation as our community of fate: a community whose members elect their representatives by universal suffrage and expect the nation-state to both ensure social cohesion and respect individual liberties. Because such expectations have not yet been rendered illegitimate (though they have been partly corroded by globalization), advocates of revamping the nation-state argue that there is no other arena in which peoples have a better chance of making their voices heard once again.[13]

Left-leaning proponents of an alignment between popular and national sovereignty certainly do not want to be conflated with right-wing nationalists. In fact, far from simply disclaiming any affinity with nationalism, they present their stance as the best antidote to the current resurgence of nationalistic sentiments: as they see it, the growing popularity of xenophobic political parties stems precisely from the decay that free-trade agreements, deregulated financial markets, and unelected supranational bureaucracies have caused to national sovereignty. The appeal of demagogues who scapegoat migrants, so their argument goes, feeds on an experience of powerlessness among citizens who feel both unprotected and unrepresented by the state officials they have elected. Symmetrically, therefore, curbing the attraction of xenophobic populism for victims of globalization depends on restoring the tools that used to give national governments control over their budget and their currency—tools, that, in turn, gave people the sense of being governed by the depositaries of their own sovereignty.

Steeped in nostalgia for the struggles and compromises of the Fordist era, the case for "democracy in one country"—to paraphrase Nikolai Bukharin—persuades many within the European Left, especially since the Greek government surrendered to the pressure of its EU partners in July 2015. The fact that the German finance minister had already warned his Greek colleague five months earlier that once treaties are signed, "elections cannot be allowed to change economic policy," admittedly casts a dark shadow over the democratic prospects of a postnational world order.[14] Yet chilling as this cautionary tale may be, the idea of staking the survival of democratic institutions on the recovery of national sovereignty raises major objections.

Patriotic fervor, arguably a volatile affect under any circumstance, proves particularly ill equipped to advance democracy in a context where the Extreme Right couches its own agenda in democratic rhetoric. Indeed, far from replicating the overt loathing of democratic institutions characteristic of its fascist and Nazi predecessors, the new breed of xenophobic demagogues, in Europe and beyond, claims that the culturally homogenous nation for which it stands constitutes the only viable abode of popular sovereignty. For the demos to regain proper protection and representation, right-wing populists profess, the territory in which it is rooted must be shielded from inflows of alien capital, commodities, and people. Because their phobia of all things foreign is ostensibly more coherent — or at least easier to grasp — than a stance that seeks to distinguish financial and commercial protectionism from inhospitality, ethnocultural nationalists are in a better position to capitalize on popular longings for sheltering borders than their progressive counterparts.

Left-leaning champions of national sovereignty may of course decide to challenge the xenophobic parties' corner on the patriotic market by echoing their worries about the "danger" of immigration. They can even try to give an anticapitalist spin to their own call for tighter border control by pointing out that employers have an interest in attracting cheap foreign labor and that Western imperialism is responsible for the swelling number of asylum seekers.[15] So far, however, such window dressing has proved far more beneficial to the legitimacy of Far Right populists, who gladly include the critique of exploitation and imperial wars into their protectionist and isolationist perspective, than to the popularity of their progressive challengers, whose willingness to dabble in fearmongering is understandably reviled by a sizable portion of the Left's electorate.

Framing the resistance to bondholders' hegemony as an opposition between national sovereignty and transnational finance is not only ethically dubious at the outset but also politically questionable with respect to its likely consequences. To the extent that it is more than an empty campaign promise, the ambition to halt financial flows at the border exposes politicians who successfully make it the centerpiece of their platform to the ostracism of bond markets. The latter are always able to anticipate a newly elected government's decision to seize control of credit institutions and capital flows—either by speculating against its treasury bills and bonds or, more radically, by excluding its debt altogether from the secondary market. Investors thus have the power to make the populations dependent on their loans pay for the audacity of having elected unfriendly representatives.

At first, governments under attack will probably enjoy the solidarity of their constituents—or at least of the majority whose mandate they honor. Sooner or later, however, as impatience grows among the population under their administration, self-declared upholders of national sovereignty may be inclined to abuse their mantle by treating protest as treason. To the extent that they indeed veer in that direction—and the record shows, most recently in Venezuela, that they often do—the same leaders who initially came to power on the promise of wresting their country's democratic institutions from the blackmail exercised by financial markets end up curtailing democratic expressions of dissent on their own accord. Elected representatives who resort to such emergency measures usually justify their authoritarian drift by claiming self-defense against the creditors who deprive them of liquidities. Yet whatever the justification, a strategy that is liable to include smothering dissent and curtailing civil liberties is arguably not well suited to resisting investors' claim on democracy.

Instead of attempting to secure a sanctuary space where representative democracy would be reempowered to work at its own pace, the alternative way of challenging the preemptive power of finance involves competing with credit providers' harassment skills. This second approach is about learning how to occupy the temporality distinctive of financial markets, rather than about creating a haven where the agency of elected officials will be wrested from investors' grip. Its practitioners are thus intent on breaking with the intermittent character of political action in the realm of popular sovereignty—that is, with necessarily sequential and finite operations, such as organizing electoral campaigns or planning marches and demonstrations.

Political activism aimed at continuous harassment found an initial mode of expression in the street and park occupations of 2011—in particular, the Spanish 15-M (May 15) and Occupy Wall Street, as well as its multiple avatars. These movements, one should remember, distinguished themselves from traditional protests against corporate and governmental power in that their specific target was the subordination of elected officials and private companies to the dictates of financial institutions—and the tragic consequences of their subordinate position once markets crashed. Those who took part in 15-M and Occupy still addressed their political representatives. But they did so only to proclaim that they did not feel represented by politicians who had not only failed to indict reckless banks but who also actually had helped them recover at the expense of their own constituents. At the same time, however, and precisely because their movements sought to question the conditions under which popular sovereignty is delegated, 15-M and Occupy activists clearly conveyed that they did not expect the radical change they called for to come from the substitution of new and truly representative leaders for the ones then in charge.

The choice made by militants in Madrid, Barcelona, and New York to occupy public space was primarily meant to enact a form of territorial secession, to define a "free zone" where indignant citizens could manifest their defection from a polity whose democratically elected leaders were doing the bidding of financial capitalists. To put it in Albert Hirschman's famous terms, 15-M and Occupy activists wanted to "voice" their "exit."[16] Yet, even more than carving out their own space, what these activists were after was the creation of a lasting movement or, better still, of an activism endowed with the capacity for continuous expression. Like their Wall Street foes, the Zuccotti Park campers sought to gain an unrelenting rating power on the choices of elected representatives. In the absence of such uninterrupted pressure, they reasoned, banks' permanent blackmail about the "systemic" consequences of their potential collapse would not only keep them immune from reform but also entrench ruling politicians in their conviction that bailing out financial institutions must take priority over compensating their victims.[17]

Despite their efforts to capture and hold the attention of the authorities, occupiers of streets and parks eventually failed to alter the direction of government policies. Fatigue, bad weather, police crackdowns, but also the sheer impossibility of living a full-time activist existence ended up exhausting these new political movements, while their adversaries in the world of finance continued their work of harassment unruffled and uninterrupted. Even so, a resolve not to abandon the monopoly of continuous activism to financial institutions has remained at the heart of the initiatives developed by the heirs and in the wake of 15-M and Occupy.

Exemplary in this respect have been the actions of the anti-eviction organization called Plataforma de Afectados por la Hipoteca (PAH) in Spain and in particular the appropriation by its members of a harassment technique originating in Argentina and dubbed *escrache*, which means "exposure" in local slang. Founded at the height of the Spanish real estate crisis in 2009, the PAH took on the mission of providing assistance to the staggeringly high number of people who were being evicted from their housing by the very banks that had encouraged them to go into debt by concealing from them the substantial risks attached to the loans they were offered. While assisting "victims of mortgage loans" (*afectados por la hipoteca*) with legal counsel and material aid, the activists gathered in the "platform" (*plataforma*) did not confine themselves to humanitarian action. In conjunction with labor unions and other components of 15-M in which they also took part, beginning in 2011, PAH organizers drafted a so-called popular legislative initiative (ILP), which called both for a change in Spanish law regarding evictions and, in anticipation of this legislative reform, a decree that would declare a moratorium on all pending evictions. The main demand of the ILP regarded the introduction of mandatory "dation in payment," which would compel financial institutions to ask for no more than repossession of the mortgaged property. Harsher than in other industrialized countries, including the United States, Spanish law allowed — and still allows — banks to go beyond repossessing the property itself if the price of the real estate being repossessed does not cover the outstanding debt at the time of eviction.[18]

Garnering nearly a million and a half signatures on a petition, and, according to all surveys, supported by a majority of the Spanish population, the ILP was nevertheless undermined by the ruling Popular Party (PP), whose candidates won a majority of seats in Parliament following the November 2011 elections. While Mariano Rajoy's new right-wing government agreed to introduce minimal improvements in the legislation on evictions in response to pressure created by the ILP's success, the piece of legislation voted on by the PP majority in 2013 ultimately did not even include the possibility of substituting dation in payment for the full repayment of the debt. And this omission remained despite rulings against Spanish laws on default and eviction by both the European Court of Justice and the European Court of Human Rights. On account of the "systemic" consequences of their collapse, the government kept debt-ridden banks afloat at the expense of its distressed constituents. Taking stock of the PP's subordination to these financial interests, PAH activists realized that by itself, popular support for their rather modest reform proposals was no match for the ability of financial institutions to blackmail public officials. Resorting to relentless nagging techniques of their own, ILP promoters thus subjected PP members of Parliament to a succession of *escraches*.

Developed in the mid-1990s by the Argentine HIJOS collective, the first *escraches* aimed to challenge the amnesty granted by President Carlos Menem to the convicted officers who had served under the regime of General Videla—in particular, those responsible for the kidnapping and murder of thousands of opponents known as *los desaparecidos*, "the disappeared." As HIJOS militants devised it, an *escrache* involved two different stages. The first was about tracking down the address of an amnestied person and dispatching a small group of activists to his home. Once under the murderer's windows, their second task was to publicize the amnestied criminal's sinister past by means of harangues, chants, placards, and brochures handed out to the public. Activists would accompany their target every time he left his house, never resorting to physical violence, but tirelessly repeating the list of his misdeeds. Decisive in the struggle against the erasure of all traces of the dictatorship, the stalking operations and incessant "outings" mounted by HIJOS made a major contribution, if not to the fall of Menem, then at least to the reopening of inquests into the disappeared after Nestor Kirchner's election in 2003.[19]

At a time when the street and square occupation movement was coming to an end in Spain, the PAH activists' deployment of *escrache* simultaneously targeted Popular Party parliamentarians who obstructed adoption of the ILP and the financial institutions to which they were submissive. As activists had done some fifteen years earlier in Argentina, the PAH sent small groups to the residence of conservative deputies to remind them, as noisily as possible and while tracking their movements, that they were responsible for the thousands of evictions that have occurred every year in Spain since 2008. In combination with the relentless stalking of PP representatives, PAH activists also organized a succession of "performances" in banks, where they would enter a branch and begin to dance, accompanied by singers who, in flamenco song, denounced the misdeeds of the establishment they had invaded.[20]

The differences between the original Argentinean *escrache* and its later adoption in Spain are not restricted to context and theme — exposing the government's submission to the military in one case and to financial institutions in the other. In Argentina, the most complex part of the activists' intervention preceded the operation itself: the preparatory work, which consisted in locating the amnestied officers and compiling the dossiers that established their involvement in the dictatorship's crimes, was arguably the hardest part of HIJOS's *escraches*. By contrast, in Spain, both the Popular Party's opposition to the ILP and the role of the banks, which pursued about fifteen thousand evictions annually, were well known. In the Spanish reprise of *escrache*, therefore, there was no great revelation to be made or memory to be refreshed: at stake in the PAH's militant actions was just the public harassment of political and financial criminals.

Taking their cue from bond markets, PAH activists sought to provide a continuous assessment of public policies. Rather than a massive but necessarily short-lived display of indignation, *escraches*, banking as they were on the popular support enjoyed by the ILP, amounted to an ongoing rating of the government's decision to let indebted owners be evicted from their homes in order to replenish the coffers of the financial institutions responsible for the real estate crisis. Thanks to operations of sufficient frequency that frayed their opponents' nerves, *escraches* organizers meant to match bondholders' ability to establish the credit, or lack thereof, of political representatives.

Whereas it is usually the lot of social movements to face exhaustion — due to the difficulty of keeping people mobilized for long periods of time—*escraches* involved small groups of militants for a limited number of hours at a time and thus aimed to tire out PP representatives first, adding to their discredit on a daily basis. And indeed, *escraches* continued to be "performed," even after and despite the refusal of the ruling party to pass the ILP into law. What eventually put an end to them was another law—the Citizens Security Law, passed in July 2015 and dubbed the "gag law" by its critics—which paid tribute to the effectiveness of PAH activists by heavily fining (between 30,000 and 600,000 euros) anyone who either attempts to prevent an eviction or takes part in an "unauthorized protest" near public institutions such as the Spanish Parliament.[21]

In a somewhat different register, a group of Occupy veterans launched the Strike Debt campaign in the United States. Two initiatives have emerged from it: the Rolling Jubilee (2012) and the Debt Collective (2014).[22] Rebelling against the deleterious consequences of massive recourse to private debt to finance the public good of higher education, Strike Debt activists not only seek to inform financial aid recipients about the system that condemns them to tailor their existence to the conditions for repayment of the loans they took out to obtain a university degree. In addition to their work as whistleblowers, which has included the publication of a *Debt Resistors' Operations Manual*,[23] they also took on the double task of wiping clean of debt a certain number of slates and of mobilizing a critical mass of debtors to turn the act of default into a political strategy.

Duly securitized—that is, converted into alienable bonds that can be repackaged and sold in the secondary market—student loans often follow former students for the rest of their lives. This is especially common, since unlike companies such as Enron or Lehman Brothers, former students are not allowed to declare themselves personally bankrupt. Securities that bundle loans for which the repayment is uncertain—a category in which student loans figure prominently because of the precariousness of employment and the ensuing devaluation of university degrees—inevitably see their market value decline, commensurate with the doubts they cast in the minds of portfolio holders. Attentive to price movements, the initiators of Rolling Jubilee endeavored to raise funds—principally through crowdfunding—to buy depreciated securities. Once acquired, the latter were consigned to a symbolic bonfire that, in accordance with the tradition of the jubilee, frees the borrowers from their debt burden. Less than two years after launching Rolling Jubilee, Strike Debt had collected some $700,000 in donations, allowing it to cancel nearly $32 million in debt.

Terminated—or at least put indefinitely on hold—on 31 December 2013, Rolling Jubilee gave way to another kind of initiative: "debt collectives." After having bought and cancelled nearly $4 million of loans advanced to students of Everest University in Florida—a member of the Corinthian Colleges Network—Strike Debt activists discovered that Everest's senior management was the subject of various legal actions for fraud. The school had attracted students through misleading promises, including the guarantee of a job at the end of the course. Everest had also increased its enrollment costs in line with the limited amount of public financial aid given to its students, thereby forcing the latter to borrow from the university at an exorbitant interest rate of nearly 15 percent. Yet while the lawsuits consigned Corinthian Colleges Network to bankruptcy, the courts nonetheless required the defrauded students to repay their loans.[24]

In that context, rather than relieving students who had been victims of fraud by buying their bonds, Strike Debt activists decided to help them launch an actual debt strike by collectively refusing to repay their loans. Initially conceived as a platform for former Everest students to meet and commune, the Debt Collective aimed to transform student debt from a sum of private misfortunes into a political weapon. The point of the initiative was to make use of student solidarity and collective refusal to honor illegally extorted commitments in order to cement a pressure group powerful enough to persuade creditors to reduce their demands in line with the depreciation of the securities in their possession. Ultimately, Strike Debt's purpose was to render the Debt Collective's threat of massive default formidable enough to convince public authorities—the Department of Education, in particular—to have a Rolling Jubilee of their own. This would happen by way of writing off, at the federal level, all fraudulently incurred and excessively burdensome student debts.

Beyond the case of Everest and other parts of the Corinthian Colleges Network, the founders of the Debt Collective have thus made it their mission to foster the aggregation of current and former students, utilizing both their mass (44 million US citizens have resorted to a loan to access higher education) and the sum total of their debt ($1.48 trillion as of May 2018) to shake off the yoke of lenders. For if borrowers unite, Strike Debt activists argue, they will be in a position to turn their resistance to repaying into a threat at least as ominous as the "systemic risk" brandished by financial institutions characterized as "too big to fail."

Obviously, the Debt Collective platform is a long way from gathering a sufficient number of supporters to compete with credit providers for influence over political decision makers. Likewise, the volume of debt wiped out by Rolling Jubilee is barely a proverbial drop in the ocean of the bond securities that structure and constrain the lives of 40 million people who have taken out student loans. Still, they have sounded the alarm, both about the criminal practices of many university establishments whose usurious loans are their principal raison d'être and about the resemblance between the financial aid "bubble" and the subprime mortgages that caused the 2008 crash. More importantly, Strike Debt's activists have managed to insert themselves into the field of continuous speculation where bondholders ply their trade.

Not content to conjure up the specter of a massive default by indebted students, the Debt Collective has endeavored to give it substance by taking action against particular establishments—the Corinthian group, but also ITT Tech and the New England Institute of Arts—and by publicizing the growing number of visitors to its platform, making it the metric of their movement. Drawing inspiration from the modus operandi of lenders—that is, constant credit rating—its organizers seek not only to mobilize collectives of students and former students against the predatory institutions that have ensnared them but above all to put constant pressure on the public authorities. In addition to calling for stricter regulation of financial aid, they want to validate the principle of free higher education. The latter is justified both for reasons of principle—access to education is a common good—and because of the likely burst of the bubble when the securitization of students finally casts doubt on the economic viability of devolving their loans to the private sector. That the proposal to make higher education free played a key role in Senator Bernie Sanders's campaign during the Democratic primaries in 2016—to the point of appearing, in diluted form, in the party platform adopted by Hillary Clinton—attests to the ripple effect of the activism spurred on by Strike Debt.

ESPOUSING POPULISM AND BENCHMARKING BANKS

Activists who aim to challenge the hegemony of financial markets by organizing at their pace—rather than by shielding the arena of political representation from investors' exigencies—are arguably more preoccupied with counteracting the way they are governed than with rehabilitating the mandate of their elected representatives. Yet giving precedence to the exercise of what Michel Foucault called governmentality over the expression of popular sovereignty does not necessarily entail forsaking or even sidestepping electoral politics. Exemplary in this regard is the case of Ada Colau, who cofounded PAH in 2009 prior to becoming mayor of Barcelona in the spring of 2015.[25] Other PAH members have joined Podemos, a political party created in 2014 in order to convert the spirit of 15-M into a winning agenda on election days. Similarly, in the United States, a number of Occupy veterans got involved in Bernie Sanders's presidential campaign. Still, regardless of whether PAH or Strike Debt activists run for office or stick to non-governmental politics, a novel relationship between the rulers and the ruled is evidenced in the platforms dedicated to mortgage-credit and student-debt activism. In order to better identify the mode of government that these activists seek to promote, we must recall how the sequel to the 2008 financial crash altered the political landscape of the developed world.

While the Great Recession damaged the standing of most incumbent heads of state or governments, it proved especially devastating for those who belonged to center-left parties. At first glance, by virtue of their Keynesian roots, liberal and social-democratic politicians seemed well placed to take advantage of a crisis widely blamed on deregulated financial markets. However, having spent the previous twenty-five years assimilating neoliberal precepts of public management, most of them did not so much as dream of calling for a directional shift—despite the fact that in the immediate wake of the crash, mainstream media pundits were not only comparing the crisis to the Great Depression but also rediscovering Keynes's critique of speculation and praising Roosevelt's New Deal.[26]

Unfit to reap the benefits of the widespread hostility encountered by unbridled financial capitalism, representatives of allegedly progressive parties turned out to be scarcely more at ease when, having weathered popular outrage and calls for change, the political leaders of the developed world agreed that the time had come to restore the regime of capital accumulation responsible for the crash. Though center-left politicians had failed to question the merit of rescuing financial institutions unconditionally—and were now backing the decision to mend the deficits created by bank bailouts with austerity measures—they still found it difficult to champion belt-tightening measures with as much gusto and self-confidence as their rivals on the center-right. Bereft of convictions of their own yet lacking enthusiasm in their defense of an agenda at odds with their traditional values, nominally liberal and social-democratic candidates were thus bound for political insignificance. For while their endorsement of "structural reforms" cost them dearly with their core electorate, they did not manage to make up for these losses by attracting more conservative voters, who understandably preferred more sanguine promoters of lean government and labor-market flexibility to their sheepish emulators.

Seemingly unredeemable since the early 2010s, the decay of center-left parties has impacted the political arena in major ways. First, their inability to distinguish themselves from their traditional rivals has reinforced the latter's legitimacy: conservative parties, on account of their proficiency in adjusting public policy to the criteria of attractiveness defined by bond markets, have become the sole home of all so-called reasonable voters convinced that, like it or not, "there is no alternative." Second, the deactivation of the time-honored center-left versus center-right polarity—supporters of embedded markets in the name of equality and solidarity versus champions of unhinged competition in the name of freedom and efficiency—has prompted the rise of a new structuring antagonism: the defenders of national identity versus the promoters of uprooting globalization.[27] Indeed, in large swaths of the developed world, the political field is now primarily divided between nationalist and neoliberal right-wing parties—with the latter increasingly striving to make up for the unpopularity of their economic agenda by emulating the latter's xenophobia.

Finally, in countries where right-wing populists have not succeeded in presenting themselves as the only credible opposition to mainstream politicians, the waning of social-democratic parties has enabled more radical versions of the Left to gain, or regain, a more substantial audience. Stimulated by the "occupation" movements of 2011, these fledgling alternatives to exhausted progressive parties have taken contrasting institutional forms: in some cases, the creation of a new party; in others, the infiltration and subsequent repurposing of an old one; and in others still, the federation of issue-specific social movements in a "citizens" platform.[28] Yet notwithstanding the room provided by the decrepitude of center-left organizations, this budding constellation of opponents to bondholders' hegemony is itself divided on the choice of foes whose strategy deserves to be imitated.

In line with the perspective articulated by the Argentinean philosopher Ernesto Laclau and furthered by the Belgian political theorist Chantal Mouffe, the first option calls for a populist conversion of the Left, the purpose of which is to challenge right-wing populists' claim on antiestablishment feeling.[29] This stance is predicated on the conviction that the votes cast for nationalist candidates are seldom motivated by deep-seated racism and xenophobia: in most cases, the populist argument goes, people who give in to demagogues' obsessions with roots and borders are merely projecting onto immigrants and minorities the anger caused by their disempowerment, instead of tracing it to their elected representatives' subservience to global finance. Therefore, rather than bolstering the resentment of these misguided yet rightfully angry citizens by treating them with contempt, Left populists seek to turn their rancor into a healthy revolt against the rent-garnering financiers to whom they actually owe their misfortune.[30]

Politicians and intellectuals who urge the Left to embrace such populism credit their right-wing rivals with a clear understanding of what Mouffe calls the "populist moment" currently affecting Western societies.[31] According to Mouffe, the sway of financial capitalism over liberal democracies has reduced the scope and stakes of political debates to little more than a competition between like-minded teams claiming to be more efficient than their rivals at attracting investors. Though this perversion of the democratic process is clearly detrimental to wage earners, Mouffe contends that it has shifted the focus of social discontent from the exploitation of labor, which traditionally fuels leftist militancy, to the suppression of popular sovereignty around which the likes of Marine Le Pen, Geert Wilders, Nigel Farage, and Donald Trump have managed to mobilize their base. Consequently, she argues, it is now incumbent on the Left to reconfigure its priorities so as to challenge the right-wing populists' hold on the project of wresting the exercise of sovereign power from unaccountable elites.

Convinced that the days of the depoliticizing alternation of center-right and center-left governments are numbered, Mouffe professes that the future belongs to those who will manage to capture the democratic demands at once thwarted and fueled by the "there is no alternative" consensus among mainstream political organizations. To prevent reactionary demagogues from reaping the benefits of the coming rebellion against investors' dictates, she encourages progressives to pivot, so to speak: instead of clinging to an increasingly blurred Right/Left axis, they should emulate the new populist Right and give precedence to a vertical divide between "the underdogs" and "those in power"—what the leaders of Podemos refer to as the "cast" and what Occupy militants used to call the 1 percent.

Giving low versus high priority over Left versus Right proves highly consequential. For the Left is, by definition, closer to the center than to the Far Right, whereas fellow "underdogs" are less far apart from each other than they both are from the establishment who deprives them of their voices—even though their voices may not utter the same grievances. This explains why progressive populists are increasingly loath to enter "antifascist alliances" with the custodians of the status quo in order to prevent the populist Right from winning elections. For the same reason, they show considerably more empathy to voters who give their support to xenophobic nationalists than to their allegedly elitist counterparts who call Trump supporters "deplorable." In the eyes of Left populists, the former are misguided democrats whose legitimate feelings of neglect just need to be redirected, whereas the latter's posture of moral superiority thinly conceals their allegiance to the ruling oligarchy.

The shift from a horizontal to a vertical axis of political polarization is not the only way in which the two types of populist movements mirror each other. Insofar as they prioritize the realm of electoral politics, populists of both the Left and the Right endeavor to "construct a people"—as Ernesto Laclau puts it—that will prove hegemonic enough to unseat neoliberal elites. Such construction involves collecting the various outcries generated by the compliance of governments with the requirements of bondholders, but also condensing these grievances in a defining antagonism between "us" and "them."

At the outset, the "us" that right-wing populists construct along ethnic lines and through the condensation of xenophobic affects is radically at odds with its progressive counterpart, which is purported to stem from the coalescence of democratic demands voiced by discriminated minorities, exploited wage earners, and increasingly disenfranchised middle classes. With regard to the mode of construction of their respective peoples, however, similarities are undeniable: not only do all populist movements stake their ascent on the popular rejection of illegitimate elites, they also share the conviction that the "us" they seek to forge can come together only when a credible foreperson is given the authority to express its sentiments, designate its adversaries, and articulate its priorities. Far from envisioning the personalization of power and the vertical organization that comes with it as another form of dedemocratization, both progressive and reactionary promoters of the coming antielitist surge predicate the construction of their "people" on the opposition between the flesh-and-blood representative of its grievances and the cold-hearted technocrats who do the bidding of financial capitalists.

That liberal institutions have failed to prevent capital markets from corroding popular sovereignty is undeniable. Yet for the Left, the illiberal turn involved in the "populist moment" hypothesis is fraught with major perils.[32] First, as already mentioned, both the urgency of seizing the populist moment and the priority given to the electoral conquest of state power rehabilitate, in the eyes of the populist Left, the legitimacy of charismatic leadership and vertical organization. Though justified in the name of efficiency, the notion that the champions of the struggle against dedemocratization should be entitled to some autocratic license arguably suffers from a dubious logic combined with a checkered historical record—recently revived by the cronyism and authoritarian drift of Left populism in South America.

Second, as a discursive strategy, resorting to the "us versus them" rhetoric originally championed by the Nazi legal scholar Carl Schmitt is clearly better suited for the purposes of a reactionary movement. Insofar as, for both left-wing and right-wing populists, the free flow of foreign commodities and capital is the means through which "they" impose their rule on "us," adding the free flow of people to the fray is arguably a more expedient move than excluding inhospitality from the protections needed by the "people from below" in order to recover their sovereignty. In other words, adding exclusionary patriotism to "we, the people" makes it easier to grasp, which partly accounts for the inability of progressive populists to snatch voters from their xenophobic rivals.

Finally, to the extent that they keep vying for those "underdogs" who heed the call of Extreme Right demagogues, the promoters of left-wing populism are bound to overlook the difference between active and reactive affects or, worse, to conflate them deliberately. Yet indignation and *ressentiment* are the affective substances of antagonistic politics. For what fuels *ressentiment* is never social injustice or inequalities, but only the feeling that undeserving others are enjoying what should rightfully be mine and that the wrong people—that is, people not like me—are on top. Though individuals may be simultaneously moved by outrage and prey to rancor, political entrepreneurs who fail to distinguish active from reactive motives are hardly less toxic for the democratic fabric of the polity than the antipopulist establishment they seek to unseat—especially when they oppose the alleged patriotism of the popular classes to the cosmopolitanism they ascribe to "out of touch" elites.

Not all segments of the antiausterity Left concur on the necessity of a populist turn in order to occupy the political space freed up by the withering away of social democracy. Exemplary in this regard is the difference between Podemos's national leadership and the citizens' platforms with which this young party is associated in many Spanish municipalities. The former is largely composed of academics turned politicians who, in keeping with Laclau and Mouffe's perspective, stake their bid for state power on the construction of a people united by its rejection of an illegitimate cast. The latter, by contrast, primarily include grassroots activists who, before running for office, belonged to advocacy groups involved with specific consequences of the financial crisis—evictions, in the case of PAH activists, but also budgetary cuts in public health, education, and welfare for those who took part in the so-called tides (*marea*). Informed by their own experience of financial capitalism, what this second breed of recent converts to electoral politics seeks to challenge and emulate is not the right-wing populists' proficiency in harnessing antiestablishment sentiment, but the banks' capacity to blackmail elected officials.

Supporters of the populist agenda defined by Laclau and Mouffe hardly underestimate the role of financial institutions in the deterioration of liberal democracies. Yet in their view, the way to keep global finance in check is to restore the ascendancy of the mandate that elected officials receive from the people over the claims of bondholders. To that end, candidates for public office are urged to personify the antielitist animus of those who experience themselves as the losers of globalization and, once elected, make use of their representativeness as a rampart against creditors' entitlements. By contrast, activists who take their cue from financial institutions care less about selecting truly representative leaders than about modifying the way in which elected officials assess the risks to which their own choices expose them. More than the Extreme Right's appeal to underdogs, practitioners of investee politics envy the liquidity providers' ability to affect the credit of governing agencies.

Progressive populists contend that while pressuring governing agencies is the role of social movements, their approach is the only one that suits the purposes of a political party focused on winning elections. However, the trajectory of some Spanish nongovernmental activists shows that prioritizing the arena of the allocation of credit and discredit in no way excludes running—and successfully, at that—for elected office.[33] What does distinguish the citizens' platforms that succeeded in conquering a majority of large cities in the Spanish local elections of 2015 is their vision of the art of governing.

Whereas Left populism urges elected leaders to use the power of their office to protect the people they represent from the injunctions of global bond markets, the mode of government championed by the mayoral teams in Barcelona, Madrid, or La Coruña primarily aims to promote alternative pressure groups stemming from civil society—whether homeowners facing eviction, medical patients, students, environmentalists, or precarious workers. Citizens' platforms assign themselves the mission of empowering these groups, of helping them compete with the blackmailing power of lenders, and by that token of modifying the conditions under which they, as public officials, are to adjudicate between the conflicting claims of creditors and activists. Thus, according to this approach, governing is less about safeguarding the people from the special interests of financial institutions than about checking the latter's influence by strengthening alternative special interests; it is less about wagering resistance to credit providers on the mandate conferred by popular sovereignty than about reconfiguring the field of credit by increasing the accountability of elected officials to rival pressure groups.

DEFECTION OF DEBTORS AND DUPLICATION OF CREDITORS

Since 2010, the consensus among G7 members to let austerity absorb the costs of bank bailouts has put the issue of debt at the heart of the critique of contemporary capitalism. While some new social movements concentrate on the havoc wrought by private debts—be it mortgage credit or student loans—others produce audits to expose the "odious" character of sovereign debts. Public debts are deemed odious when the levies required to honor them lead states to violate the social rights of their citizens, which, according to international public law, is a valid ground to demand their cancellation.[34] Drawing on both types of activism, radical intellectuals such as David Graeber, Andrew Ross, and Maurizio Lazzarato claim that the recent ascent of financial capitalism should impel its detractors to shift their attention from labor conflicts to relations between creditors and debtors.[35]

Divergences among them notwithstanding, social critics who see debt, rather than labor, as the main fuel of capital accumulation trace the ascendancy of rent over profit extraction to the exhaustion of the political technology used by postwar liberal democracies to appease the salaried classes. Until the mid-1970s, they recall, industrialized powers averted unrest by pursuing full employment, guaranteeing regular wage increases, offering relatively decent social benefits (including health care, pensions, and unemployment insurance) and facilitating access to higher education for workers' children. This mode of cooptation of wage earners reached its limits, however, when women, minorities hitherto confined to the subproletariat, and migrants from recently decolonized countries demanded their fair share of the opportunities promised by what John Kenneth Galbraith called "the affluent society."

For capital owners, shouldering the rising cost of appeasement soon became an unacceptable proposition—one that would precipitate a profit crunch, which would in turn result in a gradual socialization of the means of production. Thus, to persuade governments that the time for a change of direction had come, investors made use of the leverage afforded to them by the new regime of floating exchange rates, the liberalization of energy prices (in response to the oil crises of 1973 and 1979), and the ensuing development of derivative financial products.

Starting with Reagan and Thatcher's conservative revolution, governments followed the neoliberal playbook and established new priorities: battling inflation took precedence over securing full employment, while supply-side incentives, rather than Keynesian demand stimuli, were purported to ward off the deflationary impact of prioritizing price stability. As we have seen, the pursuit of these new goals came at the cost of indefinite wage stagnation and shrinking social benefits, thereby causing the demise of the postwar social compact. Because they were still worried that policies meant to appease empowered capital owners could raise the discontent of the wage-earning classes to dangerous levels, the leaders of the developed world looked for a new compromise—or at least for a new way of buying time, as Wolfgang Streeck puts it—by resorting both to government and private debt: they borrowed the resources required to perform their own public-service functions—instead of raising taxes or printing money—and, in the name "democratizing credit," encouraged their citizens to do the same, so as to make up for stagnating salaries. Debt thus became the new social compact's engine of growth and its main appeasement device. Although unquestionably more anxiogenic than the career prospects and guaranteed benefits of the Fordist era, the increasing accessibility of private loans—whether to acquire consumer durables or to pursue a college education—has proved formidably effective in reconciling class interests, inasmuch as it has taught the indebted that their fate is now intimately bound with bond-market fluctuations.

Households who consent to the sacrifices required to gain and maintain a reputation of solvency must tailor their plans to the preferences of lenders. Yet notwithstanding the neoliberal ideal of self-reliance, they soon learned that what is expected of borrowers—whether private citizens or governments—does not include the pursuit of financial independence. In an environment where the job market scarcely holds out the necessary prospects for self-financing, living according to the expectations of creditors involves sustaining one's standing with them indefinitely, rather than trying to get out of debt once and for all. To be deemed reputable, borrowers are not supposed to seek an escape from the spiral of indebtedness, but to elicit the kind of confidence that will allow them to file for new loans. Hence the claim made by Graeber, Ross, Lazzarato, and others that the current hegemony of financial capitalism prompts a gradual replacement of the condition of wage earner by that of debtor. This transformation occurs when the value that creditors attribute both to the assets acquired thanks to their advances (be it housing or university degrees) and the behavior liable to sustain their trust (in particular, prioritizing debt servicing over any other expenditure) prove more decisive in averting the risk of destitution than the sum of wages generated by precarious jobs and social benefits provided by lean governments.

Making credit available to the many was supposed to be a win-win process, insofar as it reconciled the purchasing power of a majority of consumers with the appreciation of their creditors' portfolios. In the end, however, this alleged "democratization" of financial services could no more escape what Graeber judiciously calls a "crisis of inclusion" than did its predecessor, the Keynesian social compromise.[36] Despite the efforts made by financial institutions and by governments subject to their demands to extend the net of indebtedness to the least solvent fringes of the population and to conceal the risks entailed in this operation, the collapse of the subprime bond market eventually revealed what underwrote the new social compact from the start: an insurmountable incompatibility between the fulfillment of promises made to borrowers (the possibility of buying a "middle-class" lifestyle on credit) and the returns to which lenders had accustomed themselves.

That the financial crisis of 2008 did not fatally damage the regime that Ross and Lazzarato, respectively, dub "creditocracy" and "governing by debt" shows the depth of the political authorities' attachments to its integrity. Called upon to arbitrate between financial institutions chock-a-block with valueless assets and households incapable of honoring debts contracted in manifestly illegitimate conditions, governments unanimously castigated the former's cupidity and assured the latter of their compassion. In practice, however, they made it their priority to refloat banks and other credit providers and to that end authorized them to seize the assets of indebted homeowners.

That public authorities chose to save mortgagees rather than borrowers can be traced to their comparative assessment of the immediate risks to which they were exposed by delinquent creditors and defrauded debtors. They reasoned that the banks were too big to fail because of the systemic consequences of their bankruptcy, whereas the borrowers were too stunned to rebel against the injustice of bailouts financed at their expense. Yet for scholars who see debt as the keystone of contemporary capitalism, the path followed by governments at that particular juncture was not merely dictated by exceptional circumstances. It was instead indicative of what their job has become. Back in the Fordist era, elected officials were to impart the lesson that decent salaries demanded hard work of laborers as well as companies profitable enough to employ them. Today, by contrast, governing is primarily about stressing to borrowers that while the renewal of their loans requires them to attend to their reputation of solvency, it is also incumbent on never letting creditors fail.[37]

Activists and social critics who advocate a shift of focus from wage labor to indebtedness not only point to debt as a new mainspring of capital accumulation and a prevalent disciplinary mechanism. Convinced that the ascent of creditors also affects the way in which capitalist predation can be resisted, they call upon debtors to emulate the unionized laborers of yore: first, by recognizing that "debtor" is indeed the name of their common condition and, second, by investing their newfound collective consciousness and solidarity to expose and reject the norms that legitimize their subjection to credit providers.

Concretely, the constitution of debtors as a socially consistent and politically conscious class should resonate with the struggle against the loan-shark practices of private lenders and the citizens' audits revealing the odious character of some government debts. These mobilizations expose systematic biases toward creditors—for instance, the fact that private borrowers are not allowed to file for bankruptcy even if they were misled by fraudulent lending practices, whereas insolvent banks are bailed out with taxpayer money—instrumental in the emergence of a debtors' class consciousness. Taking stock of the unequal standards to which borrowers and lenders are held, debtors become aware of their shared condition and the power contained in their solidarity. Reminiscent of the fear of a general strike that yesteryears' revolutionary syndicalism sought to instill in industrial capitalists and the governments favoring their interests, the mere threat of collective default has the potential of exercising formidable pressure on financial institutions and public officials beholden to bond markets.[38]

Yet according to Graeber, Ross, and Lazzarato, borrowers will not turn their state of indebtedness into a weapon unless they overcome the all too often internalized suspicion of moral failure that is attached to being indebted. The authors of *Debt: The First 5000 Years*, *Creditocracy*, and *Government by Debt* believe that what ultimately enables financial capitalism to rule, even in the wake of an event as damning as the subprime market crash, is debtors' guilt—a psychic formation that the German language emphasizes by using the same word, *Schuld*, for fault, guilt, and debt. The concept thus carries deeply moralized connotations—except when investors use it as a lever. As long as borrowing is associated with a character flaw, meeting lenders' expectations will continue to be perceived as an ethical imperative and a redemptive course. Debtors' emancipation therefore is incumbent on exposing the fallacy of such associations—just as, for Marx, workers needed to be made aware that their exploitation was predicated on being identified as the free owners of their labor power.

If borrowers are to envision a type of sociability freed from financial markets' evaluative criteria, Graeber claims, they must learn to

distinguish the loans they have contracted with rent-seeking creditors from the commitments they feel compelled to keep—whether due
to affection, loyalty, civility, or without even knowing why. Along the
same lines, Andrew Ross wagers that the appeal of social movements
mobilized against the hegemony of finance depends on their capacity
to disseminate the following conviction: mutual obligations that create
bonds between people on a daily basis are different in kind from the
debtor relations whose calculation and repayment are at the discretion
of professional lenders.[39]

Graeber and Ross further argue that one of the main accomplishments of Occupy, a movement in which they were both actively
involved, consisted in awakening its participants to the contrast
between their commitments to each other as fellow activists and their
obligations to reimburse the debts they incurred in order to study, pay
for housing, or make up for insufficient income. In their eyes, the Zuccotti Park camp and its various replicas were not only forums dedicated
to denouncing a financial system whose beneficiaries do not exceed
1 percent of the population: they were also laboratories for experiment-
ing with ways of cooperating and sharing that are at odds and thus
purport to do away with the mechanism of interest-bearing loans.

By changing the focus of their critique—from the alienation that
forces laborers to reproduce the conditions of their exploitation to the
guilt that prompts debtors to maintain their solvency—Graeber, Ross,
and Lazzarato account for a mode of capital accumulation where rent
collection by lenders takes precedence over profit extraction by employers. Moreover, stressing the antinomy between calculable debt and
authentic reciprocity enables them to delineate the prospect of a break
with financialized capitalism that remains faithful to the communist
ideals of the labor movement. Their approach, however, deserves to
be questioned on two counts: the first pertains to the heuristic value
of representing the power relations created by bond markets as a
straightforward subordination of debtors to creditors, the second to

the pertinence of an activist strategy based exclusively on the rejection of debt.

Analyzing debt solely through the lens of lenders' ascendency over borrowers misses the complexity of the triangular relationship between credit providers, elected officials who finance a large share of their budgets by issuing tradable bills and bonds, and ordinary citizens whose indebtedness increases as a consequence of their governments' efforts to remain fiscally attractive in the eyes of bondholders. We may first recall that the indignation vented during the "occupations" of 2011 focused on governments' divergent treatment of two agents threatened by bankruptcy: the financial institutions whose demonetized securities they bought and the remaining "99 percent" of private citizens whose debt cancellation was denied. In other words, the 2008 crisis revealed that all debtors are not treated equally—a point, by the way, that Graeber and Ross don't fail to underscore. Governments refloated some liquidity-deprived borrowers on the pretext that their default would imperil the world economy, whereas others enjoyed no such privilege on the grounds that their defection is proscribed by law and regarded as immoral.

The danger represented by the financial system's failure persuaded elected representatives to save the so-called systemic banks and thus induced a symmetrical inversion of roles: the taxpaying clients became the credit providers for "systemically" insolvent debtors. For the austerity measures to which governments resorted in order to cover the costs of their rescue operation effectively turned their own citizens into lenders of last resort. Initially, public officials expanded their own deficits to clean up the balance sheets of moribund financial institutions. Once refloated, however, the latter immediately displayed anxiety about the condition of their rescuers' accounts. To maintain their credit with holders of their bonds, governments rushed to draw from their citizens' resources, dramatically reducing allocations to social programs and public services. By making fiscal consolidation a permanent condition for securing investor confidence, they not only transferred the bill of a restored banking system to citizens but also assigned them the status of third-party guarantor of all future refinancing.

The period from summer 2008 to winter 2010—from the bursting of the real estate bubble on both sides of the Atlantic to the G7 meeting in the small Canadian city of Iqaluit, where the switch to austerity was decided[40]—illustrates that in critical times, the power relations between lenders and borrowers can be temporarily reversed. For while debtors deemed "too big to fail" received all the public support they requested, governing agencies eventually transferred their burden to households that, by bearing the brunt of deficit-curbing measures, were required to act as guarantors of their elected representatives' unrecoverable loans to banks in need. Of course, the time during which private citizens were forcibly recruited as lenders of last resort to restore the status quo was brief: it ended as soon as refloated credit institutions felt confident enough to go back to business.

By the time lenders reopened shop, they found that clients were already lined up. Given the sacrifices imposed on private citizens in order to consolidate the debt of their governments, wage earners and social-benefits recipients had no other choice than to solicit new loans from the very establishments that had just been rescued at their expense. In short, once the financial crisis got "resolved," creditors and debtors resumed their "normal" relations. Yet, however short-lived, this episode attests to the ambivalence of the power inherent in the notion of credit. Depending on the circumstances, credit either refers to the privileges of creditors, namely, their license to select the projects worth financing, or to the attractiveness of certain debtors, who manage to draw financial support to the detriment of other applicants.

Despite the violence of the Great Recession, once the hegemony of financial capital had been restored without undue conflict, the triangular relations assigned by the bond market underwent yet another development. In the autumn of 2010, lenders, while still somewhat cautious, had good reason to look optimistically to the near future. Not only were they refloated, but thanks to the deficits incurred in their rescue, the new order of the day involved dispelling the bond market's worries about public finances rather than imposing stricter regulations on private financial institutions. Buoyed by speculative attacks on government debts—especially those of Southern European countries—credit providers reckoned it was time to press their advantage by sending a message about austerity. They wished to convey that austerity should not be considered a temporary cure dictated by exceptional circumstances—as public officials had initially presented it—but envisioned as a *perennial* approach to public policy.

Eager to keep speculators at bay, national leaders were quick to shed all references to "momentary efforts"—whether the one they had made to avoid the collapse of the financial system or the one they had then demanded of their citizens to ward off the bankruptcy of state institutions. Instead of presenting austerity as a short-term emergency measure justified by pressing dangers, they drew on an expertise developed within international organizations—the International Monetary Fund, the Organisation for Economic Co-operation and Development, the European Commission—to argue that short of treating debt consolidation as a permanent priority, governments were actually jeopardizing the welfare of future generations.

Since the beginning of the 2010s, explains sociologist Benjamin Lemoine, elected representatives have echoed experts who emphasize that the excessive social demands of today's citizens—excessive in that satisfying them would translate into laxer fiscal policies—expose the children of these citizens to a dire fate, or if not their children, then at least their grandchildren.[41] Unless current state commitments are "structurally" reduced, the argument runs, the compounded sums allocated to pensions, unemployment benefits, health insurance, and even education will soon prove unsustainable—and all the more so as the proportion of nonactive people continues to grow in the developed world due to increasing life expectancy and longer periods of education. In other words, the bill left for tomorrow's governments would render them incapable of assuming their responsibilities toward the populations in their care, and because of their ballooning debt, incapable of attracting private investments to the territory under their administration.

That supporters of fiscal stringency would invoke their concern for future generations to back up their stance is nothing new, of course. Although such "common sense" scarcely withstands analysis, the claim that virtuous governments should follow the example of prudent heads of household, who naturally do *not* leave debts to their children, is the most traditional way of legitimizing the pursuit of balanced budgets. What is distinctive about recent advocates of fiscal hawkishness, as Lemoine stresses, is the idea of equating resources devoted to social programs with a form of state debt. Not content to sound the alarm about the impact of current deficits on the resources of future citizens, promoters of permanent austerity argue for including budgets devoted to pensions, health care, or public schooling in the "debt burden" of the state, along with loans contracted by the issuance of treasury securities.[42]

The intended purpose of reclassifying welfare-state benefits as debt is to underscore that short of drastically reducing the promises they make to their own constituents, today's elected representatives are bound to deprive their successors of the resources necessary to serve the next generations of citizens. Lumping together what public officials owe to the people they govern with what they must reimburse to the holders of their bonds thus aims to impress upon public opinion the idea that governments are dangerously overextended.

However, by equating commitments deriving from the social contract between voting taxpayers and their elected leaders with the latter's contractual obligations to lenders, advocates of perennial austerity also convey that state officials are accountable to two different types of creditors. Consequently, while conflating citizens' and bondholders' claims is designed to raise anxieties about an apocalyptic future, if current levels of public expenditure are maintained, the contention that a state's "social debt" is of the same nature as its financial debt poses the question of which debt should be honored in priority. In other words, far from providing a compelling justification for slashing social programs and privatizing public utilities in order to secure the sustainability of state finances, the representation of constituents as creditors arguably endows their expectations with as much legitimacy as those of lenders.

While governments have hardly ceased to subordinate the needs of the populations they represent to the interests of the institutions from which they borrow a large proportion of their resources, the recent history of financial capitalism shows that their relations with these two parties are far from straightforward. At times, public authorities relay creditors' demands by encouraging private citizens to go into debt and by preventing them from defaulting on their repayment obligations; at times, they rescue institutional lenders on the verge of collapse by requiring their constituents to help restore the financial system by acting as collateral; and at times, they invoke the unsustainable character of their combined commitments to subjects of social rights and holders of treasury securities to justify sacrificing the welfare of the former to the upkeep of their own credit with the latter—often in the name of future generations' well-being.

Authors who set their revolutionary hopes on default do not pay much attention to the fact that debtors are given a variety of roles, such as borrowers condemned to take out new loans, guarantors of refinancing ruined speculators, and holders of debt destined for a write-down. As they see it, all of these scenarios merely illustrate that regardless of circumstances, government arbitration always favors financial institutions. For debtors to escape their fate they must *defect*, argue Graeber,

Ross, and inheritors of Italian *operaismo* such as Lazzarato and Christian Marazzi.[43] Defecting involves recognizing and disavowing the norms that attach debtors despoiled by "creditocracy" to their condition. While Lazzarato models such disavowal on the rejection of work by "wildcat" strikers in the early 1970s, Graeber and Ross model debt-free zones on the park and square occupations of 2011. Yet whether they wish for a grand refusal or a multiplicity of local secessions—for "voice" or for "exit," as Albert Hirschman would have it—all radical critics of "government by debt" agree that debtors should strive to extricate themselves from the hold of rent-seeking lenders rather than speculate on the complexity of the "creditocratic" regime to which they are subjected.

Calling for an outright rejection of the whole set of relations deriving from the notion of credit is certainly consistent with an intransigently anticapitalist stance. For if it is true that indebtedness not only supplants exploitation as the cornerstone of capital accumulation but also exacts an even heavier toll on the lives of its prey than commodified labor, there is arguably no reason to—and no room for—compromise. Yet precisely since activists who champion this stance claim that debtors' mobilization against their condition should take its cues from the strategies of yesteryear's unions, such a "default and defect" approach prompts an objection. The unions of the bygone era, as we have already recalled, not only bet on workers' repudiation of their condition, they also called upon their members to mobilize as traders of labor power in order to fight efficiently for higher wages, better working conditions, and social insurance. Thus, if past struggles are to inform new ones, debtors should be encouraged to adopt the same dual approach to their own condition—recognize and denounce the guilt that perpetuates their subjection and, at the same time, make use of the various positions to which the vagaries of the bond market assign them in order to improve the allocation of credit.

This two-pronged relationship of the indebted to their condition is already operative in practice, most notably in the activism of the Debt

Collective. On the one hand, in keeping with Graeber's and Ross's urgings,[44] collectives of recalcitrant debtors identify themselves as such through their shared understanding and condemnation of the creditocratic regime to which they are subjected. On the other hand, however, the overriding aim of their initiatives is to endow the risk entailed by their default with a weight comparable—on the rulers' scales—to that of the creditors' looming bankruptcy.[45]

Modeled on the blackmailing power exercised by banks deemed "too big to fail"—and at the same time reminiscent of the strike notices served by trade-union organizations—the threat of default is the lever to which debtors can resort in their capacity of borrowers. However, agitating for the possibility of a "debt strike" is not the only means at their disposal to establish a less unequal balance of power with financial institutions. The other two roles assigned to indebted citizens following the 2008 crash also provide significant fulcra. The first one is the status of third-party guarantors that was foisted on taxpaying households and social-benefits recipients when governments socialized the losses of so-called systemic banks. For their awareness of being the lenders of last resort, called on by states to avert the breakdown of the banking system, entitles debtors to demand a right of inspection of the prudential rules that credit providers must obey.

It is admittedly unlikely that, in acknowledging citizens' contribution to bank rescues, regulatory authorities will invite citizens' collectives to sit on the Basel Committee on Banking Supervision—an international institution founded in 1974 and purported to "improve the quality of banking supervision worldwide." Yet from the standpoint of debtors' exculpation, which Graeber and Ross make the psychic pivot of debtors' eventual emancipation, there is undeniable merit in imparting on the indebted that they are not mere dependents of credit providers, but actually guarantors of their survival. Representing governmental austerity policies as measures enabling banks to borrow from their customers enables debtors to replace their status as morally compromised individuals whose quest for debt relief resembles a request for pardon with one of generous patrons who, as such, have a right to make their contribution to the welfare of institutional investors dependent on stricter regulation of the financial system.

Finally, though the status of social creditors derives from accounting acrobatics intended to keep governments forever lean, it also lends itself to political reappropriation. Indeed, as Lemoine indicates, activists who take on the mantle of legitimate claimants have an opportunity to challenge the primacy of the state's financial debt over its commitments to users of its services. In contrast to the reversibility of the relations between private lenders and their customers, which emerges in those critical moments when the latter are called on to help clean up the balance sheet of the former, the axis of symmetry outlined by the expanding semantic purchase of government debt can take on a different function. Debtor activism can bring out the equally legitimate character of two kinds of debt: the financial debt vested by treasury securities and the social debt that governments must honor by providing pensions, health-care benefits, and free public education. In other words, once what elected officials invest in their citizens' well-being and what they borrow on the bond market are both included in the overall debt they bequeath to their successors, the rhetoric of a "burden" on future generations can be turned back against supporters of permanent austerity. For even if we accept the argument that safeguarding the future requires political leaders to go back on some of their promises, there is no reason to suggest that protecting unborn children should involve breaching the promises made to their parents, rather than applying a haircut to treasury bills and bonds.

Like the pursuit of shareholder value by corporate management, the obsessive attention that public authorities pay to the confidence of bondholders reconfigures the field of social conflict generated by capitalism. Managers whose fate depends on the rating of their company's stock certainly leave little bargaining room for their employees. Yet as the previous chapter argued, their subordination to investors' valuations does not undermine the levers of trade unions in the labor market without turning the stock market into a space polarized by the divergent aspirations of shareholders and stakeholders.

Similarly, governments whose main concern is sustaining the trust of lenders drastically diminish the purchase of the mandate conferred by popular sovereignty. Yet while drastically reducing the incidence of their constituents' choices at the polls, their dependence on the holders of their debt turns the bond market into a zone of antagonism between creditors and debtors, provided that the latter manage to take advantage of the various roles assigned to them—that is, as "too big to fail" borrowers, as lenders of last resort, and as social creditors. Altogether, the respective ascendency of shareholders and bondholders over employers and elected officials challenges stakeholders and debtors to make up for the disempowerment of labor organizations and democratic elections.

NOTES

1. Wolfgang Streeck, *Buying Time: The Delayed Crisis of Democratic Capitalism*, trans. Patrick Camiller (London: Verso, 2014), chapter 1.

2. Benjamin Lemoine, *L'ordre de la dette: Enquête sur les infortunes de l'État et la prosperité du marché* (Paris: Éditions la Découverte, 2016), pp. 45–83.

3. Wolfgang Streeck, "The Crises of Democratic Capitalism," *New Left Review* 71 (2011), https://newleftreview.org/II/71/wolfgang-streeck-the-crises-of-democratic-capitalism; Streeck, *Buying Time*, chapter 1.

4. On the "Volcker shock," see, in particular, Greta A. Krippner, *Capitalizing on Crisis: The Political Origins of the Rise of Finance* (Cambridge, MA: Harvard University Press, 2012), pp. 116–20; Martijn Konings, "The Institutional Foundations of U.S. Structural Power in International Finance: From the Re-Emergence of Global Finance to the Monetarist Turn," *Review of International Political Economy* 15 (2008), pp. 35–61.

5. Krippner, *Capitalizing on Crisis*, pp. 86–105.

6. Streeck, *Buying Time*, chapter 2.

7. Wolfgang Streeck, "The Rise of the European Consolidation State," Max Planck Institute for the Study of Societies, Cologne, *Discussion Paper* 15/1 (2015), https://wolfgangstreeck.com/2015/02/13/the-rise-of-the-european-consolidation-state; Streeck, *Buying Time*, chapter 3.

8. See Andrew Ross Sorkin, *Too Big to Fail: The Inside Story of How Wall Street and Washington Fought to Save the Financial System—and Themselves* (New York: Penguin, 2010).

9. As Wolfgang Streeck also observes, those whom he calls "market people" (*Marktvolk*) are in fact beset by contradictory fears: anxious about the inadequate solvency of states whose leaders lack fiscal restraint, they are also alarmed by the recessive impact of the austerity policies they themselves advocate. However, far from letting their fear of the deflationary effects of endless reductions in demand mitigate their propensity to ask for ever leaner government budgets, they persist in wagering the resumption of growth exclusively on supply-side policies, including fresh tax rebates, thereby interminably fueling the sources of

their own anxiety. See Streeck, "The Crises of Democratic Capitalism" and "The Rise of the European Consolidation State."

10. On the various ways of "undoing" democracy specific to neoliberal political technology, see Wendy Brown, *Undoing the Demos: Neoliberalism's Stealth Revolution* (New York: Zone Books, 2015); Pierre Dardot and Christian Laval, *Never Ending Nightmare: How Neoliberalism Dismantles Democracy*, trans. Gregory Elliott (forthcoming, Verso, 2019).

11. See, in particular, Dieter Zinnbauer, "The Vexing Issue of the Revolving Door," *Edmond J. Safra Research Lab Working Papers* 61 (2015), https://papers.ssrn.com/sol3/papers.cfm?abstract_id=2600633.

12. On the history of the Greek crisis, see Yanis Varoufakis, *Adults in the Room: My Battle with Europe's Deep Establishment* (London: The Bodley Head, 2017); James K. Galbraith, *Welcome to the Poisoned Chalice: The Destruction of Greece and the Future of Europe* (New Haven: Yale University Press, 2016); Marie-Laure Coulmin Koutsaftis (ed.), *Les Grecs contre l'austerité: Il était une fois la crise de la dette* (Montreuil: Éditions Le Temps des Cerises, 2015); Yanis Varoufakis, Serge Halimi, Renaud Lambert, Costas Lapavitsas, and Pierre Rimbert, *Europe, le révélateur grec* (Paris: Les Liens qui Libèrent, 2015).

13. For obvious reasons bound up with the modalities of the European project, jointly inspired by Hayek (see Streeck, *Buying Time*) and German ordoliberalism (see Thomas Biebricher, interview with William Callison, "Return or Revival: The Ordoliberal Legacy," *Near Futures Online*, no. 1, "Europe at a Crossroads" [March 2016], http://nearfuturesonline.org/return-or-revival-the-ordoliberal-legacy), supporters of a democratic revival inside the perimeter of the nation-state are mainly recruited among citizens of countries in the European Union, especially the Eurozone. See, in particular, the coauthors of Cédric Durand (ed.), *En finir avec l'Europe* (Paris: La Fabrique, 2013)—Dimitris Dalakoglou, Cédric Durand, Razmig Keucheyan, Stathis Kouvélakis, Costas Lapavitsas, and Wolfgang Streeck. See also Frédric Lordon, *La malfaçon: Monnaie européenne et souveraineté démocratique* (Paris: Les Liens qui Libèrent, 2014); Lordon, *Imperium: Structures et affects des corps politiques* (Paris: La Fabrique, 2015).

14. Varoufakis, *Adults in the Room*, p. 237.

15. Particularly striking in this respect is the evolution in Germany, if not of Die Linke (the Left party) as a whole, then at least of one of its main leaders, Sahra Wagenknecht, who hit the headlines with hostile comments on Angela Merkel's policy of welcoming refugees. See, in particular, the articles by Volcker Schmitz, "The Wagenknecht Question: The German Left's Response to Right-Wing Populism Will Determine Its Future," *Jacobin*, February 2017, https://www.jacobinmag.com/2017/02/die-linke-germany-sahra-wagenknecht -immigration-xenophobia-afd, which defends Wagenknecht; and by Florian Wilde, a member of Die Linke opposed to the Wagenknecht line, but arguing for leniency toward her, "Die Linke ist mehr als Wagenknecht," *Neues Deutschland*, 16 January 2017, https://www.neues-deutschland.de/artikel/1038636.die-linke -ist-mehr-als-wagenknecht.html. Less pronounced but nevertheless significant, is the inflection of Jean-Luc Mélenchon's rhetoric in France. In the summer of 2015, the head of the *insoumis* movement likewise referred to the "irresponsibility" of German policy on migrants at the same time as its subordination to the interests of German capital. Rather than welcoming refugees en masse, he proposed to remedy the tragedy of their exile by putting an end to the wars that force them to leave home. It is in the name of this pacifist ideal that Mélenchon has called for closer links between France and Vladimir Putin's Russia, whose contribution to the "pacification" of Syria is, as everyone knows, exemplary.

16. Albert O. Hirschman, *Exit, Voice, and Loyalty: Responses to Decline in Firms, Organizations, and States* (Cambridge, MA: Harvard University Press, 1970).

17. On Occupy, see, especially, Carla Blumenkranz, Keith Gessen, Mark Grief, Sarah Leonard, and Sarah Resnick, *Occupy!: Scenes from Occupied America* (London: Verso, 2011); W. J. T. Mitchell, Bernard E. Harcourt, and Michael Taussig, *Occupy: Three Inquiries in Disobedience* (Chicago: University of Chicago Press, 2013); Michael Gould-Wartofsky, *Occupiers: The Making of the 99% Movement* (Oxford: Oxford University Press, 2015). On 15-M, see Rafael de la Rubia (ed.), *Hacia una rEvolución mundial No violenta: del 15M al 15o* (Madrid: Editorial Manuscritos, 2011).

18. Dation in payment—or *dation en paiement*—is a feature of the French *Code Civil* and also of Louisiana law. It is in act by which an insolvent debtor gives

something other than money in payment for the debt owed. In the case of unpaid mortgages, the process amounts to transferring the title of property from the debtor to the creditor. On the PAH, see Ada Colau and Adria Alemany, *Mortgaged Lives: From the Housing Bubble to the Right to Housing*, trans. Michelle Teran and Jessica Fuquay (Los Angeles: Journal of Aesthetics and Protest Press, 2014).

19. On *escrache* in Argentina, see Susana Kaiser, "Escraches: Demonstrations, Communication and Political Memory in Post-Dictatorial Argentina," *Media, Culture and Society* 24 (2002), pp. 499–516.

20. flo6x8, "Bankia, pulmones y branquias," https://www.youtube.com /watch?v=CJfeUSvRKDA.

21. On the Spanish "gag law" (*ley mordaza*), see Ashifa Kassam, "Spain Puts 'Gag' on Freedom as Senate Approves Security Law," *The Guardian*, 12 May 2015, www.theguardian.com/world/2015/mar/12/spain-security-law-protesters-freedom -expression; Jessica Jones, "The Ten Most Repressive Points of Spain's Gag Law," *The Local.es*, 1 July 2015, www.thelocal.es/20150701/the-ten-most-repressive -aspects-of-spains-new-gag-law; "Spain's Ominous Gag Law," *New York Times* editorial, 22 April 22 2015, www.nytimes.com/2015/04/23/opinion/spains-ominous -gag-law.html.

22. Strike Debt!, http://strikedebt.org; Rolling Jubilee, http://rollingjubilee .org; The Debt Collective, https://debtcollective.org.

23. Strike Debt, *The Debt Resistors' Operations Manual*, http://strikedebt.org /The-Debt-Resistors-Operations-Manual.pdf.

24. Debt Collective, "Corinthian," http://wiki.debtcollective.org/Corinthian.

25. See, especially, Jordi Mir Garcia, "A Democratic Revolution Underway in Barcelona," *Near Futures Online*, no. 1, "Europe at a Crossroads" (March 2016); http://nearfuturesonline.org/a-democratic-revolution-underway-in-barcelona- barcelona-en-comu. For a broader perspective on these Spanish citizens' platforms and their remarkable success in the 2015 local elections, see Ludovic Lamant, *Squatter le pouvoir: Ces rebelles qui ont pris les mairies d'Espagne* (Paris: Lux, 2016), pp. 29–47.

26. Until the autumn 2009, Keynesian economists—Paul Krugman and Joseph Stiglitz, in particular—were widely regarded as the mouthpieces of

common sense, while such an emblematic neoliberal figure as Richard Posner, one of the most venerable spearheads of the Law and Economics Program, solemnly announced his belated conversion to Keynesianism in his book *A Failure of Capitalism: The Crisis of '08 and the Descent into Depression* (Cambridge, MA: Harvard University Press, 2009) as well as in the article that accompanied its launching: "How I Became a Keynesian," *The New Republic*, September 2009. For his part, Martin Wolf, distinguished editorial writer for the *Financial Times*, referred to the financial crisis as a "Minsky moment," a sudden collapse of asset values, and in turn rallied to Keynes in a December 2008 article entitled "Keynes Offers Us the Best Way to Think about the Financial Crisis," *Financial Times*, December 23, 2008, http://www-personal.umich.edu/~kathrynd/files/PP290/KeynesandtheFinancialCrisis_FT_Dec2308.pdf.

27. Correlated with the gradual substitution of public debt for tax revenues, the rise of right-wing populism has certainly preceded the financial crisis and subsequent collapse of the center-left. Yet xenophobic demagogues have considerably strengthened their hold on hearts and minds since the beginning of the 2010s, owing to their ability to capitalize, successively, on the increasing precariousness of jobs caused by policies of fiscal austerity, the influx of refugees in Europe following the tragic failure of the so-called Arab Spring (whether these revolutions were crushed, as in Syria or Bahrain, or perverted, as in Egypt, Libya, and, to some extent, Tunisia), and the new waves of terrorist attacks in Europe and the Americas.

28. Syriza in Greece and Podemos in Spain are brand-new parties, even if the former was created by the fusion of several leftist formations, while Jeremy Corbyn won control of the Labour Party in the United Kingdom and Bernie Sanders tried to do the same with the Democratic Party in the United States. In the Spanish "rebel town halls" — in Barcelona, Madrid, Coruna, and Valencia — victories were not won by Podemos per se, but by composite citizens' platforms, an alloy of political and community activists. See Lamant, *Squatter le pouvoir*, pp. 151–72; Garcia, "A Democratic Revolution Underway in Barcelona."

29. See Ernesto Laclau, *On Populist Reason* (London: Verso, 2007); Chantal Mouffe, *On the Political* (New York: Routledge, 2005; Mouffe, *Agonistics:*

Thinking the World Politically (London: Verso, 2013); Chantal Mouffe and Inigo Errejon, *Podemos: In the Name of the People* (London: Lawrence and Wishart, 2016).

30. "Many of the demands that exist in a society do not have an essentialist reactionary or progressive character. It is how they are to be articulated that determines their identity." Chantal Mouffe, "In Defence of Left-Wing Populism," *The Conversation*, 30 April 2016, https://theconversation.com/in-defence -of-left-wing-populism-55869.

31. Chantal Mouffe, "The Populist Moment," *openDemocracy*, 21 November 2016, https://www.opendemocracy.net/democraciaabierta/chantal-mouffe /populist-moment.

32. For a critique of the populist strategy advocated by Mouffe, see Éric Fassin, *Populism Left and Right* (Chicago: Prickly Paradigm Press, 2018).

33. On this point, see Lamant, *Squatter le pouvoir*, p. 198.

34. See, in particular, the investigative and mobilizing work of the Committee for the Abolition of Illegitimate Debt (CATDM), http://www.cadtm.org /English.

35. David Graeber, *Debt: The First 5,000 Years* (Brooklyn: Melville House, 2011); Andrew Ross, *Creditocracy and the Case for Debt Refusal* (New York: OR Books, 2014); Maurizio Lazzarato, *Governing by Debt*, trans. Joshua David Joran (Pasadena: Semiotext(e), 2015); Lazzarato, *The Making of the Indebted Man: Essay on the Neoliberal Condition*, trans. Joshua David Jordan (Los Angeles: Semiotext(e), 2012).

36. Graeber, *Debt*, p. 375.

37. Graeber, *Debt*, pp. 376–81; Lazzarato, *Governing by Debt*, pp. 193–201; Ross, *Creditocracy*, pp. 31–67.

38. Lazzarato, *Governing by Debt*, pp. 245–55; Graeber, *Debt*, pp. 383–91; Andrew Ross, "In Defense of Economic Disobedience," *Occasion* (2014), http:// arcade.stanford.edu/occasion/defense-economic-disobedience.

39. Graeber, *Debt*, pp. 94–102; Ross, *Creditocracy*, pp. 23–29.

40. On the turn to austerity in 2010, see Paul Krugman, "How the Case for Austerity Has Crumbled," *New York Review of Books*, June 2013, http://www .nybooks.com/articles/2013/06//06/how-case-austerity-has-crumbled.

41. Lemoine, *L'ordre de la dette*, pp. 278–81.

42. *Ibid.*, pp. 281–89.

43. Christian Marazzi, *The Violence of Financial Capitalism*, trans. Kristina Lebedeva and Jason Francis McGimsey (Los Angeles: Semiotext(e), 2011).

44. Graeber was an influential founding member of Strike Debt.

45. For a stimulating introduction to the strategy of default, see Melinda Cooper, "The Strategy of Default—Liquid Foundations in the House of Finance," *ResearchGate*, January 2013, https://www.researchgate.net/publication/292970645.

CHAPTER THREE

The Appreciation of Individual Conduct

UNSHACKLING THE SELF-RELIANT AND COACHING THE DISPIRITED

The various functions that credit relations assign to private citizens—borrower, lender of last resort, social creditor—are all subject to a form of activist appropriation. As debtors, activists can brandish the threat of their default; as guarantors, they can object to having their welfare used as collateral (at least until lending institutions are reformed); and as social creditors, they can dispute the primacy of the state's financial debt over its commitments to the people in its care. Short of preventing financial capital from thriving on indebtedness, these roles enable investee activists to challenge debt consolidation policies from different angles. What still needs to be identified, however, is the lever that these various forms of debtor empowerment can press. In other words, we must still look for the equivalent, in the realm of bond market activism, of what corporate social responsibility is for stakeholder activism in the stock market—and of what wages have been for trade unions in the labor market: a mechanism purported to legitimize capitalist predation yet liable to be turned against its designated purpose.

To discover how the bondholder value of a state can become the object of counterspeculations, we should consider the residual commitments that rulers still feel comfortable making to the population they govern, once the share reserved for maintaining investors' good will has been set aside. For even if the attention of governments is now principally focused on the attractiveness of their debt in the secondary market, they cannot simply make do with reassuring investors. In order to remain competitive at the polls, they need to argue that while mindful to the rating of their treasury bills and bonds, their program still manages to reconcile the constraints imposed by lenders with the expectations of their fellow citizens.

From the end of the Second World War until the early 1980s, the leaders of the most developed countries based their legitimacy and staked their reelection on their ability to deliver careers—at least to white male natives. Stable jobs with prospects for promotion and protection against illness, old age, and unemployment formed the core of the social contract throughout the postwar period. Subsequently, however, with the decline of the Fordist mode of capital accumulation and the repudiation of Keynesian countercyclical policies, guarantees of professional and personal security gave way to different kinds of commitments on the part of elected officials. Rather than being promised gradual upward mobility with regular pay raises and vested social rights, voters have been lured by the prospect of prosperity resulting from the reduction of bureaucratic fetters on individual initiative.

With the exception of the months following the 2008 crash, the alleged wrongheadedness of governmental overreach in economic matters has remained the unchallenged doxa for almost forty years. Yet each decade has attached its own kind of vow to this lasting consensus. In the 1980s, the architects of the conservative revolution pledged to support entrepreneurial endeavors by way of granting tax breaks, removing red tape, and abolishing "privileges" hitherto enjoyed by special-interest groups. In the 1990s, the champions of the "third way" hardly stood for reembedding markets. Yet while treating the changes introduced by their predecessors as a fait accompli, they underscored the responsibility of governments to help people help themselves, which involved training them to navigate a flexible labor market and facilitating their access to commercial credit. In the 2000s—following the 9/11 attacks in New York and Washington—US and European authorities continued to preach adaptability but also tackled their constituents' growing sense of insecurity. Rather than address the anxieties raised by stagnant salaries and the erosion of the welfare state in their own right, however, they sought to subsume them under the menace of terrorism and their vow to wage a relentless and ultimately successful war against it. Finally, since the early 2010s, the development of the so-called sharing economy has prompted public officials to present the "collaborative" work provided by what is alternatively called "platform capitalism" and the "sharing economy" as a new opportunity to expand the reach of individual autonomy: for while dealing with private contractors frees recruiters from the obligations attached to employment contracts, it also allows recruited "free agents" to move beyond the subordination inherent in wage labor.

Heeding the call of Mont Pelerin luminaries, 1980s conservative revolutionaries discarded the main objective of their Keynesian predecessors: the simultaneous pursuit of full employment and rising wages. Instead, they committed the power of their office to helping taxpayers enjoy the fruits of their labor. According to neoliberal doctrine, using taxes to finance public utilities and social welfare programs amounted to a form of confiscation that eventually proved to be a disservice to all: mandatory redistribution, the argument went, not only deprives self-reliant citizens of what they have rightfully earned, but also discourages hard work and initiative on the part of its beneficiaries, thereby harming the productivity of their labor and, ultimately, their own prosperity. At the same time, neither the Reagan administration nor the Thatcher cabinet assumed that their agenda was merely about protecting a minority of Schumpeterian entrepreneurs from the envy and the sloth of the masses. Far from conceding the nonegalitarian character of tax cuts tailored for large companies and affluent households, the revolution marched under the banner of a "populist" fight against privilege.[1]

Now, contrary to the aristocracies of yore, the conservative revolution's privileged classes scarcely distinguished themselves by the purity of their blood or the size of their fortunes. Among the main objects of the "democratic" indignation branded by neoliberal populism were trade-union organizations (accused of sacrificing the general interest to the preservation of their members' advantages), civil servants (denounced for occupying posts sheltered from any competition), and recipients of unemployment benefits (rebuked for indulging in idleness at the expense of their fellow citizens). Unionized workers, government functionaries, and job seekers were presented, if not as the inheritors of the erstwhile nobility, then at least as illegitimate beneficiaries of hardworking taxpayers.

To popularize their castigation of these allegedly parasitic groups, neoliberal ideologues had no qualms occupying the terrain of class struggle, albeit not without altering its traditional terms. At a time—the early 1980s—when the inglorious decrepitude of state socialism could only damage the cause of proletarians exploited by capitalists, they strove to separate class antagonism from labor exploitation and ascribe it instead to the plundering of ordinary taxpayers by the beneficiaries of special rights. Equipped with this novel conception of social injustice, promoters of the neoliberal populist brand identified their break with Keynesianism not so much as the return to a heroic age of capitalism than as a reprise of the fight for true equality of conditions. Calling themselves conservative only to the extent that progress had become synonymous with creeping socialism, they primarily sought to reclaim the revolutionary ideals of the Enlightenment, which in their eyes were perverted by the discriminatory effects of collective bargaining and state handouts.

Though actually responsible for setting developed nations on the path to unprecedented levels of inequality, the first generation of neoliberal leaders successfully managed to make the abolition of "privileges" a cornerstone of their discursive strategy. However, by the turn of the 1990s, the deficits generated by their vow to emancipate tax-payers were met with increasing anxiety in bond markets.[2] Thus, in a context of debt consolidation and looming recession, the revolution-ary zeal represented by the Reagan administration and the Thatcher government gave way to a phase of restorative therapy whose main exponents would be Bill Clinton's New Democratic Party in the United States, Tony Blair's New Labour in the United Kingdom, and Gerhard Schröder's red/green coalition in Germany.

Advocating a third way between the old liberal or social-democratic approach and that of the neoliberal doctrinaires, the various leaders of the "new" center-left certainly had no intention of rehabilitating what the conservative revolution had destroyed. At the same time, however, they rejected their immediate predecessors' vision of a polity divided between entrenched special-interest groups and a despoiled major-ity of hardworking taxpayers. On the contrary, precisely because the benefits and protections that distinguished the postwar welfare state seemed to them to belong to a bygone era, they made it their mission to help citizens deprived of these services adapt to their new environment by encouraging and training them to make do without protected jobs and government resources.

As Bill Clinton would explain in 1996 when presenting his wel-fare reform bill, keeping the jobless in a state of dependency created by programs of unconditional assistance was not the proper way to care for them. To give people the means to escape unemployment, the New Democrat president argued, the government's task was to "help them help themselves."[3] Contrary to his Republican predecessors, Clinton did not equate welfare dependency with caste privilege: to accuse the unemployed of deliberately abusing the system was in his eyes a false and unfair aspersion. The old welfare regime deserved to be criticized and mended, Clinton explained, though not because it enabled its ben-eficiaries deliberately to take advantage of their fellow citizens. Instead of denouncing a culture of undue entitlements, third-way politicians compared the effects of unconditional assistance to the addictiveness of certain toxic substances. Like victims of alcoholism and drug addictions, the comparison went, recipients of welfare allowances are soon unable to live without their "fix." Stripped of any sense of initiative, they are caught in a vicious circle of dependency, only heightened by the disdainful resentment they perceive in the gaze of others. Discouraged and frowned upon, the unemployed thus inexorably lose their self-respect and, for that very reason, see no better option than endlessly seeking the renewal of their welfare benefits.

Breaking the vicious circle of welfare dependency thus became the priority of the New Democrats and their friends across the Atlantic. In 1997, Tony Blair stressed that unlike traditional Labour politics, his New Labour Party was no longer under a mandate to ensure the welfare of the working class. Instead, with the help of "workfare" programs, the objective he set for his government was to restore the morale and employability of the workless class.[4] In Germany a few years later, Gerhard Schröder's reforms had a similar aim. Beside curbing fiscal deficits and restoring labor productivity, this third-way pioneer pushed the so-called Hartz laws through Parliament in 2003, which were meant to help the needy rediscover the pride of not depending on state handouts by way of compelling them to accept precarious, underpaid jobs that bore no relation to their qualifications.

Because they claimed to be doing everything possible for their citizens to gain confidence in their own value, late twentieth-century proponents of therapeutic leadership could not do without funding to back up their attempts at coaching the dispirited. In particular, they ensured that new public investments were committed to education and lifelong training. Yet their efforts were not confined to enabling the gifted to discover and develop their talents. Third-way reformers concurred in regarding the human capital of their citizens as not merely a matter of innate creativity, acquired knowledge, gleaned know-how, and social relations inherited or created by interpersonal skills. For them, even the least well-endowed were capable of self-enhancement—in their own eyes as well as in their potential employers' judgment—to the extent that they compensated for their disadvantages by offering compelling evidence of flexibility and availability.[5] In other words, in the absence of a more substantial portfolio of skills, agreeing to work very long hours in conditions of maximum insecurity and for a reduced wage would be an effective way of creating a virtuous circle between self-respect and appreciation of one's value by others. Comparable to bonds, whose price increases in inverse proportion to the interest rate demanded by their buyers, the less that poor workers make do with, the more they will be appreciated.

At the end of the second millennium, third-way reformers argued that all individuals, whatever their resources, were capable of adopting conduct that would optimize—as well as mutually reinforce—their employability and their dignity. To give concrete shape to this message of hope, supporters of government coaching broke with the hostility to labor organizations displayed by leaders of the conservative revolution: instead, they called upon trade unions to collaborate with them. Labor activists were invited to drop their old role of guarantors of vested rights and convert to the new creed of center-left politicians. Rather than organizing their affiliates to resist labor-market reforms, their new role would involve helping the workforce adapt to the new conditions of employment. In other words, so as not to perish with the corporatist interests they had hitherto defended, labor unions were now given the opportunity to sponsor educational and motivational outreach programs that maximized the chances of becoming or remaining employable.

Finally, like labor unions, civil servants were no longer denigrated as unduly privileged and inefficient but incited to reinterpret their mission in accordance with the spirit and objectives of the third-way agenda. Contrary to Ronald Reagan and Margaret Thatcher, who treated the public sector as a problem to be resolved exclusively by reducing the numbers of its agents, the ostensibly inclusive and conciliatory approach of Bill Clinton and Tony Blair aimed to make state employees appreciate the perverse effects of their statutory advantage. The point was now to impart a forceful message to them: keeping their jobs shielded from competition and their pay dissociated from performance contributed in equal measure to civil servants' own lack of motivation and the resentment they often encountered. Thus, to initiate a more virtuous circle of self-respect and appreciation, third-way reformers sought to expose civil servants to methods refined by human resource departments in the private sector. State services were thus introduced to the culture of ratings and incentives characteristic of labor practices in the age of good governance—a system where promotion and bonuses, but also retention, depend on punctually achieving targets fixed by managers.[6]

In the 1980s, the conservative revolutionaries' vow to let taxpayers enjoy the fruit of their labors had induced the replacement of taxes by borrowing as the preferred mode of state finance—the transition from the fiscal to the debtor state, in Wolfgang Streeck's terminology. In the following decade, however, third-way reformers' attempt to coach so as to improve the employability of their constituents was the counterpart of their first turn to fiscal consolidation policies. The structural reforms implemented by center-left governments in the 1990s purported to reduce public deficits. Yet these were off-set by financial market deregulations, allowing former addicts of unconditional welfare benefits to soften the painful withdrawal by running up debts on their own credit cards and bank accounts. Having endowed the labor market with unprecedented flexibility, late twentieth-century "progressive" leaders believed that it was the duty of governments to help the governed borrow their way through the new environment—provided that these newly indebted citizens paid as much attention to their solvency as to their employability.

Faithful to the program devised by Mont Pelerin doctrinaires, the first generation of neoliberal governments sought to rehabilitate, but also to expand, the purchase of the meritocratic ethos blunted by mandatory redistribution and the socialization of risks. Tough love and trickling down wealth, they believed, would eventually whip everyone into entrepreneurial shape. For their part, the third-way "coaches" of the first post–Cold War decade developed a different kind of social engineering: rather than breed self-reliant entrepreneurs constantly calculating the costs and benefits of their decisions, they encouraged their fellow citizens to embrace the condition of investees—that is, of men and women capable of earning and maintaining the trust of temporary employers, lenders, or venture capitalists. Whether they requested a short-term job, a mortgage loan, or contributions to their startup initiatives, the subjects that third-way advocates simultaneously addressed and endeavored to fashion were prospective investees—projects in search of investors. As such, they differed from the typical wage earners of the Fordist period, whose security concurrently depended on state protection and corporate jobs, but also from the self-reliant entrepreneurs that early neoliberal governments had wished to mold.

While the third-way approach makes investees responsible for increasing their attractiveness in the eyes of agents entitled to judge their employability and solvency, it is incumbent on the rulers who solicit their votes to second their efforts. Governments are thus expected to invest in their citizens' continuing education and guarantee the loans they contract, but also to convert unemployment insurance into dignity-boosting return-to-work programs and let financial institutions make credit more accessible. Rather than simply occupy a middle ground between the social and economic security promised by the old center-left and the unfettering of initiative extolled by neoliberal ideologues, 1990s "progressives" sought to establish a new common ground between the expectations of their fellow citizens and that of their own creditors: the former would be provided with means to enhance their value to lenders and potential employers, whereas the latter would be given the opportunity to invest in a country where everyone is enticed to enhance his or her human capital. For making a territory attractive for investment, third-way advocates argued, is not simply a matter of lowering taxation, deregulating labor markets, and reinforcing intellectual property rights: equally important is the estimated worth of its population. Exponents of the new center-left could thus claim that their efforts to improve the citizenry's appreciation by potential investors constituted the agenda of a financially responsible welfare state.

The arenas where third-way reformers invested in the human capital of the populations they governed included education, immigration, and welfare: schools received funding so as to endow students with an appreciable skill portfolio; borders opened so as to take in foreigners whose talents promised to generate patentable ideas or whose pliability contributed to the flexibility of the labor market; and welfare services morphed into lifelong training programs so as to adapt job applicants to rapidly changing conditions of employability. Altogether, the promise to personalize public investment—to adapt government services to individual life trajectories—informed the agenda of New Democrats, New Labour, and new Social Democrats. It was a promise to the recipients of these policies that their elected leaders would do their utmost to help them cultivate their assets—but also to credit providers who could be lured only by a nation where public authorities sought to raise the financial attractiveness of its members.

REASSURING THE INSECURE AND WEEDING OUT THE DISCREDITED

In tone as well as in practice, the inclusiveness professed by third-way reformers was an undeniable departure from conservative revolutionaries' tough love for alleged abusers of hardworking taxpayers. However, the empathy displayed by the former proved insufficient to check widening economic inequalities triggered by the neoliberal turn of the 1980s. Moreover, anxieties generated by stagnating wages and precarious jobs were arguably more difficult to defuse in the 1990s than in the previous decade: on the one hand, with the end of the Cold War, leaders of the "free world" could no longer mobilize the Soviet menace to deflect social tensions; on the other hand, having renounced the populist rhetoric deployed by Reagan and Thatcher, Clinton and Blair did not have the option of imputing the hardship of common folks to the privileges of special-interest groups.

Psychologically, the commitment of center-left governments to help everyone become more appreciable made matters even worse: for while the crude meritocratic stance of early neoliberals could either be emulated or rejected as thinly veiled bias toward the rich, the third-way promotion of individualized care could only entice its beneficiaries to blame themselves if their condition did not improve. Programs designed to treat addictions to state-sanctioned handouts were meant to create a virtuous circle for their recipients, whose regained self-esteem would boost their attractiveness in the precarious markets for jobs and consumer credit. Symmetrically, therefore, failure to deliver such a result was bound to produce exactly the opposite effect, undermining the confidence and self-respect of those whose assets were not appreciated. Consequently, the new regime of public assistance infused large swaths of the population with a feeling of insecurity that was all the more insistent for being so hard to admit, since it was liable to be interpreted as the symptom of a stubborn addiction to unconditional benefits and statutory protections.

Short of altering their economic policy, public authorities soon realized that they needed to address the demand for safety welling up among their citizens most affected by welfare and labor market reforms. The pervading sense of vulnerability created by the 9/11 attacks, not only in the United States but throughout the industrialized world, provided them with an unexpected opportunity to put security at the top of their concerns. Governments threatened by al-Qaeda still remained disinclined to treat the anxieties induced by increasing socioeconomic inequalities, shrinking social benefits, and household dependency on private loans. Yet they sought to reaffirm their legitimacy by vowing to protect the populations in their care from terrorists and their putative allies. Offering such protection was all the more convenient because the fears Western leaders promised to assuage did not proceed from the implementation of their own agenda but from the fanaticism of its most implacable denigrators.

No sooner had the "war on terror" been declared than its promoters began to relax their efforts at fiscal consolidation in order to invest massively in national security. This shift, however, hardly modified the condition of "projects in search of investment" that already informed the existence of Western citizens on the eve of the Twin Towers' destruction. From the outset, in the weeks following 9/11, President George W. Bush signaled to his fellow Americans that their patriotism had to include an economic dimension. As well as demanding their unwavering support for the military operations on which he was about to embark against a new "axis of evil," Bush asked them not to let terror alter their habitual behavior, from hard work and prayer to vacationing and, especially, shopping.[7]

Thus, Americans were enjoined to aid their country by their labor, but also through their leisure activities and purchases of consumer goods. For many, no doubt, patriotic shopping was a difficult task to undertake. To finance the war against al-Qaeda and its real or alleged allies, the Republican administration was quick to reduce further the size and scope of social programs, while its ever-increasing desire to placate investors ran against the option of raising the minimum wage to stimulate household consumption. Yet the US president still needed to be spared the deleterious consequences that an economic slowdown doubtlessly would have on the popularity of his military campaigns already underway or in preparation. Thus, while not directly maintaining the purchasing power of the least affluent consumers, the Bush administration deployed unprecedented efforts to assure that a majority of the citizenry had access to the credit required to maintain "the American way of life."[8]

The years of George W. Bush's wars actually mark a turning point in the history of consumer credit—some would even say of the democratization of credit—in that they all but erased the traditional demarcation between groups entitled to borrow from private entities and those hitherto deemed insufficiently solvent to receive loans. Thanks to the carte blanche granted by a broad range of public agents, from lawmakers to central bankers and regulators tasked with controlling capital market operations, financial institutions were encouraged to cultivate their creativity with instruments capable of both disseminating and concealing risk. As the ensuing securitization of bad debts progressed, lenders were able to extend their services to the lowest income groups.[9]

With the growing market value of consumer durables acquired on credit, the popular classes' contributions to the activities of financial markets held two advantages for the "war on terror" architects. First, the profusion of high-yielding and supposedly safe liquid assets resulting from the expansion of consumer credit enticed investors to keep the economy afloat by reinjecting their cash into those economic sectors that were galvanized by the appreciation of securitized debts. In the United States, it was largely thanks to loans made to households without resources—the famous subprime mortgages, which multiplied sevenfold between 2001 and 2007—that real estate credit was able to grow at an annual rate of 13 percent during the first six years of George W. Bush's two terms.[10] Second, the economic growth generated by what the sociologist Colin Crouch has aptly called privatized Keynesianism[11]—that is, a demand stimulus in the form of expanded commercial credit—secured the citizenry's ongoing support of the military buildup required to occupy Afghanistan and to prepare the invasion of Iraq. Better still, being able and even encouraged to refinance their loans in order to defer repayment deadlines helped debtors dispel their haunting feeling of economic insecurity, or at least facilitated the projection of their anxieties onto the foreign enemy—terrorists and their sponsors—that their government had promised to defeat in battle.

Western public support for the US administration's claim to fight terror while preserving the free world's way of life began to drop with the opening of the Iraqi front in March 2003. Opposition to George W. Bush and Tony Blair's decision to fight terrorism by invading its alleged breeding ground resulted in the first instance from problems in the battlefield. Already undermined when the world discovered that they had lied about Saddam Hussein's weapons of mass destruction, the reputation of both leaders was further eroded by the accumulation of "collateral damage" that the forces occupying Iraq left in their wake, from routine massacres of civilians to systematic use of torture and the abduction of suspects. As the "shock and awe" campaign launched by the US president and his British partner turned into an awful quagmire, the coalition of the willing they had assembled soon found it equally hard to win the hearts and minds of the population it was supposed to liberate from a terrorist-friendly tyrant and to retain the backing of the democratic societies whose values it pretended to embody.

The Madrid and London terrorist attacks—in March 2004 and July 2005, respectively—only further discredited the Iraq war by way of demonstrating that, notwithstanding its imperialist character and brutality on the ground, the occupation of foreign countries did precious little to protect the capitals of the developed world. Finally, with the subprime market crash of 2008, the political failure of the military campaigns launched by the Bush administration and its allies was compounded by the collapse of the economic model that was designed to maintain popular consent during the indefinite prosecution of the war on terror.

Once hit by the financial crisis and the ensuing Great Recession, citizens of developed countries were equally disinclined to trust the efficiency of self-regulating markets and to project all their fears onto a designated axis of evil. Barack Obama's victory in the US presidential election of November 2008 reflected both disinclinations. His platform was indeed largely built on a twofold promise to regulate financial institutions and to withdraw American troops from Iraq. Yet the hopes for radical change invested in the Democratic president—in economic as well as in geopolitical matters—rapidly faded.

On the economic front, the prospect of a revived New Deal, which Keynesians had associated with Obama's victory, never materialized: modest stimulus notwithstanding, the efforts deployed by the incoming administration aimed less at subordinating the interests of Wall Street to the pressing needs of Main Street than at refurbishing the financial sector without demanding much in return—allegedly for fear that stringent constraints would prevent traumatized credit institutions from helping the "real" economy recover. On the geopolitical front, while eager to extricate US troops from the Iraqi quagmire and more generally to wrest US foreign policy from the neoconservative project of protecting the free world by "liberating" the countries where its enemies dwelled or ruled, Obama fell short of articulating, and more decisively, of implementing an alternative agenda. Hampered by the chaos that his predecessor had created in occupied Iraq and Afghanistan, his desire to disengage was further stymied by the conflicts that followed the repression of the Arab Spring—the United States reluctantly supported the 2011 Franco-British expedition against the Libyan regime as well as the 2015 Saudi-led air campaign against the Houthi rebellion in Yemen—and the rise of the Islamic State in Iraq and Syria.

Although Obama's foreign and domestic policies did not meet the expectations harbored by his most fervent supporters during his first presidential campaign, they still prompted a significant shift in the commitments that the political leaders of the developed world would make to their electorate in the following decade. First, both the absence of political benefits and the enormous human and financial cost of the post-9/11 "preventive" invasions brought the neoconservative agenda into unredeemable disrepute. In keeping with the French and German governments' warning to their American and British allies back in 2003, military interventions to spark "regime change" were now widely regarded as misguided hubris. According to the new received wisdom, formerly colonized nations, regardless of how they felt about their own rulers, were not likely to see foreign occupation as a welcome remedy to homegrown oppression. Reckoning that imperialist campaigns did not arouse gratitude on the ground, Western powers opted for a clear dissociation of the two kinds of enemies that the "axis of evil" rhetoric had conflated: while they still gave themselves license to hunt down terrorist groups wherever they dwelled, substituting friendly governments for the regimes hitherto accused of abetting terrorism was no longer part of the agenda.[12]

Conflicts of interest among them notwithstanding, the permanent members of the UN Security Council have gradually come around to what has always been the Russian and Chinese position: incumbent governments of a recognized state should be treated as legal and thus irremovable depositaries of national sovereignty, regardless of their democratic legitimacy and human rights record. Consequently, the only enemies that leading members of the "international community" are entitled to confront militarily are terrorists whose main distinctive feature is their status of nonstate actor.[13] This new doctrine does not amount to isolationism, since it allows for incursions into faraway countries where terrorists have either received safe haven or carved out an enclave by force. Major military powers thus retain considerable latitude to carry out allegedly antiterrorist operations, even in the absence of a formal seal of approval from the UN. Yet the revamped war on terror marks a radical departure from George W. Bush's and Tony Blair's ambition to get rid of tyrannical regimes: with the exception of Muammar Gaddafi, whose swift toppling was owed to very particular circumstances[14] and has been lamented ever since by all the successors of the governments involved, local state authorities are now more likely to be recruited as auxiliary forces, or at least treated as lesser-evil surrogates, than associated with terrorists.

Reckoning that imperial campaigns not only fail to win the hearts and minds of the populations they are supposed to liberate but also generate retaliations in the shape of suicide attacks back home, the governments of industrialized nations have refocused their approach to domestic security accordingly. There again, what has prevailed is the stance that Bush's defense secretary, Donald Rumsfeld, associated with "Old Europe" following Jacques Chirac and Gerhard Schröder's refusal to join the "coalition of the willing" in Iraq. Rather than staking the eradication of terrorism on hazardous military interventions purported to remodel the Middle East, both the French president and the German chancellor advocated a more defensive approach, based on multilateral police cooperation, tighter border controls, as well as closer monitoring of local minorities deemed vulnerable to the terrorists' message.

By 2008, dissociating homeland security from the imperial expansion of democracy was also about adjusting the scale of the war on terror to the compromised state of the financial system: whereas the Bush administration and its British partner saw the hunting down of enemy combatants and the valorization of their fellow citizens' assets as two missions that they could carry out simultaneously, but also independently of one another—the former through deficit spending, the latter by making commercial credit more accessible—their successors were compelled to devise a financially sustainable mode of protection against terrorism. Having successively made it their priorities to save credit institutions from bankruptcy and to placate revamped bond markets with austerity measures, Western governments could no longer afford the cost of nation building in order to make good on their promise to keep their constituents safe.

The opportunity to wage a less costly war on terror arose in the wake of the Arab Spring. Politicians faced with the Great Recession had certainly not waited for popular upheavals in Tunisia, Egypt, Libya, Bahrain, or Syria to argue that curbing immigration from the Global South would go a long way in easing their constituents' distress. Yet until 2011, the persuasiveness of such an argument was limited to voters whose xenophobic proclivities predated the financial crisis, if only because depressed labor markets are a far more efficient disincentive to economic migration than restrictive visa policies. However, once the chaos created by Gaddafi's toppling and the crushing of the Syrian revolution followed the falls of Ben Ali's and Mubarak's dictatorships, the ensuing exodus of asylum seekers gave considerable traction to the claim that an unmanageable influx of migrants was threatening the Global North—and Europe, especially. Moreover, since the so-called refugee crisis largely involved survivors of Middle Eastern and North African conflicts, tighter border controls and stricter asylum laws were soon conflated with antiterrorism, so as to become the privileged dimensions of an affordable security policy.

Remarkably, the demise of the neoconservative agenda helped Western governments justify their increasingly overt inhospitality: for once detached from the forceful democratization of the regions where terrorists had their bases, the promise to make the industrialized world a safer place no longer needed to be entangled with the worldwide promotion of human rights and humanitarianism. In other words, having wrested the protection of their fellow citizens from the ruinous imperial delusions of their predecessors, post-2008 leaders felt no more obliged to support rebellions against brutal dictatorships than to provide a shelter to their victims. (There is at least one counterexample to this change of approach: just as the 2012 Libyan expedition was a belated instance of "regime change," Angela Merkel's decision to open German borders to Syrian refugees in the summer of 2015 ran against the prevailing phobic grain. However, faced with mounting pressure both from her European colleagues and the rank and file of her own conservative majority, the German chancellor eventually agreed to scale down her "welcome" policy.)

Propitious for the adaptation of national security to the constraints of debt consolidation, the promotion of immigration as a major risk is a template of how Western governments have rearticulated the relationship between their commitments to their constituents and what they owe their creditors. As previously argued, in the 1990s, the champions of the third way had staked the reconciliation of their attractiveness in financial markets and their popularity in the electoral arena on the promise to help their constituents raise the value of their human capital. While this pledge has successively survived 9/11, George W. Bush's wars, the financial crisis of 2008, and the ensuing Great Recession, the ways in which it is honored have been decisively altered by the conjunction of the turn to fiscal austerity in 2010 and the state-sanctioned panic about refugees in the following years.[15]

With questionable good faith, but undeniable glibness, late twentieth-century leaders such as Bill Clinton and Tony Blair had professed that those who strove to enhance their own creditworthiness contributed as much to the competitiveness of their country of residence as to their own self-esteem. For that reason, fostering their employability and guaranteeing their solvency were missions that their political representatives had both a duty to assume and an interest in fulfilling. Governments today are equally concerned to make their commitments to their constituents palatable to investors and vice versa. However, the aftermath of the financial crisis has rendered them less confident in the propensity of liquidity providers to appreciate public programs designed to educate children, accommodate migrants, or motivate the jobless. While state officials remain convinced that raising the value of their nation's human capital is their best hope to meet creditors' expectations without alienating voters, they pursue their objective quite differently than early promoters of the third way: instead of wagering the valorization of the population in their care on education, training, and selective immigration, they focus on keeping the individuals whose worth is least likely to be immediately appreciated out of investors' sight.

To configure a stock of residents suitable to be submitted to creditors for evaluation, governments resort, alternatively or in combination, to several techniques. One efficient way of reducing the negative impact of allegedly nonappreciable segments of the population on the financial attractiveness of their country involves altering the criteria of eligibility and modes of control of applicants for social benefits so as to clear the registers of unemployed,[16] invalids, and disabled workers.[17] Public authorities are also keen on modifying the conditions of residence in their territory so as to repel migrants devoid of immediately appreciable resources while attracting wealthy foreigners and transnational enterprises in search of tax havens. In some cases, especially during the Great Recession, governments also have actively encouraged the emigration of their own nationals, especially young graduates whose skills were not rated highly enough on the domestic market.[18]

Efforts to enhance a territory's value by ridding it of those residents least attuned to market expectations were especially marked in Europe as a response to the government debt crisis and the influx of refugees. Yet the same practices can be found in differing degrees throughout the industrialized world—with regard to inhospitality, Australia arguably surpasses all its partners—and most notably in the United States following Donald Trump's election. Weeding out the discredited so as to valorize the ratio of human capital per capita of a population has the dual advantage of pleasing increasingly impatient lenders and, thanks to the conflation of immigration with public safety risks, of aligning budget-consolidation constraints with national-security concerns.

PRECARIOUS WORKERS AND FREE AGENTS

To maintain the financial attractiveness of the territory over which they preside, political leaders have become more inclined to dispose of—or at least conceal—those citizens and denizens who seem to lack valuable assets, rather than invest in their skill sets. To improve the per-capita valuation of their nation's human capital, governments currently seek to decrease the denominator rather than increase the numerator. Designed to enhance the creditworthiness of the population at a competitive cost, such social policy is not reducible to its quantitative dimension, however. While weeding out the discredited takes multiple forms, including limiting access to disability programs, making job seekers disappear from unemployment statistics, denying asylum and residency to most applicants, and in some cases pressuring young graduates to emigrate, it also involves repurposing Bill Clinton's old commitment to "help people help themselves."

Back in the 1990s, pioneers of the so-called new economy were already hailed as role models: "to bring back the will to win," as Tony Blair had put it, everyone, the "workless class" included, was invited to emulate start-up founders, whose positive energy and innovative spirit managed to attract venture capital. Practically, however, the vast majority of prospective investees addressed by third-way governments were wage earners looking for temporary jobs to make do in an increasingly flexible labor market and for renewable commercial loans to make up for welfare reforms and slashed social programs. As critics on the Left emphasized, New Labour and New Democrats' coaching primarily targeted the "precariat" created by earlier neoliberal reforms. A notion coined at the turn of the 1990s, the precariat comprised an atomized salaried class whose prospects, or lack thereof, were shaped by unstable job offers, receding social benefits, and weakened labor organizations.[19]

Two decades later, by contrast, public policies targeting investee projects in search of investor payments no longer presume these will be salaried jobs. This new governmental outlook is not primarily premised on the soaring proportion of self-employed relative to wage earners. Slightly up in some industrialized countries, including France, the United Kingdom, and the Netherlands, the share of independent contractors actually shrank a little in the United States between 1994 and 2014 and still accounts for less than 15 percent of the active population in the Organisation for Economic Co-operation and Development as a whole.[20] The hypothesis of a trending decline in the wage-earning class derives most of its plausibility not from statistical evidence, but from the rise of "platform capitalism," a framework that owes little to statecraft, but that goes some way in exempting governments from the responsibility of fostering their citizens' "employability" in the traditional sense of the word.[21]

Two decades ago, entire careers pursued in the same company were already a rare holdover from the Fordist era. Pressured by impatient shareholders to concentrate on their "core business"—that is, the immediately appreciable fraction of their capital—firms strove not only to outsource their other activities (whether by subcontracting, hiring temporary workers, or relocating to regions where production costs were lower) but also to reorganize internally.[22] The pyramidal structure of the vertically integrated corporation—typical of industrial capitalism's golden age, as described by Alfred Chandler—gave way to a modular organization. Whereas the Fordist firm relied on rigid hierarchies, proprietary technologies, and employers' loyalty, its modular successor is composed of relatively autonomous components, each centered on projects of scheduled maturity implemented by ad-hoc teams and for that reason easily detached and jettisoned when the results of the "module" cease to meet investors' expectations.[23]

As even high-paid corporate employment involved more project-based and thus fixed-term hiring than lifelong careers, the post-Fordist labor market became increasingly polarized. While some workers changed employers because of their sought-after skills, others bore a heavy burden of irregularity and mobility. Often interspersed with long stretches of unemployment, members of the precariat had access only to temporary jobs, with virtually no prospects of advancement. While scarcely vouchsafing the emancipation heralded by third-way coaches and self-improvement gurus, they increasingly realized that flexibility and availability were indeed the preconditions of their employability.[24]

Epochal as the change from Fordism to post-Fordism was for management and employment, the advent of platform capitalism prompts yet another, possibly even more "disruptive" transformation. This is because the phenomenon commonly called "Uberization," as Gerald Davis argues in *The Vanishing American Corporation,* involves the programmed decline of jobs themselves in favor of an economy based on a trade in tasks—that is, on services sold (as it were) by the unit.[25] Advocates of this brave new world, which they adorn with terms such as the "sharing" or "collaborative" economy, present the emergence of Uber-like platforms as the ultimate actualization of Adam Smith's vision of the market. According to them, these virtual interfaces bring disintermediation to an unprecedented level by allowing providers and seekers of services to connect without the proverbial "middle man," whether the service supplied and demanded is taking a trip in a car with a driver, ordering a home delivery, resolving a computer problem, finding accommodation for a temporary stay, designing a website, drawing up an architectural plan, or even being diagnosed and prescribed drugs by a certified doctor.[26]

However, as attested by the formidable rent they extract from the connections they facilitate, platforms such as Uber, TaskRabbit, Airbnb, the Mechanical Turk of Amazon, or Upwork are clearly not reducible to a digital prosthesis of the invisible hand. Moreover, some of them do not merely offer a meeting and negotiating space for their users. Contrary to how classical liberals envisioned the function of a market, as a neutral space where traders and their customers freely manage their transactions, these digital interfaces actually monitor the labor and fix the remuneration of the service providers who use their platform. The drivers that Uber enables to pick up fares, for instance, are subject to strict control and pressured to conform to the preferences inscribed in the platform's algorithm. The routes they take are dictated by GPS, while their efficiency, availability, and interaction with passengers are systematically rated to determine their retention in the ride-hailing "fleet."[27]

Ultimately, all that survives of the Smithian vision of the market in the "collaborative economy" is the commercial—as opposed to waged—character of the relationship between the company that owns the interface and the service providers themselves. Even when the latter have little leeway, as in the case of Uber drivers, the platform that thrives on the services they supply does not hire them as employees but only as private contractors. Proponents of Uberization claim that short of fully emancipating those who sign them, these commercial contracts constitute a welcome alternative to the uneven supply of precarious jobs. Unlike wage earners, the argument goes, self-employed service providers are not compelled to conform to the working hours fixed by their employer—they are in control of their schedule and availability, even if such freedom is largely offset by the fact that a poor rating of the way they use their time is likely to precipitate the termination of their contract.

In a majority of cases, far from improving the condition of precarious workers, settling for a "partnership" with a platform leaves them in a situation that combines the constraints of wage labor with the risks of being self-employed. For while the rating system that prevails in the sharing economy can prove at least as stifling as the subordination inherent in salaried work, the commercial nature of the contracts signed by "partners" exempts platforms from the social contributions incumbent on actual employers. In Uber's case, the subterfuge is so patent that a number of courts have identified and condemned it—even in the United Kingdom, the country of "zero hour" jobs, where the employer is not obliged to provide any minimum working hours—to the point of compelling the company to recognize that drivers affiliated with its site are indeed its employees.

Despite such reversals suffered by the most brazen platforms, the "gig economy"—a phrase that is both more precise and less distorted than the "collaborative" or "sharing" economy—seems inevitably set to expand rapidly in the near future. In accordance with Law and Economics precepts, the flagships of the gig economy are no more than a set of interlocking commercial contracts between a "principal" authorized to make decisions in the name of the company—or better still, the company's stock—and a multiplicity of "agents" mandated to valorize its capital.

Back in 1937, Gerald Davis recalls, the jurist Ronald Coase already argued that entrepreneurs do not become employers until the "transaction costs" of constant recourse to the market gave them no other choice.[28] For this pioneer of neoliberal thinking—and in particular of the agency theory of the firm, which is at the heart of the Law and Economics doctrine—what originally compelled companies to hire workers on a regular basis (to rely on employment contracts, rather than purchase services by the unit) was the practical difficulty and cost involved in organizing auctions for every task. The author of "The Nature of the Firm"[29] thus argues that the wage relation was always a second best for capitalists: were the transaction costs of relying on the price mechanism to diminish, entrepreneurs would rather go back to the market in search of a better deal than retain the same service providers for the duration of the employment contract. Industrial development, Coase added, made employing indispensable, but also increasingly burdensome for employers, for wage earners took advantage of their decreasing substitutability to demand higher pay and greater protection.

However, thanks to information and communication technologies whose impact neither Coase, in 1937, nor even agency theorists of the 1970s could imagine, platforms such as Amazon's Mechanical Turk and Upwork have succeeded in drastically reducing the transaction costs of recourse to the market price mechanism. Rather than hiring employees, calling on subcontractors, or even relying on temps, the firms that use these platforms can create competition among a considerable number of candidates for the performance of a single task. Above all, they can repeat the operation at an unrelenting pace with no costs apart from the rent owed to the interface. The rise of platform capitalism is thus purportedly set to multiply and possibly generalize partnerships, based on a purely commercial relationship between suppliers and purchasers of services, at the expense of employment contracts.

The constraints involved in transporting material commodities and the relatively high cost of 3D printers still limit the extension of this new economic model to the sector of nonrival goods, that is, goods, intangible for the most part, that can be replicated at no cost and possessed or consumed by multiple users. For their part, extractive and manufacturing industries, as well as agriculture, can hardly do without the labor of wage earners. Nonetheless, given the increasing automation of the most repetitive work, the advent of a world of partners brought together for the duration of a gig and with no mutual obligations beyond provision and remuneration of a single task is already sufficiently plausible as an eventuality to inflect both business management and public policies.

The prospect of a gig society translates into the growing attention that legislators and public administrators pay to the condition of the "self-employed." Should we infer that the dream of the founding fathers of neoliberalism—the dream of a society dubbed "de-proletarianized" by Wilhelm Röpke in the 1950s—is coming into being? Are we witnessing the conversion, in terms of both status and psychology, of the former wage-earning classes to generalized entrepreneurship, a conversion regarded by the 1974 Nobel Prize–winning economist Friedrich Hayek as necessary to avert socialism? Does the status of "self-entrepreneur" (*auto-entrepreneur*), introduced into French administrative law in 2008, illustrate the analysis of Michel Foucault, who in his 1979 lectures on neoliberalism cast the "entrepreneur of oneself" as the subject whom Chicago School economists were endeavoring to fashion?[30] The recent adjustment of legislation to technological and managerial innovations would undoubtedly be to the taste of founders of the Mont Pelerin Society in 1947. However, a closer examination of today's "free agents" and their mode of existence scarcely suggests that their privileged habitat, the capitalist platform, is gradually universalizing the entrepreneurial condition.

Whether desirous of "sharing" their do-it-yourself talent thanks to TaskRabbit, their apartment on Airbnb, their car with Lyft or Uber, or their model-making skills on Upwork, the self-employed status of service providers by the unit implies that the latter are both free from the bond of subordination represented by wage labor *and* deprived of the guarantees that come with it. On this twofold basis, Uberized contractors seem like the epitome of neoliberal subjects: liberated from the yoke and deprived of the protections inherent in the wage-labor condition. It would seem that their fate depends solely on their work and savings. Yet in reality, gig seekers owe more to the web of connections they prove capable of weaving than to their ability to pull themselves up by their own bootstraps. More precisely, both the exploitation of the resources they possess and the coverage of the risks to which they are exposed depend on the credit that they manage to accumulate.

On the one hand, it is certainly by advertising the skills and other assets they seek to "share" on the relevant interface that service providers succeed in finding customers. Yet successful self-marketing actually requires that the free agents' first clients appreciate them well enough to rate their services favorably. Building a digital reputation—manifested by scores, "likes," friends, and followers—is thus the primary concern of independent contractors. On the other hand, in the absence of benefits associated with the salaried condition, the accumulation of a reputational capital—which includes a decent credit score reflecting a past of loans without default—is also how self-employed gig seekers win the confidence of bankers and private insurers. Altogether, therefore, the sustainability of their operations depends far more on the appreciation of sponsors, whether customers or backers, than on the self-reliance that neoliberal ideologues present as the core of the entrepreneurial ethos.

Despite being self-employed, the typical addressees of the gig economy diverge from the profit-seeking (and for that reason debt-averse and tax-averse) entrepreneurs hailed by the neoconservative revolution. Yet they do match the profile of the credit-seeking investees molded by third-way reforms and rhetoric in the following decade. If anything, the advent and proliferation of digital interfaces devoted to professional and social connection perfects the 1990s vision of "projects in search of investment" by way of facilitating the integration of their various resources in a multidimensional portfolio. Along with offering them a site where they can connect with one another, platforms endow their users with a specific set of continuously rated assets that they can combine, cross-reference, and manage as so many components of their reputational capital.

Enlightening in this respect are the prophecies of Rachel Botsman, who defines herself as a global authority on the collaborative economy. In a Ted Talk dating from 2010, the coauthor of *What's Mine Is Yours*[31] forecasts that in the near future—which she definitely sees as bright—the main resource people will have to cultivate will be their reputational capital.[32] Soon, Botsman imagines, everyone will have some kind of Facebook hyperpage where the various appreciations of friends, lovers, mentors, creditors, customers, and service providers will be displayed side by side. This open portfolio, she adds, will make it possible to evaluate the attractiveness and reliability of the person on display, as well as to assess the development of her reputational value and thus to determine her suitability for a task, a line of credit, or an intimate relationship.

Rachel Botsman certainly recognizes that her prophesized mechanism raises some questions, especially regarding the protection of people's privacy. But in her view, the disadvantages of overexposure are positively offset by the management power that each individual will be able to exercise over her profile. To avoid embarrassment, is it not enough to reconfigure the page where a reputation is exposed to inspection, even if it means investing in more presentable conduct and company or, if need be, in acquiring positive reviews?[33] Like a company buying back its own shares to avert a drop in their price or a central bank resorting to quantitative easing in order to appease bondholders, the private asset managers fashioned by the development of platform capitalism are invited to speculate or, more precisely, to fuel speculation on their own reputational capital.

The enthusiasm of its promoters certainly offers no guarantee that in its current form, the "collaborative economy" is destined for a radiant future. Yet in a number of developed countries, the erosion of the wage-labor condition, or at least the impending decline of the wage-labor society, is deemed plausible enough to inspire multiple think tank reports and, in some cases, already to affect public policy. Up until now, governments have largely confined themselves to a laissez-faire attitude, albeit sometimes combined with moral reservations, vis-à-vis the gig economy. Conscious of the fears aroused by the Uberization of work yet at the same time anxious not to deprive themselves of the economic activity generated by Uber, Amazon, and others, politicians are happy to venture harsh criticisms of the "partnerships" that platforms impose on service providers, going so far as to express their approval when a court decision condemns a blatant denial of employment, but are careful not to ban recourse to partnership by legislative or regulatory paths.[34]

It is unlikely that such a wait-and-see attitude can last, however. For in devolving the responsibility to rule on platforms' labor practices to the courts, elected representatives expose themselves to a no-win situation: faced with accusations of negligence and subservience when predatory sites emerge unscathed from legal proceedings against them, they also risk watching the giants of the gig economy desert their territory if a judgment requiring the redefinition of partnerships as employment contracts sets a precedent. We might therefore predict that the authorities' current passivity will soon give way to a supportive approach of the character already prescribed by several think tank reports.

Purported to calm people's anxieties about a pervasive Uberization of work yet equally careful to ward off the exodus of major platforms, upcoming reforms are likely to be two-pronged. On the one hand, governments will be receptive to the complaints of service providers such as drivers and couriers who resent having to be self-employed in order to be recruited by ride-hailing or food-delivery companies. Short of making the conversion of commercial contracts into employment contracts mandatory, as is increasingly required by the courts, public authorities seem poised to endow independent contractors with a modicum of the rights and protections granted to actual employees. Though platforms may resist such adjustments by threatening to move their operations elsewhere, the fear that, wherever they go, court rulings could prove more stringent than moderate legislative reforms is bound to persuade platforms to come to terms with more protective partnerships.

On the other hand, wage earners will likewise see their status change. In line with the trend that has been affecting labor law ever since flexibility became a cornerstone of public policy, champions of further reforms call for yet another adaptation of legislation to the evolution of the market. For an ever-increasing proportion of the working population, their argument goes, professional trajectories not only comprise a multiplicity of jobs—fixed term or part-time, successive or cumulative—but also an alternation and sometimes a combination of actual employments and gigs. Thus, as these contingent workers become more "autonomous" with every passing day, or at least less dependent on just one employer, there is no reason to maintain a clear distinction between their statutory rights and the new protections that are about to be afforded to the self-employed.[35]

Altogether, and ultimately, reformers want to pave the way for the replacement of both partnerships and precarious employment contracts with a single regime of professional activity. For political leaders still committed to facilitate the valorization of their citizens but faced with bond markets wary of states' "social debt," the inclusion of all contingent workers in the same status of partial self-employment has a double advantage. First, in accounting terms, the standardization of guarantees will convey that elected officials are striving "to do better with less"—a motto that bondholders never fail to appreciate. But over and above its positive impact on fiscal consolidation, the emergence of a post-wage-labor condition also enables public officials to amend their pledge to their fellow citizens: while not reneging on their promise to help everyone become more appreciable, they will no longer be held accountable for their constituents' employability, in the narrow sense of the word.

It is important to emphasize that there is nothing inherently regressive about including wage earners and independent contractors in a single regime of legal guarantees. On the contrary, combining the protections won by the former with the autonomy enjoyed by the latter—when self-employment is their choice—could result in a status that would remedy the subordination that comes with being employed as well as the precarious conditions under which most free agents sell their services. Yet in a context where social reforms are primarily meant to accommodate the wishes of liquidity providers, the chances that contingent workers will experience the upcoming single regime of professional activity as a "win-win" improvement on freedom and security are extremely slim.

COMPENSATED SUBORDINATION AND SPONSORED INTERDEPENDENCE

For more than two decades, the governments of industrialized nations have tried to retain the confidence of both creditors and voters by vowing to help the latter become more attractive in the eyes of the former. Initially formulated by third-way politicians in the 1990s, at a time when an already expanding derivatives market encouraged households to run up debts, the project of enticing citizens to enhance their creditworthiness has continued to inform public policy ever since. Yet the way in which governments attend to their mission has evolved, especially over the last decade. As already mentioned, optimizing the per-capita value of a nation's human capital now proceeds as much from a reduction in the ratio's "denominator" by way of the actual banishment and statistical erasure of groups deemed financially unattractive as from an increase in the "numerator" by way of investing in education and training as well as welcoming skillful and/or pliable migrants. Moreover, even among the individuals who are still eligible for incentives to make themselves more appreciable, employability is no longer what public policies necessarily seek to foster: thanks to the emergence of platform capitalism and its economic model, all that governments need to offer are resources enabling their beneficiaries to manage more effectively the asset portfolio that underpins their reputation.

The support that public authorities still extend to the valorization of their citizens is informed by two complementary preoccupations. The first one is sticking to frugal promises. Already part of Bill Clinton's pledge to "help people help themselves" and Tony Blair's commitment to motivate the "workless class," such a concern has been considerably reinforced since the beginning of the 2010s, when debt consolidation came back, so to speak, with a vengeance. Governments' second preoccupation is protecting themselves from the hostility induced by their frugality. They usually tackle this by stressing the burden of allegedly undeserving claimants, thereby turning their efforts to discriminate among credit seekers on the basis of "assets" such as nationality, race, pliancy, and flexibility into a potentially popular move. Popular, that is, with white "natives" who feel grateful to be appreciated for their roots and skin color.

Third-way leaders of the 1990s celebrated the globalization of all types of exchanges. The free movement of capital, goods and, to a lesser extent, people, was deemed necessary to build a peaceful "international community," whose member states would rely on a blending of skills and cultural hybridization to compete more successfully for investors' favors. Two decades later, however, mainstream politicians are no longer inclined to announce the advent of a world without walls. Indeed, most of them have used the failure of the Arab Spring and its consequences—an influx of refugees and a recurrence of terrorism—as justifications not only to reinforce border controls but also to showcase their economic patriotism and invite their fellow citizens to reappraise national identity as a precious facet of their human capital. While hardly intent on regulating capital movements, present-day governments are careful not to treat unregulated financial operations as just one dimension of a desirable cosmopolitan order allowing liquidities, commodities, and people to move freely across national borders. On the contrary, they endeavor to dispel the unpopularity of their persistent dependency on financial markets by raising fears about migrant invasions and, in some cases, by calling for the restoration of trade protectionism.

Although eulogies of halcyon globalization are no longer fashionable, elected representatives remain convinced that incentivizing their creditworthy constituents to invest in their human capital is what they must do to secure the trust of markets without losing too many votes. In their view, it is a commitment that both voters and investors can come to terms with: the former because they no longer have much faith in the resumption of strong economic growth that sustained stable employment throughout the Fordist era; the latter because once dissociated from the promise to guarantee employability for all, pledges to help people increase their attractiveness to recruiters and lenders delineate the kind of social policy that bondholders can support.

In that respect, public officials' concern for the per capita value of their nation's human capital is analogous to the attention that corporate managers pay to their firm's social responsibility: in both instances, governing is primarily about persuading financial backers that their funds are invested in valuable assets. As we have seen in the first chapter, CEOs well versed in the pursuit of shareholder value are aware that if they don't want to raise investors' eyebrows, they can't present socially and ecologically responsible practices as a regrettable but unavoidable drain on future dividends. Keeping shareholders confident requires that virtuous actions are not perceived as additional costs, but rather as a significant component of the equity appreciation that good governance is meant to deliver. In other words, it is incumbent on corporate managers to argue that because they have been appointed to sustain the credit of the firm, tending to the company's good reputation (with regard to employees rights, environmental conservation, consumer health, or ethical rules) is an integral part of their remit. Only on this condition will the sums committed to acquiring a CSR (corporate social responsibility) label represent a sound investment.

For their part, elected officials, whose priority is maintaining the confidence of bond markets, are likewise required to cast their social policy in win-win terms. On the one hand, to endow their territory with the business-friendly climate that will enable them to keep borrowing at a reasonable rate, they must: draw up budgets as rigorous about spending as they are compassionate about taxing, attend to the ever-increasing flexibility of the labor market, and offer the private sector secure property rights. On the other hand, however, to prevent such measures from backfiring on the electoral front, governments do their best to convince investors that the competitiveness of a country is also a function of its citizens' productivity. They therefore advertise programs for training and maintaining human capital that will be judged attractive not only by virtue of their moderate cost, but also because they produce the skills, flexibility, and availability that make a population financially attractive.

Because "good" governance treats CSR as a facet of a firm's share value, and thus as an asset conducive to stock market speculation, we have argued that stakeholder activism should appropriate it for its own purposes: to speculate against the stock of socially or environmentally irresponsible companies. The analogical reasoning behind the present book would thus suggest that legislative reforms purported to substitute semi-independent service providers for wage earners are likewise liable to appropriation by activists. In other words, just as *stakeholders* must challenge the power of *shareholders* to define what counts as CSR, citizens, or better still, *social creditors*, are to lay siege to and speculate on the incentives to human capital appreciation that governments sell to their *financial creditors* as an attractive substitute to employment-based protections and benefits. As for corporate social responsibility, what is at stake in this strategic reappropriation is not simply to denounce the regressive character of public policies that seek to encourage their citizens to constitute themselves as portfolios of valuable assets. While exposing the rationale behind the substitution of partnerships for employment contracts is essential to mobilize investees, the activism of social creditors is ultimately about modifying the conditions of asset valorization and credit allocation.

As they currently stand, the reform projects aiming to include all contingent workers in a single status are designed to meet the expectations of financial markets. Far from delineating a condition that would combine autonomy with decent risk coverage, they merely foreshadow another stage in the process that has made the lives of wage earners increasingly more precarious since the turn of the 1980s. And indeed, most labor unions are wary of the prevailing trend in labor law reform.

Save for so-called reformist labor organizations—the ones that have adopted the coaching role assigned them by third-way leaders in the 1990s and thus make it their mission to help their members adapt to the transformation of the labor market—union leaders concentrate their efforts on preserving whatever they can of the social rights conquered by previous generations and thus on resisting the Uberization of work that they consider inherent to the decline of the wage-labor society.

Now, if we focus on the mobilization of the Uberized themselves rather than on the labor movement's charge against the ongoing deterioration of salaried labor, we realize that while obviously outraged by the predatory practices of capitalist platforms, these workers are not after the restoration of the postwar employee status. It is true that until now, the demonstrations and court cases pursued by car drivers and food delivery couriers have been about reclassifying the services they provide as employment.[36] Yet even when these actions prove successful—and they often do—they merely represent a necessary tactical step rather than a strategic objective. In other words, the fact that gig-economy workers challenge the legality of dressing up jobs as partnerships in order to obtain minimal rights and protections does not mean that assimilating into the wage-earning class is their ultimate goal.

Significant here is the argument of Jérôme Pimot, organizer of a couriers' collective in France. In an interview given to the French online daily *Mediapart*, the delivery-cycling activist explains that like others resisting Uberization, he and his comrades turned to the courts to request that their work be reclassified as waged employment: in France as elsewhere, home delivery platforms require the people they recruit to be registered as *auto-entrepreneurs*, independent contractors.[37] Yet Pimot adds that beyond obtaining compensation for aggrieved deliverymen and deliverywomen, the purpose of taking their case to court is predominantly symbolic, that is, insofar as favorable court decisions serve to expose the duplicity of the food tech industry. To the extent that these rulings create a precedent, however, they are unlikely to provide couriers with lasting jobs.

Indeed, Pimot further observes that despite their objectionable practices, home delivery platforms operate largely in the red. Faithful to the typical economic model of start-ups, they enhance their attractiveness to investors by luring them with the prospect of cornering the entire market, but for that reason they also ask backers to be patient and endure long periods of losses. The same applies, for instance, to the carpool giants whose impressive valuation is accompanied by sizeable deficits: $4.5 billion for Uber and $600 million for Lyft in 2017. Since gig-economy platforms are already in jeopardy when they have practically no employees who are recognized as such, there are good reasons to believe that the additional cost of reclassifying "partners" as wage earners would soon prompt investors to lose their patience.

Should we conclude that case law upholding the demands of the bike couriers and hybrid car drivers offers nothing but a Pyrrhic victory? Hardly. For both Pimot and his Belgian colleagues mobilized by the collapse of the Take Eat Easy brand see the failure of their "employer" as an opportunity to reinvent their own status and activity. They argue that the bankruptcy awaiting the food tech predators, should the courts compel them to employ their couriers, would offer the latter an opportunity to occupy the space that has been vacated. More precisely, the judicial coup de grâce delivered to the brands could pave the way for their replacement by cooperatives whose delivery workers would assume the role of management and share the income. As suggested by the Belgian think tank Hackistan, we can also envisage new entities bringing together couriers and the restaurateurs whose meals they deliver. After all, platforms owe their success to the disintermediation they pride themselves on fostering.[38] If the service they deliver essentially resides in connecting suppliers and purchasers of services, it is perfectly conceivable, technically and legally, that rather than paying an often exorbitant rent to their platform's shareholders, users of these interfaces could take them over for their own purposes.

Outside the world of couriers, such cooperative sites already exist. The Green Taxi Cooperative of Denver, Colorado, owned and governed by some eight hundred drivers, competes with Uber as well as with traditional taxis.[39] More recently, in France, a collective called Coopcycle has developed software exclusively devoted to worker-owned home delivery cooperatives that "enables customers to have their orders delivered by bicycle."[40] Similar initiatives are also found in other segments of the "sharing economy," such as the private housing rental sector and e-commerce, as exemplified by the Hôtel du Nord cooperative in Marseille[41] and the German platform Fairmondo,[42] respectively.

The cooperative movement obviously has a long history. While its merit as a mode of resistance to capitalism has been a subject of fierce controversy from the start—Marx claimed, contra Proudhon, that the expansion of the market economy would soon vanquish mutualism—the same technologies responsible for the advent of platform capitalism have arguably also offered cooperativism a new lease on life. Predatory digital interfaces such as Uber, Deliveroo, TaskRabbit, and Amazon Mechanical Turk certainly play a decisive role in the corrosion of the salaried condition. At the same time, the world of service providers and users created by their mode of operation also enables its denizens to link up, network, and take control of their transactions.

Strategically, the social and political agenda foreshadowed by French and Belgian courier activists echoes the approach of revolutionary labor unions in the industrial age. Convinced that short of constantly cutting wages, capitalist ventures could not survive for very long—thanks to the tendency of the rate of profit to fall, which Marx called "the most important law of political economy"—members of the International Workingmen's Association (1875–1876) argued that negotiating higher salaries was not tantamount to legitimizing wage labor. On the contrary, they saw bargaining with their exploiters as the proper way to hasten the final crisis of capitalism. Similarly, when delivery workers

facing Uberization ask courts to reclassify their activity as employment, the strategic purpose of their action is not to obtain the status
of wage earner but to precipitate the collapse of the brands whose economic model is predicated on recruiting independent contractors.

That today's independent contractors are as determined to take
advantage of their exploiters' weaknesses as the communist industrial workers were in the second half of the nineteenth century does
not mean that they share the aspirations of their predecessors. Because
the imagined outcome of a struggle is largely shaped by the mode of
government that it confronts, the new cooperative ecosystem that
may germinate out of the ruins of platform capitalism is unlikely to
resemble the collectivization of the means of production that was supposed to seal the demise of industrial capitalism. At the same time,
what the scholar-activist Trebor Scholz calls "platform cooperativism"
may share some features with the self-managerial ideals of 1970s social
movements.[43]

The struggles waged by contingent platform workers are still young
and marginal. For that reason, it is still difficult to assess their significance and eventual impact, especially with respect to the viability
of the cooperative venues that they see as an alternative both to their
current Uberized condition and to secure employment contracts. At
this stage, the main challenge faced by the proponents of "platform
cooperativism" pertains to its economic model. For in order to compete with the capitalist enterprises that dominate the so-called collaborative economy, cooperative interfaces must constitute themselves as
actual investees, that is, as projects worthy of investment. To that end,
they have to become attractive enough to raise the funds necessary for
their operations, but they also have to develop a network of sponsoring
customers and partners that will advertise their existence and enhance
their reputational capital.

The main backers of the gig economy are venture capitalists (VCs)
obsessed with breeding "unicorns"—the code name for start-ups

valued at more than one billion dollars. VCs are thus on the lookout for "visionaries" whose skill consists not so much in resolving a problem or satisfying an existing need as in imagining a market that can be created and then conquered by their project. "Business angels," as flushed start-up creators tenderly call their VCs, readily understand that devising cost-effective ways to satisfy a hitherto unexpressed demand on a scale large enough to ward off competitors is an endeavor requiring patient shareholders. Breeding a unicorn involves not only enduring long periods of losses but also deferring dividend distribution once their protégés become profitable: for refusing to show revenues, to the extent that it conveys monopolistic grand ambitions, is a key element in a start-up's credit.[44] At the same time, however, VCs want to make sure their "angelic" patience is not confused with foolishness: they thus request that their money goes exclusively to the "vision" that the company stands for, at the expense of wages and benefits for substitutable service providers.

Cooperative platforms, it is safe to say, exhibit none of the features that VCs find attractive. First, to the extent that they are owned by workers, their primary concern is the welfare of all the people involved in their operations. (Business angels, by contrast, consider minimizing labor costs as the proper way to express gratefulness for their generosity.) Second, to the extent that sharing benefits is more expensive than relying on Uberized "partners," cooperative platforms can survive only if they forfeit the broker's fee that enables digital interfaces to display "visionary" ambitions and by that token lure venture capital. Third, to the extent that the economic model of cooperative platforms impels them to build their reputation locally rather than seek global market dominance, they may generate modest revenues at an early stage, which, as we have seen, is not what VC culture appreciates.

Does this mean that for want of meeting the criteria for venture capital allocation, digital coops do not represent a viable answer to

Uberization? Before denying platform cooperativism any capacity to take root alongside or even at the expense of its capitalist nemesis, it is important to recall that the activists who endeavor to escape enforced self-employment without returning to the bosom of wage labor belong to the category of *investees*—bearers of projects in search of investment. As such, the fate of their initiatives depends primarily on whether they succeed in earning the confidence of individuals or institutions capable of sponsoring them. Yet the fact that good credit, moral as well as financial, is the fuel of successful ventures does not imply that success is incumbent on conforming to a profile that creditors currently deem appreciable. Indeed, experts in the art of breeding unicorns are the first to stress the point: altering the laws of attraction of capital, rather than meeting the same expectations as their predecessors, is what turns start-up founders into "disruptive" innovators.[45] Do cooperative platforms have the wherewithal to "disrupt"? That is, are they capable of modifying the conditions under which credit is allocated? Though few business angels would agree—but then again, disruption is by definition what most observers can't foresee—we will argue that they stand a fighting chance.

First, as far as economic sustainability is concerned, digital-age cooperativism does not suffer the handicaps that put a fatal strain on former experiments in self-management, such as the watchmaker Lip in Besançon (1973–1977) and the appliance company Numax in Barcelona (1977–1979). In both cases, workers attempted to ward off closing their factory by taking control of production and management, but, unable to raise sufficient funds, they eventually failed to save their jobs.[46] Unlike their predecessors of the late Fordist era, however, today's cooperative platforms are less vulnerable to capital flight: insofar as they operate in the service sector and target populations with Internet access, they can rely on relatively cheap technologies and readily available customers. Thus, even without an infusion of venture capital, a skillfully conceived application accompanied by minimal upfront investment—in some cases, obtained through crowdfunding—often suffices to launch a project.

Second, cooperatives are not necessarily ill equipped when it comes to competing with the social-networking power of digital predators. For the system of cross-referenced ratings to which platform users are exposed can serve another purpose than enforcing the criteria of good conduct defined by the likes of Uber, Amazon, and TaskRabbit. Given that users and providers rate as much as they are themselves rated, and given that the credit to which everyone aspires is subject to speculation, cross-referenced ratings are a resource that the Uberized can appropriate and use to affect the reputations of others—the customers for whom they provide services, the sites on which they advertise their skills and wish to supplant, but also their peers whose assets they wish to commend.

The burgeoning activism among independent contractors affiliated with Amazon's Mechanical Turk clearly illustrates these different ways of politically and economically investing the ratings field. As reported by the essayist Paul Hampton, the first militant initiative by MTurk workers took the form of a third-party service called Turkopticon, launched in 2013 and intended to evaluate the providers by listing bad payers and stigmatizing abuses. Next came Dynamo, in 2015, a collective grafted onto the experience of its predecessor, but more ambitious because it undertook to formalize the work of Turkopticon by drafting a code of correct practice for service purchasers and to secure better treatment from Amazon by a massive, widely publicized dispatch of complaints directed to its CEO. While this initial campaign ended in failure—far from agreeing to the Turkers' requests, Jeff Bezos penalized them for their audacity by raising the site's access costs—the reprisals suffered by the Dynamo activists led them to envision another strategy. Riding on the outrage created by the response of the platform's owner, they started circulating the idea that instead of "voicing" unheard complaints, Turkers should challenge Amazon's

Mechanical Turk by "exiting" and pooling their networks of clients to create their own cooperative platform.[47]

As this still-budding initiative indicates, coalitions of gig-economy workers do not exactly follow in the footsteps of industrial-era labor unions. Rather than pressure the platforms on which they sell their services in order to obtain better working conditions, they seek to appropriate the rating system that these predatory interfaces thrive on to build their own credit at their expense. Digital interfaces, after all, do not encourage the users of their sites to rate each other without constituting them, potentially at least, as sponsors of each other's performances. Contracted tasks, to the extent that suppliers and clients rate their experience, contribute not only to the income but also to the credit of all the parties involved—including the platform owners. With Trebor Scholz, we can therefore stake the development of platform cooperativism on the formation of an ecosystem composed of worker-owned outfits engaged in different activities (deliveries, passenger transportation, housing rentals, but also agricultural production, design, fair trade, and so on), yet set on establishing preferential links with each other. Thanks to mutual sponsoring, the members of each cooperative in the network would contribute to the reputation and, by that token, to the economic viability of their partners.[48]

Finally, as service providers take on the management, share the fruits, and build up the reputation of their professional activities, they can present the development of their ecosystem as a potentially popular political cause. To understand why public authorities may be enticed to support a cooperative alternative to capitalist platforms, another look at the latter's strategy is in order. As we have seen, to draw the attention of venture capitalists, start-ups with unicorn ambitions point to the existence of a hitherto ignored source of demand and claim to have discovered the algorithm to tap it. Once investors are hooked, they must make the case that to create and conquer this market to be, a relatively extended period of investment without any returns is unavoidable.

VCs are usually all the more willing to be patient, since for rapidly growing start-ups, a balance sheet in the red tends to result in share appreciation. Yet they still need to feel that their money is invested in the construction of a monopoly market. As already mentioned, slashed labor costs figure prominently among the signs of "earnestness" that business angels require. Equally important, however, is their protégés' commitment not to spare any effort to avoid taxes and dodge regulations in the countries or cities where they do operate. This is why public authorities are often ambivalent when capitalist platforms set foot in their territory.

On the one hand, the eagerness of governments to create an attractive environment for investors entices national and local rulers to welcome platform capitalism's contribution to the flexibility of the job market. On the other hand, however, they not only resent the tax-evasion schemes that gig-economy giants specialize in but are also aware of the social repercussions and inconvenience that some "sharing" sites cause to local communities—for instance, the impact of Airbnb on real estate prices. They also worry about the impact that these agents of disintermediation have on the economic sectors they purport to "disrupt," whether tourism with Airbnb, transportation with Uber, or retail commerce with Amazon.

Though elected officials rarely go so far as to banish the spearheads of platform capitalism, they can arguably be persuaded that it is in their own interest to frustrate the monopolistic ambitions of predatory unicorns. Subjected as they are to the strictures of debt consolidation, states, regions, and municipalities are admittedly unlikely to challenge global platforms fed on massive doses of venture capital with public rivals financed by tax revenues. On the other hand, proponents of platform cooperativism can make a case for the establishment of a regulatory framework designed to curb tax evasion and make companies accountable for the negative externalities created by their mode of operation. Having capitalist platforms abide by stricter rules regarding fiscal contributions, environmental preservation, urban zoning, and labor practices would go some way, if not in jeopardizing their financial attractiveness, then at least in giving local cooperatives a chance to compete with them in terms of the price and quality of services.

Some cities have already started down this road. In Barcelona, especially, where the mayor and her team hail largely from social movements, the municipal government uses its regulatory prerogatives to facilitate the development of cooperative service providers in key economic sectors such as transportation, energy, and telecommunications. In committing to backing cooperatives, progressive elected officials indicate their refusal to devolve disintermediation—the removal of intermediaries in a supply chain—to predatory interfaces domiciled in tax havens. At the same time, opting to facilitate the emergence of worker-owned and self-managed ventures constitutes a departure from the paths traditionally identified with the Left—keeping utilities and services in the public sector and making wage-labor protections the main tenet of social policy.[49]

For their supporters, coop-friendly regulations are not merely meant to create a niche for contingent workers' projects, leading at best to a modest expansion of the so-called social and solidarity economy (SSE) sector. Convinced that the renewal of cooperativism is a more credible challenge to Uberization than the restoration of the postwar social compact, where workers' welfare depended on secure wages and social benefits guaranteed by the state, gig-economy activists also see their demands as a blueprint for a new political engagement with governments. Rather than simply asking for legal or statutory protections against exploitative recruiters, promoters of cooperative platforms urge public authorities to act as "incubators" of their own initiatives. Ultimately, they want their political representatives to provide a "platform" for their platforms: more than as a bulwark against predators or a substitute for market mechanisms, governments should act as a facilitator of their incipient cooperative ecosystem so as to enhance its competitiveness.

As salaried work dissolves into gigs, the champions of cooperative platforms neither settle for the dire autonomy of independent contractors nor strive to reinstate the compensated subordination of yesteryears' wage earners. Instead, they seek to lay the ground for a sustainable regime of horizontal interdependence predicated on mutual sponsorship and favorably tilted regulations. While their advocacy arguably speaks to certain categories of contingent workers—mostly young, urban, and technologically savvy—what still calls for further examination is the potential reach not only of platform cooperativism's business model but also of the social imaginary and political agenda that its development would entail. The answer to this question largely depends on whether one believes in the widespread, yet controversial claims about the impending "end of work" or at least about the waning of the wage-labor society.

It is primarily on the Left that pronouncements about the unavoidable ebb of employment opportunities are held to be a fable. Whether Marxists, post-Keynesians, or members of the Regulation School,[50] a number of heterodox economists view the allegedly epochal crisis of wage labor as an ideological tale designed to obfuscate the role of financial capitalism in the constant deterioration of working conditions. As they see it, the increasing flexibility and segmentation of labor markets are hardly inevitable consequences of technological progress and globalization. There is, of course, no denying that in combination, information and communications technologies, robotics, and skilled labor streams facilitate the polarization of the workforce between a small minority who, on account of their highly rated skills, either enjoy stable positions or are free to choose (upward) mobility and an increasingly vast majority who must settle for impermanent and precarious jobs, from fixed-term contracts to stints at temporary work agencies and gigs. According to many progressive economists, however, segmented labor markets proceed from the sway of investors' expectations over employers' choices—from the fact that the former judge the latter's performance on their ability to raise the asset-to-labor ratio of their company's operations—and not from some quasi-natural law of economic evolution.[51]

Prophecies about the end of work as we know it, their Left critics further charge, also serve to justify the subjection of public policies to the concerns of bondholders. Orthodox economists, who are the main proponents of this omen, argue that job markets contain two heterogeneous dividing lines: one is the inevitably growing but economically justified partition between the appreciated few and the substitutable many; the other is an outdated and unjustified division between protected and marginalized workers. Dubbed "insiders," protected workers are said to enjoy advantages obtained at a time when the merits of flexibility were not yet recognized: they include, above all, civil servants and holders of permanent contracts that are difficult to terminate. Contingent workers, dubbed "outsiders," are not only relegated to jobs with no future, but also, and above all, excluded from the comfort zones carved out by trade-union corporatism and tenure.

For elected representatives eager to maintain the confidence of their creditors, subscribing to such a picture has considerable advantages. In declaring that outsiders suffer from the guaranteed status enjoyed by insiders, public authorities can legitimize bundling the aid they give the former with eroded protections offered to the latter—and even present the rolling back of vested social rights as an act of fairness. Instead of expanding their social programs to make up for the deteriorating labor conditions caused by shareholders' demands, they blame the damage caused by their own debt consolidation policies on insiders' "privileges," and by that token they manage to conduct their race to the bottom in the name of equality.[52]

For its progressive critics, the dominant view of labor market divides is not only ideologically motivated: it also has a specific political purpose. Claiming that the growing gap between globalization's winners and losers is legitimate and unbridgeable, whereas the residual advantages of insiders over outsiders are unjustifiable and obsolete, is meant to advance the project of gathering wage earners and independent contractors in a single status of professional activity. While the advent of this common condition would hardly affect the compensations and guarantees afforded to the indispensable few, their contingent counterparts would be condemned to a permanent state of (semi-) Uberization.

Heterodox economists thus contend that the much-heralded waning of the wage-labor society is not, as their orthodox rivals would have it, the accurate description of an ineluctable process to which private companies, governments, and job seekers must adapt but a politically motivated proposition intended to consummate the ascendancy of financial capital and its prerequisites. Conversely, in their view, resisting the dictates of investors requires denouncing the tales that confuse their incidence on business management, statecraft, and individual lives with the implacable way of the world. What such resistance logically implies, therefore, is that a different way of managing firms and governing states would make it possible, if not to restore the wage-labor society characteristic of late Fordism, then at least to propose a modernized version of it. In other words, to dispel the myth of a shortage of jobs, it would be enough for managers to refrain from sacrificing wage earners' interests to the pursuit of shareholder value, for elected representatives to stop subordinating their voters' well-being to the approval of bond markets, and for both to agree on countering growing inequalities by sharing work and covering risks more evenly.[53]

Regardless of whether the working conditions and welfare provisions constitutive of the postwar social compact could actually be restored, one may wonder about the existence of social agents at once capable of prompting the required volte-faces and willing to do so. Labor unions, whose task it would be to alter corporate management's options, owe their particular loss of influence to shareholders' sway over corporate strategy—or, as we put it earlier, to the preemption of labor market negotiations by stock market speculations. Similarly, voters who remain presumably entitled to impose their collective will on their representatives must reckon with the subordination of their sovereignty to the valuations of their country's debt in the bond market. Moreover, their own priorities are gradually altered by the conditions under which they access commercial credit, which has become their only way of offsetting increasingly precarious working conditions. For that reason, obstacles to the restoration of the relatively protective wage-labor society of yore include not only the political weakness of its supporters but also their declining number.

Progressive detractors of the end-of-work rhetoric are certainly right to recall that the ascendency of investors' expectations over the conduct of firms, public officials, and private citizens does not pertain to the unstoppable movement of technological progress and its inescapable socioeconomic consequences. For what finance's stranglehold on the concerns and options of all economic agents primarily attests to are the political defeats suffered by labor unions and the Left over more than three decades. Even so, there are good reasons to question the relevance of a strategy that predicates the renewal of social movements on the hope of rewinding history.

Instead of exhorting contingent workers to reject ideological pronouncements about the waning of wage labor and revive the demands of earlier generations, wouldn't it be more effective to bank on activist appropriations of the investee condition, one shared by political personnel, the managers of transnational firms, and even investment bankers? Such, at any rate, is the proposal advanced in this book. Although the constitutive stakes of this alternative strategy are no longer the conquest of wage earners' rights—whether to hasten capitalism's final crisis or merely to improve workers' lot—we have argued that they echo the dual relationship of the labor activists with their wage-earning condition—a condition that they denounced as the subjective formation responsible for their exploitation yet at the same time endorsed in order to negotiate better salaries, shorter workdays, a safer working environment, and more decent benefits.

In past decades, the regime of capital accumulation unwittingly unleashed by neoliberal reforms has proved equally capable of withstanding the inequality it creates and the financial bubbles it inflates. Given this remarkable resilience, neither stressing the contingency of the policies that paved the way for investors' hegemony (the substitution of asset price for monetary inflation and of supply-side incentives for demand stimuli) nor exposing the fables proclaiming the irreversibility of current trends (especially with respect to the fate of work) are likely to mobilize investees against their condition. In a world where both legal entities and physical persons are enjoined to devote themselves to improving their credit, challenging creditors' rating power primarily involves *counterspeculating* so as to alter the conditions under which creditworthiness is defined and distributed.

While the investment relation is asymmetrical, we have already argued that virtually every economic agent alternatively assumes the functions of investor and investee. For instance, hedge fund managers are investees insofar as they depend on the confidence of their shareholders, whereas friends and customers of a cooperative behave as investors—more precisely, as sponsors—by virtue of enhancing the reputational capital of the project they support. The preceding pages have successively examined three types of investees: corporations determined to provide what their shareholders value, governments obsessed by the attractiveness of their policy to bond markets, and individuals seeking to exhibit behavior likely to be sponsored. In all three cases, the pursuit of credit is the prevailing preoccupation. Now from the perspective of investee activism as we have defined it, there is an important difference between the last type of project in search of investment and the other two.

When activists contrive to speculate against a corporation's social and environmental irresponsibility or to increase the risks of fiscal austerity in the eyes of holders of government debt, their campaigns target projects with which they are associated—as stakeholders of the firm whose practices they rate or citizens of the states they threaten with default—but that they don't identify as their own. By contrast, collectives of service providers who organize themselves into cooperatives are only indirectly concerned with influencing the valuation of other investees. Though they certainly seek to damage the reputation of the capitalist platforms dominating their sector and for that purpose petition public authorities for tighter regulations, their main ambition is to improve the credit of their own initiatives.

Contingent workers organizing against their own Uberization are certainly not the only social group dependent on the evaluations of their own project. As industrialized societies have increasingly resorted to private and public loans to compensate for wage stagnation and declining tax revenue, respectively, a growing proportion of their members has been compelled to stake their prosperity and sometimes their economic survival on the reputational capital extended by lenders, insurers, and potential recruiters as well as by government agencies tasked with weeding out allegedly undeserving benefits recipients. Firms vow to reduce labor costs by offering increasingly precarious jobs and outsourcing everything outside their core activity, while states endeavor to consolidate their budgets by abolishing civil service posts and privatizing utilities. In this environment, free agents emerge as the investees par excellence, pushed to the verge of wage labor and its attendant protections. For that very reason, therefore, it is particularly noteworthy that their mobilization does not ultimately aim at the guarantees enjoyed by so-called insiders—workers whose employment contracts still come with health care, welfare, and pension provisions.[54]

Skeptics will certainly doubt the advisability of forsaking traditional employee demands, especially if they believe that reports of wage labor's impending death are greatly exaggerated, and they may even suspect contingent workers who nurture the prospect of setting up their own shop of buying into the neoliberal ideal of entrepreneurship for all. Because investee politics exists solely in an experimental state in all its dimensions—stakeholders' activism, social creditors' claims, and cooperativism's renewal—assessments of its potential and relevance pertain to speculation in every sense of the word. Regarding the specific fate of post-wage-labor activism, the main pending question is whether it can mobilize around other categories than service providers affiliated with digital interfaces such as Uber, Airbnb, Task-Rabbit, or MTurk.

Beyond the realm of platform capitalism, the prospect of Uberization is already haunting a wide variety of professions. Casualization is increasingly widespread in higher education and research, freelancing prevails in the culture industries,[55] and vast numbers of journalists, translators, designers, and artisans are paid on piecework.[56] To offset the isolation and vulnerability characteristic of this new professional environment, engaging in the formation of freelancers' collectives increasingly seems more promising—more realistic, as well as more desirable—than petitioning public or private institutions for more permanent employment contracts.

That cooperative solutions to job insecurity are on the rise is both corroborated and made possible not only by the growing attention they receive from foundations but also by the rapid development of crowdfunding platforms. The latter are admittedly neither equipped to compete with venture capital, bank loans, and financial markets nor primarily focused on worker-owned endeavors. Yet their surge evinces a widely shared desire to develop new fund-raising venues and, by that token, to modify the regime of accreditation hitherto dominated by institutional investors. Given how professional liquidity providers select the projects submitted to their attention—and how their criteria of valuation impact the availability of jobs and public funds—there is arguably a strong correlation between the rapid growth of participatory finance and the ideal of interdependence hailed by post-wage-labor activists.

While employers' and governments' subservience to creditors is undeniably a factor in the nascent revamping of cooperativism, contingent workers who opt to explore the cooperative path are no more intent on eschewing state support than on establishing autarchic communities at the margins of markets. Initially at least, their more modest goal is to inflect public policies so as to improve the competitiveness of their business model in their chosen market. They thus want their elected representatives to tilt regulations in their favor as well as to adapt risk-coverage mechanisms to their specific needs. Instead of keeping social protections attached to wage-earning jobs, which became the norm under the Fordist social compact, post-wage-labor activists ask for universal and unconditional guarantees. The "enabling" state—rather than the welfare state—presaged by their demands attests to the resonances between cooperativism and two other social as well as intellectual movements whose champions set themselves the tasks of rethinking, respectively, the protective and the regulatory functions of the state.

The first of these movement advocates "universal" or "basic" income, the purpose of which is to combine security with autonomy. The creation of a basic-income mechanism purports to free its recipients from the sway of shareholders' valuations over employment opportunities and of bondholders' priorities over social programs.[57] It does so by guaranteeing a modest but unconditional source of revenue, rather than by making the accessibility of social benefits conditional on either having or seeking a wage-earning job.

Unlike the negative tax famously championed by Milton Friedman and revived by some of his followers—as well as by some Silicon Valley tycoons—the progressive version of universal income is not intended to reduce the social safety net to a single allowance at the expense of

health care, pension, and welfare provisions. In the eyes of its supporters, the objective is not to trade vested rights for a meager stipend—low
enough, Friedman would add, not to encourage sloth—but to grant
people the means to broaden and weigh their options. Thanks to this
afforded respite, the reasoning goes, basic-income recipients will be
able to garner more influence over the evaluation of their own existence. To the extent that universal income is not used as a substitute for
employers' social contributions, it represents not only an alternative to
the convergence of wage labor and self-employment in a single professional activity status but also the kind of financial base that contingent
workers need in order to give cooperative projects a chance to material-
ize and take off.

Equally resonant with cooperativism are the research and social
experiments revolving around the notion of the "commons."[58] Despite
its kinship with communism, the term refers less to the final stage in
the collective appropriation of the means of production than to a reappropriation of the kind of support that twenty-first-century governments
pride themselves on extending to their citizens. Recall that once subjected to the pressure of bond markets, political leaders reacted by substituting the pledge of making their constituents employable for that of
securing stable jobs. Then, when even employability became too expensive a vow, they opted for the somewhat looser commitment to help their
citizens valorize their assets. While these rhetorical shifts have invariably translated into a relaxation of lending, hiring, and firing regulations, governments still claim to be accountable to their citizens. Short
of guaranteeing professional security for all or even for those who work
hard enough to deserve it, they still promise to facilitate people's access
to the resources required to improve their credit. Though hardly swayed
by this new agenda, advocates of the commons are in a good position
to challenge its promoters on their own turf. This is because commons
activism operates precisely in the register of *accessibility*—including
access to resources such as air, water, land, and knowledge.

Indeed, what the commoners' opposition to "enclosures" entails is the recognition of a right of access. The latter sometimes legitimizes intrusion into legally appropriated domains (whether protected by fences, patents, or copyrights) and sometimes rigorously demarcates the domain of what can be appropriated. Reclaiming the commons is thus less about instituting some new property regime alongside or in lieu of private and public ownership than about using the right of access as a tool to limit the reach and dent the exercise of property rights. Urging legislators and governing bodies to institute the required measures for increasing the accessibility of resources—at the expense of their proprietors' privileges—is thus an integral part of commoners' activism. Because reforms of this nature are bound to level the playing field between venture-capitalized projects and their less well-endowed challengers, they are also an essential tenet of the regulatory environment that the development of cooperativism necessitates.

Although they do not necessarily work together or even agree with each other's advocacy, supporters of an unconditional living income, of unrestrained access to vital resources, and of a cooperative response to the Uberization of work form a coherent constellation of post-wage-labor activists. It is true that so far, these causes primarily appeal to young, urban, and college-educated members of the precariat. However, it is also worth remembering that when Marx elected the "free laborer" as the protagonist in the coming revolution, the proletariat (formed by industrial wage earners) represented only a minority of the popular classes, as is the case with today's contingent workers. Though historical analogies are not always good predictors, comparing the budding activism of today's service providers with the struggles of the labor movement in the second half of the nineteenth century at least reminds us that staking social change on relatively marginal and disempowered groups is not necessarily wrongheaded—especially when these groups seem to indicate where capitalism is heading.

Now, this is precisely why many on the Left are suspicious of calls to institute a universal basic income, to circumvent property rights, and to revive cooperativism: loath to let capitalism's new turn dictate the agenda of its critics, they urge fellow progressives to fight instead for the restoration of a decent social safety net provided by a refurbished welfare state and attached to protective employment contracts. In their view, resisting the social and environmental havoc wrought by financial capitalists and their criteria of attractiveness involves preserving what they endeavor to undo, not taking them at their word that it is already and irrevocably undone. For the most part, these detractors of a Left *aggiornamento* do not challenge Marx's characterization of wages as inherent in workers' exploitation and thus of emancipation as the demise of wage labor. However, as the new regime of capital accumulation tends to substitute independent contractors for wage-earning employees, they find themselves in the paradoxical situation of calling for the rehabilitation of the very condition that they eventually seek to abolish.

In contrast, post-wage-labor activists have no qualms about playing the part assigned to them by creditors' hegemony. Their stance thus resonates with a different reading of Marx, one that stresses the ambivalent relationship of wage earners to their condition. The liberal anthropology underwriting industrial capitalism, Marx claimed, enticed workers to identify as utility-maximizing traders seeking to sell their labor power at the optimal price. While this identification was alienating, insofar as it normalized and legitimized the capitalist extortion of surplus value created by labor, once appropriated by the labor movement, it enabled "free laborers" to improve their negotiating power and eventually to conquer the social rights that are now taken away from them. Integral to the defeats suffered by the labor movement in the last three decades is the fact that financialized capitalism no longer has much use for utility-maximizing labor traders. As we have seen, investors only have eyes for credit-seeking projects. The question post-wage-labor activists seek to address, then, is whether this new subjective formation can be the matrix of a renewed resistance but also of fresh aspirations.

Although fashioned by creditors' expectations, prospective investees are not mere cogs in the current regime of capital accumulation. The constant and multiple ratings to which they are subjected are certainly meant to teach them the proper criteria of attractiveness and to pressure them into conducting their lives and configuring their hopes accordingly. Yet however constrained by what credit providers deem appreciable, investees are still endowed with an agency—rated as it were—that empowers them not only to invest in their own reputational capital but also to speculate with other like-minded investees on what assets should be recognized as appreciable and thus on who deserves to be called creditworthy. Similarly, the labor movement of yore managed to appropriate and reconfigure the self-interested and utility-maximizing condition to which wage earners were assigned. While assuming that workers were motivated by the pursuit of their interests, labor activists demonstrated by their political demands and industrial actions that interests are not individual and impervious to social change but collective and determined by the history of class conflicts.

Now the analogy between employees and investees' strategic appropriation of their respective conditions also points to substantial differences between the adversaries they confront, the grievances around which they rally, and the desired outcomes of their struggles. In other words, social and political aspirations are bound to vary according to the challenges from which they arise and the subjective formations responsible for their elaboration. Just as socialism and communism were free laborers' dreams, it is now up to investee activists to imagine and construct their own vision of a post-wage-labor society. That their initial outlines draw more closely on the experience of the appreciable projects endeavoring to conceive it than on their predecessors' utopias is hardly surprising.

1. On the "populist" character of the rhetoric used to sell Reagan's fiscal policy, see Monica Prasad, *The Politics of Free Markets: The Rise of Neoliberal Economic Policies in Britain, France, Germany and the United States* (Chicago: Chicago University Press, 2006), pp. 45–82. On the discursive strategy of the Thatcher government, see Christopher Payne, *The Consumer, Credit and Neoliberalism: Governing the Modern Economy* (London: Routledge, 2012); Stuart Hall, *The Hard Road to Renewal: Thatcherism and the Crisis of the Left* (London: Verso, 1988).

2. Wolfgang Streeck, "The Crises of Democratic Capitalism," *New Left Review* 71 (2011), pp. 7–9.

3. On 22 August 1996, when signing the Personal Responsibility and Work Opportunity Act (PRWORA) that he had called for during his 1992 presidential campaign, Bill Clinton stated, "Today the Congress will vote on legislation that gives us a chance … to transform a broken system that traps too many people in a cycle of dependence to one that emphasizes work and independence, to give people on welfare a chance to draw a paycheck, not a welfare check." "Text of President Clinton's Announcement on Welfare Legislation," *New York Times*, 1 August 1996, https://www.nytimes.com/1996/08/01/us/text-of-president-clinton-s-announcement-on-welfare-legislation.html. See also Jamie Peck, *Workfare States* (New York: Guilford Press, 2001), pp. 97–126.

4. "Earlier this century leaders faced the challenge of creating a welfare state that could provide security for the new working class. Today the greatest challenge for any democratic government is to refashion our institutions to bring this new workless class back into society and into useful work, and to bring back the will to win." Tony Blair, speech at the Aylesbury Estate, June 1997, quoted in Peck, *Workfare States*, p. 261.

5. On the intellectual and discursive framework of the "third way," see, especially, Anthony Giddens, *The Third Way: The Renewal of Social Democracy* (Cambridge: Polity, 1998), followed by *The Third Way and Its Critics* (Cambridge: Polity, 2000). On third-way social policies, see, especially, Anne Daguerre, *Active Labour Market Policies and Welfare Reform: Europe and the US in Comparative Perspective* (Houndmills: Palgrave, 2007); Jingjing Huo, *Third Way Reforms:*

Social Democracy after the Golden Age (Cambridge: Cambridge University Press, 2009); Peck, *Workfare States*, pp. 261-340.

6. The conversion of unemployment insurance into return-to-work programs and measures to drive up the efficiency of civil servants became major objectives of government policy before the final decade of the twentieth century. In the United States, workfare permeated legislation from the start of Ronald Reagan's mandate—particularly with the Omnibus Budget Reconciliation Act (OBRA) of 1981—while, in the United Kingdom, New Public Management principles informed the civil service reform implemented by Margaret Thatcher between 1979 and 1990. Unlike the spearheads of the conservative revolution, however, the "progressive: leaders who succeeded them were careful not to associate budget consolidation measures with a war on overprotected categories.

7. See Andrew Bacevich, "He Told Us to Go Shopping. Now the Bill is Due," *Washington Post*, 5 October 2008, http://www.washingtonpost.com/wp-dyn/content/article/2008/10/03/AR2008100301977.html.

8. On the articulation of the Bush administration's domestic and foreign policies, see Wendy Brown, *Edgework: Critical Essays on Knowledge and Politics* (Princeton: Princeton University Press, 2005), pp. 37-59; Brown, *Undoing the Demos: Neoliberalism's Stealth Revolution* (New York: Zone Books, 2015), pp. 126-69.

9. Such, in particular, was the impact of credit default swaps (CDS), which, via payment of a periodic premium, protected their holders from potential default on repayment of a bond. Even more than other jewels of financial engineering—e.g., collateralized debt obligations (CDO) and mortgage backed securities (MBS)—these contracts of insurance against the insolvency of defaulting borrowers did not take long to establish themselves as the main vehicle to include the poor in the credit spiral. While the invention of CDS by employees at J. P. Morgan dates only from 1997, a mere ten years later they represented a market valued at $62,000 billion—more than the sum total of the stock market. On the invention and fate of the CDS, see Gillian Tett, *Fool's Gold: The Inside Story of J. P. Morgan and How Wall St. Greed Corrupted Its Bold Dream and Created a Financial Catastrophe* (London: Free Press, 2009).

10. See Robert Shiller, "Historic Turning Points in Real Estate," *Cowles Foundation Discussion Paper* 1610 (June 2007), cited in André Orléan, *De l'euphorie à la panique: Penser la crise financière* (Paris: Éditions rue d'Ulm, 2009), p. 18. On the development of the crisis of subprime bonds, see particularly Payne, *The Consumer, Credit and Neoliberalism*, pp. 150–84; Jennifer S. Taub, *Other People's Houses: How Decades of Bailouts, Captive Regulators, and Toxic Bankers Made Home Mortgages a Thrilling Business* (New Haven: Yale University Press, 2014).

11. Colin Crouch, "Privatised Keynesianism: An Unacknowledged Policy Regime," *British Journal of Politics and International Relations* 11.3 (2009), pp. 382–89.

12. Among the most powerful members of the so-called international community, the rebellion of the Syrian people gradually reversed the perception of the relationship between regional potentates and terrorist groups dwelling in their vicinity. Instead of being lumped together in one and the same opprobrium, as Saddam Hussein and Osama Bin Laden had been in their time, local tyrants were for the most part clearly distinguished from nonstate enemies. In particular, Bashar al Assad was begrudgingly recognized as an unappealing, but indispensable subcontractor in the fight against the Islamic State, even as he staked his survival on the conflation of the terrorists he never fought with the popular resistance he strove to crush. In many ways, the geostrategic goals that the leaders of the industrialized countries currently claim to pursue recall the time of the Cold War. Regional stability and national sovereignty have decidedly taken precedence over human rights and humanitarian issues, state apparatuses are treated as legitimate representatives of the civil societies they rule, regardless of how they came to power, and democracy is once again considered a luxury to which a majority of peoples may not yet aspire.

13. Thus they grant one another the right to accuse popular opposition to regimes they support of terrorism and, consequently, to aid the latter, including militarily, to maintain themselves in power at any price.

14. French president Nicolas Sarkozy, who pressured his US and British partners into mounting a massive military campaign against Gaddafi's government and army, had personal reasons to seek regime change in Libya: not only

was he eager to compensate for the fact that his government had initially stood on the wrong side of the Tunisian insurrection against Ben Ali's rule, but more importantly, he wanted to get rid of a man who, before becoming a pariah in the eyes of the international community, had been a major, albeit covert contributor to Sarkozy's electoral campaign in 2007.

15. On the evolution of immigration and asylum policy in Europe since 2011, see, especially, Charles Heller and Lorenzo Pezzani, "Ebbing and Flowing: The EU's Shifting Practices of (Non-)Assistance and Bordering in a Time of Crisis" and Bernard Kasparek, "Routes, Corridors, and Spaces of Exception: Governing Migration and Europe," both at *Near Futures Online*, no. 1 (March 2016), "Europe at a Crossroads," http://nearfuturesonline.org. See also the reports of the Migreurop association at http://www.migreurop.org/rubrique418.html?lang=fr.

16. Three major techniques are used, alternatively or in combination, to reduce the official number of unemployed people. First, employment seekers can be given another status and thus be removed from unemployment statistics: for instance, according to the French employment office, any job seeker who has recently worked for a short period of time or who is currently holding an unpaid internship immediately ceases to be included among the unemployed. Second, insofar as the International Labor Office defines unemployment as the condition of a person who does not have a job but is actively looking for one, the civil servants in charge of receiving and guiding job seekers have been tasked with showing that the people who come to their office are often insufficiently motivated in their search to retain the right to call themselves unemployed. The criteria that can be invoked to expose a damning lack of motivation include missing an appointment with one's employment officer, regardless of the circumstances, and refusing a job offer, even when the pay, location, and job description do not fit the profile of the person to whom it is offered. Third, when employment seekers cannot be forcibly removed from the unemployment registers—whether by putting them in another category or by depriving them of the status and benefits that the unemployed are entitled to claim—the most expedient way to proceed is to persuade them to remove themselves. Inducing discouragement, or better still, self-depreciation—is another mission, and perhaps the most important

one, that employment offices expect their staff to fulfill. To that end, the officers in charge of managing the unemployed are incited to send the people under their care to job interviews that they have no chance of passing successfully, thereby imparting to them that they are unfit for the job market.

17. In Sweden, the Netherlands, and Britain, the long-term unemployed were customarily converted into invalid status, until the governments of these countries realized that the pensions they needed to pay to those they declared to be invalids clashed with the budgetary cuts they were expected to make. For instance, in the winter of 2012, David Cameron realized that while beneficial with respect to unemployment statistics, turning aging and long-term employment seekers into invalids proved too costly in terms of public finances. Thus, he decided that, having lost their positive effect on the creditworthiness of the country, invalids' pensions should not be granted too easily. To justify his decision, the British prime minister argued that many pension recipients were not really invalids, thereby shortchanging those who really were and abusing the generosity of public authorities. Although the British Department of Labor and Pensions contested Cameron's allegations, showing that abusive claims amounted to £2 million at most, about 1 percent of the available funds, the conservative prime minister remained undeterred. In order to identify fake claimants, the government hired a private company, Atos Healthcare, with the assignment of testing potential pension beneficiaries and delivering "Work Capacity Assessments" based on those tests. Atos Healthcare's bill amounted to £400 million—200 times more than the abuses the company was meant to check. Though expensive, the procedure truly diminished the overall number of discredited citizens: 1,300 people died soon after being tested by Atos Healthcare—strokes and suicides were among the most frequent causes of death. See David Stuckler and Sanjay Basy, *The Body Economic: Why Austerity Kills* (New York: Basic Books, 2013).

18. In Ireland, for instance, a country with a population of 4.6 million people, more than half a million nationals have left in the wake of the 2008 crisis—an increase of 289 percent compared with the previous six years. The summer of 2013, the moment when emigration peaked, saw sixteen thousand Irish citizens

emigrating every week. Eighty-seven percent of the half million emigrants were less than forty-four years old when they left, and according to a study published by the University College of Cork, 67 percent had at least a college degree. Irish public authorities have not simply been acknowledging the situation. Far from passive, they have actively supported the new trend, both through indirect stimulation and direct encouragements, going as far as providing explicit encouragements to putative emigrants: in 2013, the Irish employment office sent more than six thousand letters to young employment seekers about job offers in Australia, the United States, Canada, and the United Kingdom. See Irial Glynn, Tomás Kelly, and Piaras MacÉinri, *Irish Emigration in an Age of Austerity,* The Irish Research Council, University College Cork, 2013, https://www.ucc.ie/en/media/research/emigre/Emigration_in_an_Age_of_Austerity_Final.pdf. Until 2016, when a left-leaning government came to power, Portugal followed in Ireland's footsteps, with similar results: in 2012, the year after encouraging emigration officially became a public policy, about ten thousand people were leaving every month—from a country with a population of 5.6 million people, half of them under thirty and highly skilled.

19. The view of the precariat as an expression of the disintegration of the wage-labor society was forwarded by the sociologist Robert Castel in *From Manual Workers to Wage Laborers: Transformation of the Social Question,* trans. Richard Boyd (New Brunswick: Transaction Books, 2002) and, more explicitly, in "Au-delà du salariat ou en deçà de l'emploi? L'institutionnalisation du précariat," in Serge Paugam (ed.), *Repenser la solidarité* (Paris: Presses Universitaires de France, 2007), pp. 416–33. For the sociologist Patrick Cingolani, by contrast, the precariat evinces the emergence of a new form of social subjectivity, rather than only the decline of a status. See Cingolani, *La précarité* (Paris: Presses Universitaires de France, 2011); *Révolutions précaires: Essai sur l'avenir de l'émancipation* (Paris: Éditions La Découverte, 2014). See also Guy Standing, who associates the precariat with the emergence of a new "dangerous" class in *The Precariat: The New Dangerous Class* (London: Bloomsbury, 2014).

20. See Jacques Bathélemy and Gilbert Cette, *Travailler au XXIe siècle: L'ubérisation de l'économie?* (Paris: Odile Jacob, 2017), pp. 71–91. See also Philippe

Askenazy, *Tours rentiers!: Pour une autre repartition des richesses* (Paris: Odile Jacob, 2016), pp. 158–62.

21. See, especially, Nick Srnicek, *Platform Capitalism* (Cambridge: Polity, 2017); Arun Sundararajan, *The Sharing Economy: The End of Employment and the Rise of Crowd-Based Capitalism* (Cambridge, MA: MIT Press, 2016).

22. Gerald F. Davis, *The Vanishing American Corporation: Negotiating the Hazards of a New Economy* (San Francisco: Berrett-Koehler, 2016), pp. 115–26. See also William Lazonick, "Evolution of the New Economy Business Model," *Business and Economic History On-Line* 3 (2006); Lazonick, "The Financialization of the American Corporation: What Has Been Lost, and How It Can Be Regained," *Seattle University Law Review* 36 (2012), pp. 857–909.

23. Alfred D. Chandler, *The Visible Hand: Managerial Revolution in American Business* (Cambridge, MA: Harvard University Press, 1977); Olivier Weinstein, *Pouvoir, finance et connaissance: Les transformations de l'entreprise capitaliste entre XXe et XXIe siècle* (Paris: Éditions La Découverte, 2010), pp. 141–50; Timothy J. Sturgeon, "Modular Production Networks: A New American Model of Industrial Organization," *Industrial and Corporate Change* 11.3 (2002), pp. 451–96.

24. Gerald Davis quotes "Neutron Jack" Welch, former boss of General Electric and peerless practitioner of "good governance," addressing the students of Harvard Business School in 2011: "You can give lifetime *employability* by training people, by making them adaptable, making them mobile to go other places to do other things. But you can't guarantee lifetime employment." Davis, *Managed by Markets: How Finance Reshaped America* (Oxford: Oxford University Press, 2009), p. 91. See also Colin C. Williams, *Rethinking the Future of Work: Directions and Visions* (Houndmills: Palgrave, 2007), pp. 205–19.

25. Davis, *The Vanishing American Corporation*, pp. 145–50 and 172–75.

26. Abby Goodhough, "House Calls: Skype Chats and Fast Diagnosis," *New York Times*, 11 July 2015, cited in Davis, *The Vanishing American Corporation*, p. 173.

27. Patrick Cingolani, "Ubérisation, turc mécanique, économie à la demande: Où va le capitalisme de plateforme?," *The Conversation*, August 2016, https://theconversation.com/uberisation-turc-mecanique-economie-a-la-demande-ou-va-le-capitalisme-de-plateforme-64150.

28. Davis, *The Vanishing American Corporation*, p. 172.

29. Ronald Coase, "The Nature of the Firm," *Economica*, new series, 4.16 (1937), pp. 386–405.

30. On "the entrepreneur of oneself" as the realization of Gary Becker's version of *homo oeconomicus*, see Michel Foucault, *The Birth of Biopolitics: Lectures at the Collège de France 1978–1979*, ed. Michel Senellart, trans. Graham Burchell (New York: Palgrave Macmillan, 2008), p. 226. Most analyses of the neoliberal subject drawing inspiration from Foucault's lectures revolve around this page.

31. Rachel Botsman and Roo Rogers, *What's Mine Is Yours: How Collaborative Consumption Is Changing the Way We Live* (London: Collins, 2011).

32. Rachel Botsman, "The Case for Collaborative Consumption," TEDxSydney lecture, May 2010, https://www.ted.com/talks/rachel_botsman_the_case_for _collaborative_consumption.

33. There is indeed a more or less informal secondary market in positive opinions. Thus, in June 2016, the *Financial Times* reported the story of Mark Cowper, who had had the idea of buying expressions of enthusiasm and "followers" on Twitter for Social Bite, his online catering service in Sydney. Such was the success of the operation that Cowper soon received a prize for the city's best online service. However, Social Bite had a purely virtual existence: the site did exist, but there was no business and there were no customers. See Frederica Cocco, "How a Bogus Business Became an Online Sensation," *Financial Times*, 16 June 2016, https://www.ft.com/content/f5203ac4-2f33-11e6-a18d-a96ab29e3c95 (subscription required).

34. During the taxi mobilization against Uber in Paris in June 2015, Bruno Leroux, then president of the Socialist group in the National Assembly and deputy for Seine-Saint-Denis, harshly criticized the enterprise and its supporters on the LCI TV station: "I am especially shocked that some people defend those who do not want to respect any rules," and "this is undeclared work. What they are doing is illegal activity, social dumping, wage dumping. It's everything we reject in our country."

35. Exemplifying such a horizon is the project developed by Jacques Barthélemy and Gilbert Cette in *Travailler au XXIe siècle*, pp. 85–129. On contingent workers in the United States, see David Weil, *The Fissured Workplace: Why Work Became So Bad for So Many and What Can Be Done to Improve It* (Cambridge, MA: Harvard University Press, 2014), pp. 271–74. According to the Census Bureau, a "contingent" worker is one who does not have "an implicit or explicit contract for long-term employment." Contingent workers account for no less than 30 percent of the workforce in the United States.

36. In this regard, the most significant victory to date is doubtless the judgment delivered by the London Employment Tribunal in October 2016. It denied Uber the right to treat two drivers affiliated to its site as self-employed partners. The barrister for the plaintiffs succeeded in persuading the judge that the control and subordination to which his clients were subject made them employees. As such, they could not be paid below the minimum wage or deprived of paid holidays and insurance coverage. If upheld on appeal, this decision should apply to some forty thousand drivers in the United Kingdom who use the Uber app. The number of such trials is multiplying throughout the world. In France, the national health care service is suing Uber to get it to reclassify its self-employed drivers as wage earners. In the United States, Uber has paid $100 million to put an end to two class-action suits, in California and Massachusetts, that aimed at a change of status for its drivers. Uber is not the only platform affected by such sanctions, for in January 2017, once again in London, the City Sprint platform, which runs a network of bike couriers, was also mandated to reclassify its "partners" as employees. The multiplication of such trials has eventually impelled the British government to undertake a comprehensive review of working practices and conditions in the gig economy. The purpose of the inquiry was to pave the way for the development of the partially self-employed status referred to above.

37. "Le travail ubérisé, par ceux qui le vivent," Jérôme Pimot interviewed by Mathilde Goanec, *Mediapart*, 30 January 2016, https://www.mediapart.fr/journal/france/300116/le-travail-uberise-par-ceux-qui-le-vivent?onglet=full. The case brought by Pimot and his collective involved couriers who were deprived of income by the collapse of the Tok Tok Tok brand and who retrospectively sought to obtain the compensation that would be owed to wage earners.

38. "La startup Take Eat Easy échouée, une résurgence coopérative possible: Vers un changement radical d'investissement et de fonctionnement," a text from the think tank of the Hackistan collective, coauthored by Pierre-Alexandre Klein and Raphaël Beaumond, 1 August 2016, https://www.scoop.it/t/anders-en-beter/p/4067264437/2016/08/06/hackistan-vers-un-changement-radical-d-investissement-et-de-fonctionnement.

39. See Nathan Schneider, "Denver Taxi Drivers Are Turning Uber's Disruption on its Head," *Nation*, 7 September 2016, https://www.thenation.com/article/denver-taxi-drivers-are-turning-ubers-disruption-on-its-head.

40. See https://coopcycle.org/en and https://newsroom.rei.com/coopcycles. See also: "Coopcycle, le premier coup de pédale," *Mediapart*, 16 March 2018, https://blogs.mediapart.fr/coopcycle/blog/160318/coopcycle-le-premier-coup-de-pedale.

41. Hôtel du Nord is a "patrimonial cooperative" formed by inhabitants of Marseille's northern districts in 2011. With a network of fifty rooms in the homes of private individuals who open the door of their flat or villa to travelers, its social objective is "developing the hospitality and natural and cultural heritage" of these districts.

42. The Fairmondo platform aims to be an alternative to the giant Amazon and comprises a network of cooperatives owned by their local users. See https://www.fairmondo.de/global.

43. Trebor Scholz, *Platform Cooperativism: Challenging the Corporate Sharing Economy* (New York City: Rosa Luxemburg Stiftung, 2016); Scholz, *Uberworked and Underpaid: How Workers Are Disrupting the Digital Economy* (Cambridge: Polity, 2016); Scholz, with Nathan Schneider (eds.), *Ours to Hack and to Own: Platform Cooperativism—A New Vision for the Future of Work and a Fairer Internet* (New York: OR Books, 2016).

44. On a first analysis, a start-up's economic model differs radically from that of a corporation subject to the rules of "good governance." Far from being gauged by the prospect of generously distributed short-term dividends, the attractiveness of a prospective unicorn is based on the promise of deferred hegemony—a project of domination in a market where the winner takes all. This is

a neo-Schumpeterian business model based on the daring of the entrepreneur and the flair of the investor of venture capital. However, unlike the enterprise head of the heroic age, but like firms made to pursue shareholder value, it is not the enterprise's income that seals the success of the adventure but precisely its capital value—that is, the estimated price of the start-up's shares should its creators decide to make it an incorporated company. In this light, losses, to the extent that they attest to the magnitude of the conquest underway, are an important asset. To understand the spirit of this type of capitalism, readers are referred to a remarkable scene from the TV series *Silicon Valley*: http://www.youtube.com/watch?v=BzAdXyPYKQo.

45. For an exemplary presentation of the art of disruptive innovation by its most ardent propagandists, see Jeff Dyer, Hal Gregersen, and Clayton M. Christensen, *The Innovator's DNA: Mastering the Five Skills of Disruptive Innovators* (Boston: Harvard Business Review Press, 2011).

46. On Lip, see, especially, Frank Georgi, "Le moment Lip dans l'histoire de l'autogestion en France," in Chantal Mathieu and Thomas Pasquier (eds.), *Actualité juridique de l'action collective: 40 ans après Lip, Semaine sociale Lamy*, supplement to no. 1631, 19 May 2014, pp. 65–72; Georgi, "'Vivre demain dans nos luttes d'aujourd'hui': Le syndicat, la grève et l'autogestion en France (1968–1988)," in G. Dreyfus-Armand, R. Frank, M.-F. Lévy, and M. Zancarini-Fournel (eds.), *Les années 68: Le temps de la contestation* (Brussels: Éditions Complexe, 2000), pp. 399–413. On the Numax experiment, readers may watch Joaquim Jordà's documentary *Numax presenta*, made in 1979: https://vimeo.com/199546260.

47. Paul Hampton, "As 9-to-5 Jobs Vanish, Look Who's Reinventing the Working World," *Yes Magazine*, August 2016, http://www.yesmagazine.org/issues/the-gig-economy/for-40-percent-of-us-the-future-of-work-has-already-arrived-20160825.

48. Scholz, *Platform Cooperativism*, pp. 21–26.

49. See Mayo Fuster Morell, "Barcelona as a Case Study on Urban Policy for Platform Cooperativism," *P2P Foundation*, https://blog.p2pfoundation.net/mayo-fuster-morell-barcelona-as-a-case-study-on-urban-policy-for-platform-cooperativism/2017/02/23; Stacco Troncoso and Ann Marie Utratel, "The Commons Collaborative Economy Explodes in Barcelona," *Commons Transition*, April 2016, http://commonstransition.org/commons-collaborative-economy-explodes-barcelona.

50. Founded in the 1970s by French economists—Robert Boyer, Michel Aglietta, and Alain Lipietz, among others—the Regulation School is one of the main branches of heterodox economics, alongside the post-Keynesian and Marxist schools of thought. A singular synthesis of Marxian, Keynesian, but also Institutionalist and Annals School perspectives, it focuses on regimes of capital accumulation—their structures, their histories, their crises—and emphasizes the necessity of an interdisciplinary approach to economics. For a comprehensive overview of the "regulationist" perspective, in France as well as in the Netherlands, Germany, and Scandinavia, see Bob Jessop (ed.), *Regulation Theory and the Crisis of Capitalism*, 5 vols. (Cheltenham: Edward Elgar, 2001)

51. See, especially, Askenazy, *Tous rentiers!*; Les Économistes atterrés, *Changer d'avenir: Réinventer le travail et le modèle économique* (Paris: Éditions Les Liens qui Libèrent, 2017), pp. 12–196. For Askenazy, the announcement of the death of the wage-labor society is an idea intrinsically bound up with the notion of equal opportunity developed by third-way think tanks. Askenazy, *Tous rentiers!*, pp. 154–56.

52. *Ibid.*, pp. 51–53.

53. *Ibid.*, pp. 151–53; Les Économistes atterrés, *Changer d'avenir*, pp. 141–55.

54. On the specificity and originality of the forms of socialization, but also politicization of contingent workers, see Cingolani, *Les révolutions précaires*, pp. 85–116.

55. In France, the demands and practices of contract workers in cultural industries have for several years been a favorite topic in studies of the precariat. See Antonella Corsani and Maurizio Lazzarato, *Intermittents et précaires* (Paris: Éditions Amsterdam, 2008); Cingolani, *Révolutions précaires*, pp. 59–84.

56. Frédérique Roussel, "Les pigistes la jouent collectifs," *Libération*, 10 May 2010, http://www.liberation.fr/medias/2010/05/10/les-pigistes-la-jouent-collectifs_625165.

57. See, especially, Philippe van Parijs and Yannick Vanderborght, *Basic Income: A Radical Proposal for a Free Economy and a Sane Society* (Cambridge,

MA: Harvard University Press, 2017); Ariel Kyrou and Yann Moulier Boutang, "Les clés d'un nouveau modèle social: La révolution du revenu universel," *La vie des idées*, 28 February, 2018, http://www.laviedesidees.fr/Les-cles-d-un-nouveau-modele-social.html; Yves Citton, "Revenu inconditionnel d'existence et économie générale de l'attention," *Multitudes* 63 (2016), pp. 59–71.

58. Foundational in the growing literature about the commons is Elinor Ostrom's book *Governing the Commons: The Evolution of Institutions for Collective Action* (Cambridge: Cambridge University Press, 1990). See also James Boyle, "The Second Enclosure Movement and the Construction of the Public Domain," *Law and Contemporary Problems* 66.33 (2003), pp. 33–74; Boyle, *The Public Domain: Enclosing the Commons of the Mind* (New Haven: Yale University Press, 2008); Benjamin Coriat (ed.), *Le retour des communs: La crise de l'idéologie propriétaire* (Paris: Éditions Les Liens qui libèrent, 2015); Michel Bauwens, *Sauver le monde: Vers une économie post-capitaliste avec le peer-to-peer* (Paris: Éditions Les Liens qui libèrent, 2015); Gaëlle Krikorian and Amy Kapczynski (eds.), *Access to Knowledge in the Age of Intellectual Property* (New York: Zone Books, 2010). From a different perspective, see also Pierre Dardot and Christian Laval, *Commun: Essai sur la révolution au XXIe siècle* (Pars: Éditions La Découverte, 2014).

Coda

Throughout capitalism's golden age, corporations identified success with sustained profitability, national governments obsessed about economic growth, and private citizens were expected to pursue their own interests, whether they perceived such a pursuit as an individual matter or the cement of class solidarity. With the ascendancy of financial institutions, however, a new order of priorities has emerged. Firms primarily care about the rating of their stock, public officials do whatever it takes to maintain the trust of bondholders, and households mainly attend to the value of their assets.

On the whole, for both natural and artificial persons, generating unrealized capital gains takes precedence over maximizing revenues. As economic agents have been enticed to meet these new expectations, the stakes of social conflicts have shifted accordingly—or at least so this book has argued. Whereas in the past, the labor movement chiefly fought for the redistribution of the surplus value created by workers and appropriated by capital owners, the focus of today's struggles is on the allocation of credit.

To claim that the current regime of capital accumulation subordinates yield to valorization is to take exception with two common assumptions about the nefarious effects of neoliberal reforms. According to their detractors, these reforms are responsible not only for exacerbating individualism, thereby leaving people insulated and forced to fend for themselves, but also for "economizing" virtually every domain of activity, thereby subjecting life itself to purely utilitarian assessments. While consistent with the professed intentions of neoliberal reformers, both aspersions are belied, or at least mitigated, by the unexpected consequences of their actions.

Dissolving class consciousness—what Wilhelm Röpke called "deproletarization"—certainly was an essential tenet of the agenda devised by neoliberal social engineers. For that reason, the adoption of their prescriptions by corporate managers and public officials is generally associated with fashioning self-interested individuals whose only option is to rely on their own enterprising spirit while competing fiercely with one another for scarce resources. However, as the successive assaults of neoliberal reformers on managerial capitalism, labor unions, and the welfare state paved the way for the hegemony of investors, creditworthiness has become the main object of socioeconomic pursuits.

Being deemed creditworthy can translate into loans, venture capital investments, buzz, material support, confidence, and other forms of empathy. Yet regardless of the kind of leverage it offers, credit, by definition, can be granted only by others. Rather than the deserved reward of the self-reliant, credit is a function—as the CEO of Facebook never ceases to profess—of our ability to connect and share.[1] Now, reckoning with the obvious fact that all credit is social credit hardly makes our financialized capitalist world a better place. Nonetheless, the substitution of credit-seeking asset managers for profit-seeking entrepreneurs does challenge the common assumption that prospective investees must wager the attractiveness of their projects on their ability to pull themselves by their own bootstraps.

Coupled with the charge of corroding social bonds, the neoliberal mode of government has been accused of compelling the governed to envision their existence in purely economic terms. Enticing people to treat life as a business was undoubtedly what neoliberal reformers had in mind. Chicago School economists argued that human behavior can always be accurately described as choices determined by the availability and relative prices of a person's preferences, and thus they urged governments to help their constituents maximize their utility.[2] Given that "competitive markets satisfy consumer preferences more effectively than monopolistic markets, be it the market for aluminum or the market for ideas,"[3] as Gary Becker claimed, public policies were to provide an environment where everyone's options could be accurately compared and priced.

Although governing agencies largely heeded the neoliberal call to turn social interactions and political campaigns into optimal shopping experiences, the outcome of their efforts did not exactly match the plan. Portfolio appreciation—what firms, states, and private citizens are now expected to pursue—does not square with the economization of human life that Becker and his colleagues sought to forward. Instead, it attests to the breakdown of a time-honored partition between self-interested and disinterested pursuits. In other words, what the rising sway of financial capital has prompted is not the expansion of the domain of tradable commodities at the expense of all realms where value used to be immeasurable; rather, it is the advent of a culture no longer predicated on the opposition between economic and noneconomic concerns.

As already mentioned, appreciation comes in several flavors: funding, reputation, and trust are all manifestations of creditworthiness. Financial markets, rating agencies, collaborative platforms, and social networks are all in the business of measuring credit. But we should remember that rates are not prices expressing the current state of negotiations on the exchange value of commodities. Rating instead contributes to the dynamic of speculating on the attractiveness of projects—individual as well as collective, moral as well as financial.

Once again, there is nothing intrinsically comforting about the discrepancy between the utility-maximizing entrepreneurs that neoliberal reforms purported to deliver and the speculating investees they actually fashioned. Yet to stress that these reforms have effectively blurred the distinction between economic and noneconomic aspirations, instead of having reduced the latter to the former, is to contend that the ascent of credit should not be treated as a curse to reverse so much as a challenge to meet. To put it bluntly, creditworthiness is worth vying for, lest we leave it to investors to determine who deserves to be appreciated and for what motives.

The US presidential election of 2016 tragically illustrated the political prominence of speculative accreditation. More than by promising to deliver jobs and higher wages to average Americans, Donald Trump earned the undying support of his core voters by vowing to valorize some key components of their portfolio. The Republican candidate persuasively conveyed that under his administration, being or standing by a nationalist, gun-carrying white male would become a truly valuable asset. In the words of his erstwhile advisor Steve Bannon, Trump was and remains committed to raising "the citizenship value" of his electorate.[4]

Xenophobic populists are not the only ones to stake social change on the reallocation of credit, however. Indeed, the most vibrant movements involved in resisting the American president's agenda, from Black Lives Matter and #MeToo to the March for Our Lives, are equally focused on the valuation of the traits and conduct that constitute people's human capital. Though hardly indifferent to specific reforms regarding police practices, workplace environment, pay gaps, and gun control, the activists involved in these movements primarily seek to "change the terms of the debate" by way of producing and circulating their own rating system. Their purpose is not only to discredit behaviors hitherto protected by institutional privilege, gender norms, legal standards, and powerful lobbies but also to reappraise the lives that these behaviors depreciate.

At odds with the Left populist strategy that wishes to convert white male rage against women, minorities, and foreigners into righteous indignation directed at unaccountable elites, Black Lives Matter, #MeToo, and the March for Our Lives unapologetically speculate against the various facets of the "citizenship value" that Donald Trump promised to raise. Far from sacrificing substance to symbolism or concentrating on symptoms to the detriment of structural inequalities, these movements reckon with the fact that the allocation of moral, social, and financial credit has become the decisive stake of social struggles.

Exemplary in this respect was a brief Twitter confrontation between David Hogg, a Parkland high school shooting survivor and spokesperson for March for Our Lives, and Laura Ingraham, a Fox News radio host and prominent member of the ruling Far Right.[5] After the latter tried to damage the reputational capital of the former by claiming that his antigun activism was just a way of whining about his poor academic record, Hogg, instead of protesting or, indeed, whining, simply published a list of the companies sponsoring the Laura Ingraham radio program and asked his "followers" to contact them. In a matter of days, eleven out of the twelve advertisers exposed by David Hogg's tweet withdrew their support from the show, compelling Ingraham to suspend her program for a week. Anecdotal as this episode clearly is, the seventeen-year-old eloquently illustrated the centrality of credit in contemporary struggles. For investee activists, *another speculation is possible* may be an apt rallying cry.

Paris/New York, April 2018

1. "At Facebook, we build tools to help people connect with the people they want and share what they want, and by doing this we are extending people's capacity to build and maintain relationships." Mark Zuckerberg, "Founder's Letter, 2012," https://www.facebook.com/zuck/posts/10154500412571634.

2. What Gary Becker called his "economic way of looking at life" did not merely apply to how entrepreneurs devise their business plans and how consumers choose among various commodities: as he saw it, assessing the costs and estimating the future benefits of a course of action within a context of relative scarcity and imperfect information is how a virtually infinite number of human decisions should be understood, from waging war to doing one's homework, proposing marriage to renouncing an addictive habit, applying for a job to engaging in a criminal activity, refusing to hire someone on account of his race or her gender to giving one's time or fortune to a charity. See Gary S. Becker, "The Economic Way of Looking at Life," revised version of the 1992 Nobel Lecture, in Becker, *Accounting for Tastes* (Cambridge, MA: Harvard University Press, 1996), pp. 139–61.

3. Gary S. Becker, *The Economic Approach to Human Behavior* (Chicago: University of Chicago Press, 1976), p. 6.

4. Steve Bannon's address to the congress of the French Front National, in March 2018, can be viewed at: https://www.youtube.com/watch?v=ue9PNeFUoOo.

5. See "Fox News: Ads Pulled from Laura Ingraham Show for Mocking Parkland Survivor," *The Guardian*, March 29, 2018, https://www.theguardian.com/media/2018/mar/30/fox-news-ads-pulled-from-laura-ingraham-show-for-mocking-parkland-survivor.

Acknowledgments

This book owes its existence to the generous and indefatigable midwifery exercised since the onset of the project by Wendy Brown, Judith Butler, Éric Fassin, and Aurélie Windels, whose constant scrutiny and meticulous research clarified and enriched my argument.

Along the way, I have also benefited from the attentiveness, criticism, and suggestions, often provided at key moments, of Ivan Ascher, William Callison, Jacques-Olivier Charron, Melinda Cooper, Jonathan Crary, Hal Foster, Carles Guerra, Andreas Gurewich, Vladimir Gurewich, Daniel Heller-Roazen, Thomas Keenan, Gaëlle Krikorian, Jonathan Levy, Fabian Muniesa, Ramona Naddaff, Alexandra Oeser, Martha Poon, Paul Preciado, Camille Robcis, Emily Rosamond, Christian Salmon, Kendall Thomas, and Eyal Weizman.

For the French original edition, I am very grateful to Hugues Jallon, who agreed to publish my manuscript at Éditions La Découverte, despite the fact that, for longer than I wish to remember, he had been expecting another book altogether. I also thank my editor Rémy Toulouse for graciously enduring an especially prickly author.

As far as the English version is concerned, I am eternally grateful to William Callison, my Zone Books editor Ramona Naddaff, as well as to Bud Bynack and Peter Sahlins, all of whom so carefully read, edited, and improved the numerous revisions of this manuscript (after it was thoroughly translated by Gregory Elliott). The same undying gratefulness extends to my friends and partners at Zone Books: Meighan Gale, who weathered my moods and kept the project on track, Kyra Simone and Jeremy Wang-Iverson, who took on the task of launching this book into the world, and Julie Fry, who, once again, produced an amazing cover design. My deepest thanks also go Max de Estaban and Danai Anesiadou, for letting us reproduce their striking work.

I further wish to thank the colleagues and friends who kindly invited me to present my work in progress: Irit Rogoff, Eyal Weizman, and Susan Schuppli at Goldsmiths, University of London, Hal Foster and Daniel Heller-Roazen at Princeton University, Paul Preciado at the Independent Studies Program (PEI) of Barcelona, Jonathan Levy at the University of Chicago, Fabian Muniesa at MINES ParisTech, and Adi Ophir at Brown University.

Finally, I dedicate this book to the people who shore me up and put up with me on a daily basis: Amanda Bay, Laszlo Feher, Milena Feher, and Gabor Feher.

Index

Near Futures series design by Julie Fry
Typesetting by Meighan Gale
Printed and bound by Maple Press